D0362513

BISON
BOOKS

ACTORS AND SINGERS

Richard Wagner

TRANSLATED BY
William Ashton Ellis

University of Nebraska Press
Lincoln and London

Manufactured in the United States of America

♾ The paper in this book meets the minimum requirements of American National Standard for Information Sciences—Permanence of Paper for Printed Library Materials, ANSI Z39.48-1984.

First Bison Books printing: 1995
Most recent printing indicated by the last digit below:
10 9 8 7 6 5 4 3 2 1

Library of Congress Cataloging-in-Publication Data
Wagner, Richard, 1813–1883.
[Literary works. English. Selections]
Actors and singers / Richard Wagner; translated by William Ashton Ellis.
p. cm.
Originally published: Richard Wagner's prose works. Vol. 5, Actors and singers. London: Kegan Paul, Trench, Trübner & Co., 1896.
Includes index.
Contents: To the German army before Paris (poem)—A capitulation—Reminiscences of Auber—Beethoven—The destiny of opera—Actors and singers—The rendering of Beethoven's ninth symphony—Letters and minor essays—Bayreuth.
ISBN 0-8032-9773-4 (pbk.: alk. paper)
1. Music—Philosophy and aesthetics. 2. Music—19th century—History and criticism. I. Title.
ML410.W1A1266 1996
780—dc20
95-30854
CIP
MN

Reprinted from the 1896 translation of volume 5 (*Actors and Singers*) of *Richard Wagner's Prose Works*, published by Kegan Paul, Trench, Trübner & Co., Ltd., London.

CONTENTS

TRANSLATOR'S PREFACE.

LLOWING that it is an advantage to have the individual volumes of a longish series distinguished by appropriate titles, even though it be impossible to thus suggest the nature of all their contents, some people might have preferred that the fifth volume of these translations should be entitled "Beethoven." Against that course there stood the serious objection that Mr Edward Dannreuther had already published an excellent English rendering of the great article in question; to repeat its name, would have given rise to much confusion. On the other hand, though "Beethoven and Shakespeare" would have expressed the main gist of the thoughts embodied in a large portion of this volume, that title would have departed from the impersonal system hitherto adopted. Unable to draw upon the one of the two chief essays in this book, I was driven to select the other; for not only is the article on "Actors and Singers" the actually longest single essay included therein, but many of the shorter articles are virtually devoted to the same subject, the art of the "ideal mime."

For once this volume corresponds—I might almost say, by accident—with an entire section of the *Gesammelte Schriften*, owing to the fact of the ninth volume of the latter containing none of the author's dramatic works. The period covered is also more homogeneous than that of its two immediate predecessors, Vols. III. and IV., since it lies between the winter of 1870 and the spring of 1873—for Richard Wagner a period big with hope and full of stir. The unexpected re-awakening of the German people to a sense of its due place among the nations had revived in Richard Wagner's breast that confidence in his countrymen which before had been so sorely shaken. Scarcely had the Franco-German War been brought to end by the victories in the full flush of which the closing pages of his "Beethoven" were written, than the author began his preparations for crowning the military triumph of his nation by a triumph quite as glorious on the field of art. In the spring of 1871 (April 17) he made his first visit of inspection to Bayreuth; on April 24, 1872, he settled in that town for good; on May 22, of the same year, the foundation-stone of the Festival-theatre was laid; and on August 2, 1873—just three months after the dedication of the last essay in this book—the topmost rafter of that building's roof was christened in due German fashion. With the delays that arrested the progress of a work so expeditiously begun, delays occasioned by deficiency of funds and only to be finally overcome in August 1876, I have no need to deal at present, as the author's own account thereof will appear in Volume VI.

After leaving Munich at the end of 1865, Richard Wagner had been allowed by Fate a nearly five-years' spell of peace and rest, the greater part of that time being spent in musical composition at Triebschen near Lucerne. This almost solitary interval of tranquilness, in a life filled full of toil and worry, was already drawing to its close when he penned the essay on "Beethoven." In 1871 began a period of renewed contact with the larger world of Germany; to produce his "Ring des Nibelungen" not only had the money, but the artists to be found. Thus we find him commencing in the spring of that year a series of journeys of inspection, of concerts in aid of the building-fund, of semi-public speeches and business negotiations of all kinds. The tranquillity of Triebschen was a thing of the past, and the only wonder is how Wagner could have found the time, amid this turmoil, to complete the 'orchestral sketch' and a great part of the scoring of *Die Götterdämmerung* before the date with which the volume terminates.

In the preface to "Beethoven" the author tells us that he had written that essay as if it were "a speech to be delivered at an ideal feast in honour of the great musician, though the speech was not to be delivered in reality"; it is somewhat singular that so soon thereafter he should have repeatedly been called upon to speak in public. Although his enemies have often since upbraided him with a "love of speechifying," his own feelings upon such occasions may easily be gathered from his "Letter to an Actor," where he alludes to the "shyness of all retiring men, about making a so-called public appearance." Coming so shortly after a time of much compulsory speech-making, preceded by a period of the greatest seclusion, it is impossible not to treat this sentence as of directly personal application; indeed the reluctance with which he addressed a company of strangers is distinctly traceable in many of the later essays in this book. The contagious example of other speech-makers, whom he necessarily met at these festal gatherings, cannot have remained without its influence on a mind so extremely impressionable as that of Richard Wagner; and we all know the circumlocution indulged in by the average German after-dinner orator. This, coupled with a constant intercourse and correspondence with the ordinary German man of business, concerning the project and plans of the special theatre for the *Ring*, has made the style of some of these essays peculiarly complicated and hard of rendering. With none of the previous volumes had I found it possible to depart from an almost absolutely literal translation, without destroying the author's meaning; with the present one not only have I been obliged to omit many an "I venture to think," but even to re-construct or paraphrase a good number of the sentences, though in no case departing from Wagner's intention, so far as it had become clear to me. In all such cases, however, I have been guided by the principle laid down in his article on the Ninth Symphony (page 248), namely that "nothing is so worth the utmost study as the attempt to clear the meaning of a phrase, a single word, in the message handed down to us by genius." The time absorbed in this attempt must be my apology for the delay in completing a volume which bears the date of 1896 though its later sheets have not been issued until 1897.

I have dwelt upon the difficulties peculiar to the present instalment of Wagner's prose-works, but, although I may not have been able to clear them all aside, the reader must not hasten to the conclusion that this volume is by any means behind the others in interest. Apart from the historical account of the origin and foundation of the Festival-theatre, the "Capitulation," "Auber," "Beethoven," "The Destiny of Opera," and "Actors and Singers," are each of them works of first-class importance.

As to the first-named, "A Capitulation," sentimental reasons might have dictated its omission; for never was there penned so scathing a satire on the manners of a neighbouring people. Those who can see no farther than their noses have attributed this attack to personal pique, to revenge upon the French for the failure of the author's Paris production of *Tannhäuser* in 1861: that Richard Wagner ever battled for his personal interests, instead of for the broad idea involved, I have not as yet seen proved by a single instance. Here, even had we not his own word for it, it is obvious that the ridicule cast upon the French is meant as a more effectual mode of shaming their German imitators: the closing section of the "Beethoven" essay (pp. 113 *et seq.*) and the last two pages of the volume establish this beyond all cavilling, to say nothing of the whole drift of "German Art and German Policy" (Vol. IV.). From the very first essay he wrote at the age of twenty-one, down to the last at that of close upon seventy, Wagner's one cry to the German was "to be *original*," to develop his own gifts and aptitudes, not squeeze himself into garments measured for a narrower waist. That the French should take the pasquinade without offence, was scarcely to be expected; a nation so outspoken in its political caricatures—I well remember the revolting cartoons exposed at all the kiosques at the height of the Boulanger fever—had far too keen a sense of ridicule not to feel the smart of so apposite a double-handed blow. It was a clear case of the biter bitten, and in England we have no particular reason for salving the sufferer's amour-propre. To have omitted the "Capitulation"—which, by the way, is a capitulation of the Germans, not the French—would have been to erase a pregnant chapter in the international history of its author's art. It also would have been, to deprive the reader of a scintillating parody, brimful of apt allusions.

I have no intention of detaining that reader by comments on all the articles included in the following pages; but the essay on "Beethoven," and one other, demand a brief remark or two.

It is not at all necessary either to be a Schopenhauerian, or even to have read a line of that philosopher's works, to appreciate Richard Wagner's superb prose-poem "Beethoven"; yet a couple of words explaining Schopenhauer's system, with an extract from his writings relative to the Platonic "Idea," may assist the uninitiate. Kant, pursuing the arguments of his predecessors to their legitimate conclusion, had arrived at the demonstration that Time, Space and Causality were merely *a priori* forms of knowledge, i.e. that they were as much dependent on the structure and peculiarities of our brain as the ideas of Colour on the physiological action of the retina and optic nerves—colour-blind people taking red for green, and so forth. Thus Time, Space and Causality were shewn by Kant to be mere "semblances" or shadows: what the substance might be, that underlies these *phenomena*, Kant declared to be inscrutable, simply calling it the Thing-in-itself, *das Ding an sich.* Searching for the nature of this Thing-in-itself, Schopenhauer believed he had discovered it in the Will, as the only common property of all creation, tracing it even in the stone, as secret of the law of gravity: all the forms of mind and matter he held to be due to the manifestation of this Will as the Will-to-live, the Will dividing itself into separate units, at war with one another. The suffering consequent on the internecine warfare of this Will, divided into countless individuals, he concluded to be remediable by nothing but the perception that every unit was merely a differentiation of the All, i.e. that the ills one put upon another were put upon a portion of one's Universal-self. Thus his moral deduction was summed up in *Mitleid* (sympathy, compassion or fellow-suffering—with-suffering); and as it was the Will-to-live that caused this suffering, his final word became Denial of the Will-to-live, admittedly the same thing as Nirvana.

Arguing on these lines, Schopenhauer regarded Art as a practical religion, since it opened up to us an avenue by which to look into the nature of this Thing-in-itself, to recognise that Universal Will through apprehension of its most immediate emanations, the Ideas; only one thing did he account of higher value, the *example* of the saint or mystic. His views on dreams and second-sight were merely tentative, and may be upheld or rejected without affecting his broader system: as they are dealt with at some length in this "Beethoven" essay of Wagner's, I may briefly say that Schopenhauer put forward the hypothesis that in this state of "in-turned consciousness" the barriers parting the separate units into which the Will "appears" divided were more or less thrown down, bringing our minds into closer contact with the Thing-in-itself than was possible to the waking consciousness of everyday—an idea which Wagner has pursued as suggesting an analogy between the dream-vision and the artistic image.

In the above paragraph it will be noticed that I have used the word "idea" in two different senses. I have done so intentionally, with the object of shewing at what a disadvantage we lie through having no indigenous equivalent for those admirable German terms "*Begriff*" and "*Vorstellung*," the former of which can only be rendered by "abstraction" or "concept," as meaning the attributes *selected* from a group of objects by an artificial process of generalising *in vacuo*, so to speak, whereas the latter, *Vorstellung* (? notion), signifies the living concrete "idea" which the object would leave behind it after being *brought before* the senses: *Begriff* might thus be compared with a figure in Euclid, *Vorstellung* with a moving coloured statue. Yet even *Vorstellung* does not convey the whole meaning of Plato's "Idea"; so that I am obliged, as said, to appeal to Schopenhauer's *Welt als Wille und Vorstellung* (Book III., § 49):—

"The object of art—that object whose portrayal is the artist's aim, and whose apprehension must therefore precede his artwork as its fount and origin—is nothing more or less than an *Idea*, in Plato's sense: not the single thing, the object of common knowledge, nor the abstraction (*Begriff*), the object of rational thought and science. Though *Idea* and *Begriff* have this in common, that both are units representing a plurality of actual things, yet their difference is great and manifest. . . . The *Begriff* is abstract, discursive, quite indefinite *within* its sphere, only defined by its boundaries, seizable by everyone who has but logic, communicable by words without any further intermediation, entirely to be exhausted by its definition. The *Idea* on the other hand, albeit definable as adequate representative of the Begriff, is thoroughly intuitive (*anschaulich*), and, though it represents a multitude of single things, defined throughout: by the Individual as such it is never cognised, but only by the mind that has risen above all will-ing, above all individualism, to the state of pure Subject of cognition: thus it is only attainable by the genius and those who temporarily are in a similar mood through an exaltation of their purely cognitive powers, for the most part stimulated by the works of genius. Hence it is not communicable outright, but merely conditionally, the Idea conceived and reproduced in the artwork appealing to each person according to the measure of his intellectual capacity; wherefore it is precisely the most excellent works of every art, the noblest creations of genius, that remain closed books forever to the dull majority of men, divided from them by a yawning gulf, as inaccessible as is the company of princes to the rabble. . . . To freely recognise and willingly acknowledge others' worth, one must have worth oneself. . . .

"The *Begriff* is like a dead receptacle, in which whatever one has put into it still lies there side by side, but out of which one can take no more than one has already put in: the *Idea*, on the contrary, develops in him who has seized it conceptions (*Vorstellungen*) that are new to the Begriff of similar name: it resembles a living, self-evolving organism, endowed with power of propagation, which brings forth what had not been lain therein.

"Consequently the Begriff, useful as it is for life, and resultful, necessary for science, for art is ever barren. The conceived Idea, on the other hand, is the true and only source of every genuine artwork. In the might of its originality it is only drawn from life itself, from Nature, from the world, and only by the sterling genius or the man inspired for the moment to the pitch of genius. Only from such immediate conception do genuine works arise that bear immortal life within them. Just because the Idea is intuitive, and remains so, the artist is not conscious *in abstracto* of the aim and purpose of his work; not a Begriff, but an Idea is hovering before him: hence he can give no account of what he is doing: he works, as the saying is, from pure feeling, unconsciously, instinctively. Copyers, mannerists, *imitatores*, *servum pecus*, on the contrary, derive their art from the Begriff: they take stock of the pleasing and effective points in genuine works, assemble them in a Begriff, i.e. abstractly, and deliberately copy them, either openly or in disguise."

As it thus will be seen that even Schopenhauer cannot define in terms of abstract reason so purely intuitive a thing as the Platonic "Idea," I must be permitted to make one further quotation, from § 34 of the same book, where he gives us an almost pictorial image thereof:—

"When, uplifted by power of the spirit, man casts adrift the ordinary mode of observation, ceases to pry into the relations of things to one another—an inquiry whose ultimate goal is always their relation to our personal will; when he thus no longer searches for the where, the when, the why and wherefore of things, but solely for their *what*; when he lets no longer abstract thinking, the Begriffe of ratiocination (*Vernunft*), usurp his consciousness; but gives his whole force of mind to beholding (*Anschauung*), plunges himself therein entirely, and lets his whole consciousness be filled by tranquil contemplation of the Object present to him at this very moment—be it a landscape, a tree, a rock, a building, or what not; when he *loses* himself completely in this object, i.e. forgets his individuum, his will, and remains nothing but pure Subject, clear mirror of the object; so that it is as if the object were there alone without an observer, and one thus can no longer part the contemplator from the contemplated, for both have become *one* through the domination of the whole consciousness by one single visual image; when accordingly the object has passed from all relation to anything outside it, the subject from all relation to the will:—then that which is thus apprehended, no longer is the single thing as such; 'tis the *Idea*, the everlasting form, the direct objectification of the Will at this its stage: and precisely for that reason the man lost in this contemplation is no longer Individual, but pure will-less, painless, timeless *Subject of cognition*. . . . In such a contemplation the single thing becomes at one blow the *Idea* of its species."

With this magnificent description of what one perhaps might call the *archetype*, I may leave the "Idea" to those who must often have felt its influence, though they scarcely could convey that feeling to another through the medium of mere abstract terms.

The other article to which I alluded on page x as calling for a word of comment, is the "Letter to Friedrich Nietzsche."

A little over a year ago the *Fortnightly Review* brought out an English rendering of Nietzsche's "The Case of Wagner." The German original of that lamentable squib had appeared in 1888, causing some little sensation at the time, as the author had once been Richard Wagner's most eloquent advocate; within six months F. Nietzsche was confined to a lunatic asylum, where he still remains, hopelessly insane—a fact publicly acknowledged by the editor of his collected works. Not only did the "Case of Wagner" appear (curtailed) in the *Fortnightly* of September 1895 without a word of warning as to the condition of mind in which Nietzsche must necessarily have been when it was written—seven years before—but the issue of an English translation of his works commenced soon after with "volume *eleven*" (!), that volume containing the "Case" and another article "Contra Wagner," with little else. No more unfortunate selection could have been made, in view of gaining for Friedrich Nietzsche that consideration which all earnest men desire from serious thinkers, or even of securing his works an English popularity at all. A second random volume has since been published, but I have not yet heard of the issue in English of what constitute the *first* volume of Nietzsche's collected works in the German, namely "The Birth of Tragedy" and the "Untimely thoughts" (*Unzeitgemässe Betrachtungen*). I only wish I had, that I might commend my readers to a truly noble and original book by this most polished of German prose-writers.

As "The Birth of Tragedy" is referred to by Richard Wagner in that "Letter to Friedrich Nietzsche" of 1872, I need no apology for here alluding to it, as also to the relations subsisting between the two authors at that epoch, and perhaps it will be best to commence with the latter point. Friedrich Nietzsche, born in 1844 near Lützen, studied classical philology at the Universities of Bonn and Leipzig, and was appointed to the University of Bâle as Professor of that science towards the end of 1868. On the 16th Jan. 1869 he writes to a friend, "To my greatest delight, Richard Wagner has lately sent me his greeting by letter. Lucerne is now no longer beyond my reach." Nothing could be more eloquent of the young man's ardour to meet the dramatist of *Tristan* and *Die Meistersinger*. At the end of 1871 he writes the preface to his "Birth of Tragedy," a dedication to Richard Wagner, from which I may quote the following: "To enable me to write the introductory words of this essay with that calm delight whose marks it bears on every page, as the distillate of good and elevating hours, I picture to myself, my highly honoured friend, the moment when you will receive it: how, perchance returning from an afternoon's excursion in the winter-snow, you will read my name upon the title-page and be convinced at once that, whatever the book may contain, at least its author has something earnest and urgent to say; that in all his thinkings he has communed with you as with a person present, and could only pen what accords with such a presence. And you will remember that at like time with the origin of your glorious monograph on Beethoven, i.e. amid the horrors and sublimities of the war then just outbroken, I was bracing my mind for this task. . . . To all who take life in earnest let me say that I consider Art the highest object and the true metaphysical pursuit of that life, in the sense of him to whom, as my exalted leader on this path, I dedicate the following essay."

From these words of Nietzsche's, at the age of twenty-seven, it is evident how intimate had been his communion with Richard Wagner; how stimulating that communion had been to himself, is obvious to anyone who reads "The Birth of Tragedy." Here is a work that pulses with the warm blood of genius from end to end. For Wagner always had the faculty of bringing out the best that lay in the natural gifts of his disciples; we have seen it in the case of Uhlig, the young Bülow, Tausig, Stein, and many another; we see it still more markedly in that of the young Nietzsche. And perhaps this "Birth of Tragedy" affords us even better testimony than the same author's "Richard Wagner in Bayreuth," since the main body of the work is not concerned with the Wagnerian Drama, save prophetically, and only toward its close do we obtain a direct allusion thereto. But this "Birth of Tragedy" is so drenched with the Wagnerian spirit, so full of sentences recalling passages in Wagner's own prose-writings—those which came after, as well as those which came before—that it gives us a far livelier picture of the brilliance of the master's conversational intercourse than any of the countless "reminiscences."

Soon after the publication of Nietzsche's first work, "The Birth of Tragedy," the author's distinguished "friend and leader" left Switzerland for good. The tie of immediate personal relations thus was severed, and it is noteworthy to find at once a falling-off in Nietzsche's literary standard: the style of the two succeeding essays, *Unzeitgemässe Betrachtungen*, 1 & 2," is polished and coruscating enough, but the grasp is narrowing, the ordinary German polemist is coming to the front. These works were written in 1873; in 1874 they were followed by the third *Unz. Betr.*, "Schopenhauer as educator," and in 1876 by the fourth, "Richard Wagner in Bayreuth." In the two latter essays we find again the glow of the enthusiast, that glow without which no work can ever hope for immortality; but to me it seems that already the author "doth protest too much," that he indulges in extravagance of praise, as if to keep his panegyric to the boiling-point by sheer weight of fuel. In fact the essay on "Richard Wagner" was begun in Feb. 1875, laid down in May, resumed in September and set aside in October of that year, with only eight chapters composed; Nietzsche then resolved in May 1876 to publish the unfinished work in time for the Festival at Bayreuth, but at the last moment he added to it three chapters, written in two days of June. In view of subsequent events, it is impossible not to see in this spasmodic hot-and-cold a token of the coming change.

And within six weeks the change had begun, with the jotting down of the first aphorisms for "*Menschliches, Allzumenschliches*" ("Human, All-too-human"), which, when finished in 1878, was dedicated to Voltaire (!), and wherein Nietzsche begins his "breaking of his idols." We are informed by the editor of the fourth edition (1895) of the last-named work that its author went to Bayreuth in the middle of July 1876 to be present at the final rehearsals of the *Ring*, but left towards the end of the month "profoundly estranged by all that surrounded him," though he returned for almost the whole of August. In what this strange "estrangement" may have consisted, it is difficult to guess: it cannot have been caused by the hero-worship inevitably practised by those surrounding Wagner, for Nietzsche must have witnessed the same kind of thing when he assisted at the laying of the foundation-stone in 1872—an event he records in no discouraged tones in his "Richard Wagner in Bayreuth." Can it have been that the practical details of the scene-shifter offended his hypersensitive idealism? Or that, like Elsa, the Ideal was only an ideal to him before its realisation; that Wagner's "tragedy of the artist of the present" had come true once more? A more likely explanation of the change, is that Friedrich Nietzsche would presumably have then been made acquainted with Wagner's immediate intention of writing his *Parsifal*, that work on which the later Nietzsche cannot pour too much scorn. In any case the "estrangement" must have been due, not to Nietzsche's "surroundings at Bayreuth," but to a purely subjective cause; for not only does he one by one cast off his Schopenhauer, his Wagner, Schiller, Plato and the rest, but eventually no hero remains at all for him save Friedrich Nietzsche. The melancholy end I have already mentioned; but from 1876 onward he never wrote a single work of connected thought, for all his voluminous effusions: nothing but aphorisms, glittering, acid, eccentric, sometimes startling and suggestive, but as unnutritious to the reader as a diet of chopped straw or a dinner composed of hors d'œuvres.

In a preface to a volume of translations from Wagner's prose it may appear out of place to have devoted so long a notice to another author, an author of whom the Bayreuth master makes no further mention, though we shall find him combating some of Nietzsche's later tenets in the volume next to appear. But the case of Nietzsche "contra Wagner" has been so sensational, the change of front so striking, that they could not well be passed without some explanation. It would be easy to fill page after page with parallel passages from the earlier and the later Nietzsche which contradict each other flatly; yet when the reader knows that Kant, Schopenhauer, and almost all the great men of the past were repudiated by this automaniac, I fancy it will suffice to relieve him of all anxiety lest Wagner's cause should suffer from the gross attacks of a phenomenal apostate.

One word upon the volumes to succeed the present one.—Volume VI., to be issued during the present year, will contain what may be called the Bayreuth papers, as most of them originally appeared in the *Bayreuther Blätter*, the editor of which journal collected them after Richard Wagner's death to form the tenth volume of the *Gesammelte Schriften*; prominent among them is the splendid essay on "Religion and Art." Volume VII., for 1898, will consist of the writings previous to 1849. Volume VIII., to be published in 1899, will comprise the absolutely posthumous publications, and will complete the series.

WM. ASHTON ELLIS.

January, 1897.

TO THE GERMAN ARMY BEFORE PARIS.

(January 1871.)

Why silent stands the German poet's-grove?
"Hurrah Germania!" has lost its love?
Lulled by the Liedertafel "Wacht am Rhein,"
"Lieb Vaterland" now sleeps without a sign?
    The German guard
stands there in boastful France's heart so vaunted,
    by battle scarr'd
it pours its blood in hottest stream undaunted,
    with silent might,
    in trust of right,
    fulfilling deeds beyond all weening,—
too great for you to even guess their meaning.

The empty word, it knew full well to strut *
when nothing came to stir its ancient rut:
the German's foolish sing-song, so men thought,
would scare away the French or e'er they fought.
    Thou faithful host,
what rule of art have thy new vict'ries broken,
    that now at most
in halls of politics thy name is spoken?
    The lofty psalm
    of triumph's-calm
    is hushed by voices diplomatic
attuned to peevish counsels democratic.

* "Das wusste freilich Rath"—an obvious word-play on the German poet Freiligrath, whose national verses had made him very popular at the beginning of the Franco-German war; the third stanza contains an equally obvious allusion to Worth the costumier.—Tr.

"A truce to victories! Your aims confine!
Appease yourselves with modest Watch on Rhine!
Leave us Paris, the gayest spot on earth,
and rest contented with the fight of Wörth!"—
        But undeterr'd
thou fightest on thy way in silent earnest,
        things ne'er yet heard
to shape to deeds thy manly valour burnest.
        Thine own best lay
        in peace or fray,
        my glorious Folk, thou'lt ever find thee,
tho' many a poet's fame grow faint behind thee.

That song, if I but view thy ev'ry deed,
its sense methinks I cannot help but rede;
'tis somewhat: "Courage glows in e'en the Turk,"
then comes: "Obedience is the Christian's work."—
        The ruler calls:
the weapons of a whole great race attend him,
        the braggart brawls
of threat'ning arrogance o'er there to end him.
        Its muscles strain,
        with might and main
        it falls upon the hect'ring foemen:
our Germany alone breeds men not women.

So, shall a German too bear Cæsar's name,
in Latin land be consecrate the claim:
who staunchly his probation-task hath plied,
to him the meed of valour's acts confide!
        Once from us reft,
of all earth's diadems the crown most royal,
        the crown uncleft
shall sit upon the brow of faith most loyal.
        This the glad psalm
        of Triumph's-calm
        by deeds of German warriors written.
The Kaiser nears: in peace the pact be smitten.

A CAPITULATION.

Eine Kapitulation.

Lustspiel in antiker Manier.

Though written in the winter of 1870-71, "Eine Kapitulation" was not published until its appearance in Vol. ix. of the Gesammelte Schriften, 1873. *The original is partly in prose, partly in verses of irregular length and metre (the so-called "Knittel-vers"). In the translation I have not deemed necessary to give each verse a fresh line of type, or to render the occasional French words and sentences into English.*

Whatever may be thought of the expediency of publishing such a satire upon a neighbouring nation, no unprejudiced person can dispute its entire freedom from spitefulness and ill-feeling; as the author observes, the Germans themselves are here castigated almost as much as the French,—at least in the eyes of anyone who has read "Deutsche Kunst und Deutsche Politik." The parody, though wellnigh as harmless as an Epilogue at the Westminster Latin Play, reminds one very forcibly of the grim humour of Aristophanes, upon whose "Birds," "Frogs" &c., the subsidiary title would suggest its having been founded. With a little skilful management and the "appropriate music à la Offenbach," we can imagine what an uproariously comic effect the skit would produce on the stage.

TRANSLATOR'S NOTE.

PREFACE TO "A CAPITULATION."

N the early days of the beleaguerment of Paris by the German troops, towards the end of 1870, I heard that the wit of German play-wrights was seeking to exploit our enemy's discomfitures by setting them upon the Folk-stage. I could find so little to object to in this, especially when I remembered how the Parisians had burlesqued our prognosticated defeat before the war began, that I even nursed a hope that some clever head would at last succeed in imparting a little originality to the popular treatment of this class of subjects; whereas all previous efforts, even in the lowest sphere of our so-called Folk-theatre, had theretofore proved nothing but bad imitations of the French. In time my lively expectation grew into impatience: in a jovial hour I sketched myself the plan of such a piece as I had wished, and in a few days of relaxation from more serious labours I had worked it out sufficiently to be able to hand it to a young musician, then staying with me, for provision of the needful music. The piece was rejected by the large outlying theatre at Berlin to which we offered it anonymously: an event which relieved my young friend from great anxiety, for he confessed to me that he would have found it impossible to concoct the music à la Offenbach the satire really needed; and that taught us, in turn, that everything requires true genius and a natural gift, both of which we gladly accorded to Herr Offenbach in this department.

If I now issue the text to my friends, it certainly is with no idea of making the Parisians look ridiculous after the event. My subject exhibits the French in no other light than one under whose reflected rays we Germans really present a far more laughable figure; for in all their follies the French have always shewn themselves original, whereas our odious imitation of them falls far below the point of ridicule. If this unpleasant theme, whose constant recurrence has spoilt me many an earnest day, shall have displayed itself for once in the mirth-provoking light of harmless satire, may it not displease the friends to whom I now hand my playful poem (for which we certainly did not succeed in finding the appropriate music) that I should try to wake in them the same brief feeling of detachment that I myself experienced in its composition.

DRAMATIS PERSONÆ.

VICTOR HUGO.

CHORUS OF THE NATIONAL GUARD:

- MOTTU, Commander of Battalion.
- PERRIN, Director of the Opera.
- LEFÈVRE, Diplomat.
- KELLER, DOLLFUSS, Alsatians.
- DIEDENHOFER, from Lorraine.
- VÉFOUR, CHEVET, VACHETTE.

(Chorus-leaders.)

JULES FAVRE, JULES FERRY, JULES SIMON, GAMBETTA, Members of the Government.

NADAR.

FLOURENS, MÉGY, and TURCOS.

RATS OF PARIS.

Paris, late Autumn, 1870.

SCENE.

The proscenium represents the square in front of the Hôtel de Ville in Paris; occupying the anterior half of the stage, in course of the piece it is used in the manner of the antique "Orchestra." At its centre stands an Altar of the Republic with the Jacobin Cap and the "Fasces" upon it, in lieu of the "Thymele"; in front it has an opening, giving it the appearance of a prompter's box turned toward the audience. Antique steps, leading from either side to the elevated hinder stage, represent the balcony of the Paris town-hall; together with the lower storey, they form the only remaining portion of the building. Above there is nothing to be seen but the sky, in which loom forth the spires of Nôtre Dame and the dome of the Pantheon. To right and left the foreground is shut in by the colossal statues of Strassburg and Metz.—Daybreak. From all sides comes the sound of drums beating the reveille.

VICTOR HUGO

(lifts his head out of the opening in the Altar, and works his way up as far as the elbows. He groans and wipes the perspiration from his brow).

Ha! Breathe I thee once more, thou sacred city's air? Paris, o my Paris, thou need'st no more despair! I come, nay, I have come, and here I am at last; full soon will I describe what perils through I've passed!— —

My God!—I'm spouting Alexandrines! How came I by this Classical relapse, I whose each breath exhales the spirit of Romance? Only in my remarkable prose can I do justice to the wonders of my journey. "*Les misérables*"! —Eh, what I there described, have I in person now passed through! Incredible! I alone could do its like. Behold the use of inspiration wed to close research! My careful study of the sacred city's sewers has placed me on the path of rescue for the Civilisation of the world!—

See here the road from outlawry to home, for thy stupendous poet, "*France*"! Dread throes of bliss convulse me still, when I think of that journey through thy bowels, o Paris! I knew the inlet as none other: one magic touch of my wizard hand has lain it open for me: and I am here, not through the Prussian ranks, but underneath them. Prodigious! But one must have genius, self-sacrifice too—my cherished passion, as witness all men!—But what am I babbling? Best save it all for my next romance! "*Dieu*"! What a tale 'twill be: I've matter for 120 volumes, merely from this quite fabulous return to Paris.—Look round thee, Victor. Thy instinct led thee true; this must be the Place de Grève; from below I plainly traced the spot where Esmeralda was hanged. (Àpropos: no one will ever write a thing to equal that,—not even Gutzkow or Laube.) Yet, no digressions! My mission is a holy one, as I myself throughout. (He stretches his head out farther, and looks around.) But where on earth am I? What's that above my head? No gallows! A scaffold though, perhaps a holy guillotine? —Hm! Is that the Place de Grève? — — Well, well!—But I don't quite know myself: surely the Hôtel de Ville had upper storeys?

MUFFLED VOICES FROM BELOW (through speaking-trumpets). Victor! Victor! Join with us!—

HUGO. Ha, what's that? some one calling from the sewers? (He turns his head back and looks down.) Who's below there?—

VOICES. We. One and the other. The genuine guardian spirits of Paris!

HUGO. No?—By God, your voices have a sympathetic twang! But what are your names?

A VOICE. Flourens, you speak!

FLOURENS' VOICE (below). Victor! Victor! I tell you, stick to us! Don't trust the air, 'twill make you dizzy! Stay with us; we're the bowels of Paris, and have something to eat too!—

HUGO. I'm dragged both ways! If only I could cut myself in two!—(A military band, playing a merry march, approaches from the distance.) Hark! Isn't that the Marseillaise?—

FLOURENS' VOICE. What's the matter with you? Leave the boobies!—

HUGO. O sounds of joy! Musical am I not, but I know the Marseillaise at four miles distance! I must, I must ascend!—

VOICES. Come down to us! It's not time yet!—

HUGO. Yes, yes! I'm with you, bowels! Only let me just listen to the inspiriting strains so long denied me.—

CHORUS OF THE NATIONAL GUARD (enters with a lively band of music. During the following chant it marches round the Altar of the Republic):

Republic! Republic! Republic blic blic!
Repubel Repubel Repubel blic blic! etc.
Repubel pubel pubel pupubel pupubel Replic! etc.

MOTTU. *Halte!—Hommage à Strasbourg!*

(The Chorus wheels to the statue of Strassburg.)

HUGO (watching with curiosity). Ah, but there's a noble side to these antique customs!

MOTTU. *Présentez l'arme!—Où est l'Alsacien pour chanter l'hymne?*

KELLER (corporal). Here.

MOTTU. *Avancez! Chantez!*

KELLER (steps forward and sings in Alsatian dialect). "O Strassburg, o Strassburg, thou fairest of all towns" etc.

(Meanwhile the Chorus files before the statue: each member of the Guard draws a bouquet of flowers out of his gun-barrel, and throws it gracefully into the statue's lap.)

MOTTU. *A présent: jurez!*

KELLER. Schuré isn't here.—

MOTTU. *Bête d'Alsacien!—Le jurement!*—

KELLER. Himmel—Kreuz—Dunner—tusig—sakerlot!

HUGO (as before). How Romanticism transfigures Classic tedium!—

MOTTU. *Répètons!*—

CHORUS (with fearful effort and distortion). "Himmel—Kreuz—Dunner—tusig—sakerlot!"—

MOTTU. *Bien ! Serrez vos rangs ! Marchons sur Metz !—*

(The Chorus files before the statue of Metz, and deposits bouquets once more.)

MOTTU. *Où est le Lorrain ?—*

KELLER (shouts down the line). Diedenhofer, forward !

DIEDENHOFER. Here.—

MOTTU. *Thionvillier ! Jurez en Lorrain !—*

DIEDENHOFER. Hagel—Bomben—Schock—Schwere-noth !

HUGO (ducking his head). Oh that *is* strong !—

MOTTU. *Répètons !—*

(The Chorus repeats the oath as before.)

MOTTU. *Citoyens Grenadiers !—Imprimez-vous bien ce que vous venez de jurer, c'est à dire: de défendre ces deux villes jusqu' à la dernière goutte de votre sang, et de ne jamais souffrir qu' une seule pierre en soit prise par l'ennemi barbare.—*

DIEDENHOFER. Mayn't I sing a little song too ?—

MOTTU. *Assez de chants frivoles ! La situation est trop sérieuse.—Dansons autour de l'autel de la république !—*

THE CHORUS (marches once more to the altar of the Republic, and executes a warlike dance around it, breaking out, at a few expressive situations, into the leg-flinging characteristic of the Cancan). "Republic ! Republic ! Republic—blic—blic !" etc.

MOTTU. *Attention !—Maintenant, entrons en conseil de guerre !—*

KELLER (in dialect). Citizens, I propose a plainer mode of speech. We should remember that all Europe is watching us : and, as we still are playing Theatre, we really ought to address ourselves to the Germans in particular, and make them clearly understand what's going on, and especially what ardent Frenchmen we Alsatians are !—

PRIVATE LEFÈVRE. *Pas si bête ! Vraiment,* we're playing to the German public.

PRIVATE DOLLFUSS. *Quant à moi, je ne saurais plus deutsch spreken !—*

DIEDENHOFER. We shall see !—

MOTTU. *Bien*! *Bien*!—for the German public!

HUGO (as before). My heart is bursting! On what immense expansion of the stage shall I stand, if I but break forth and inspire them all!—

CHORUS. Whose voice?—Some one's calling from the drains.—

HUGO (stretching still farther out). Ye know me not?—'Tis I!—Victor—Victor——

VOICES (from below). Stop! Don't get out!—

HUGO. O fate!—

CHORUS. A spy!—

HUGO. Know ye no better this giant head?—This brow?—The Titan?—The Prometheus? He who wrote abysmal romances, while ye were rotting in your shallows?—

VOICES (from below). Madman! Down!—

PERRIN (lieutenant). Ha! That nose!—I know him!—

HUGO (defending himself from those below). Who chid the tyrant? Who unveiled Tropmann? Whilst all ye were dancing, as now before the altar of the Republic, I sat alone upon an islet in the sea, and bared the horrors of the ocean's depth. Whilst ye let the barbarians starve you out, I bravely creep along the sewers, to bring to you the scent of victuals. Ye know me not?—(Turning back.) Oh, do leave hold of my coat-tails!—

VOICES (from below). Down! You are ours!—

PERRIN. Citizens, this is either the Devil or Victor Hugo himself!—

CHORUS (with shouts of joy). Hugo! Hugo!—Come out of the hole!

FLOURENS (below). Pull away! We've got him fast!

HUGO (facing backwards). Relentless demons! Let me but ask one other question.—

VOICES (from below). Look sharp, then!—

HUGO. O friends! I still have important business to transact below. I'll come again, my word upon it, and surely with the most almighty succour.—But tell me, quick, a thing that racks my brain. What changes have been effected here? Why remains there nothing of the town-hall save its balcony?

LEFÈVRE. That the Government mayn't hide from us: whenever we wanted to change it, it persisted in rushing off to the rambling upper storeys; so we've taken them away.

HUGO. But where does it govern?

VOICES (from below). Ha ha ha!—

LEFÈVRE. There on the balcony: and sleeps below it—

HUGO. 'Tis sleeping now? I nowhere see it.—

VOICES (from below). Chatterbox! Now you're coming down!—

LEFÈVRE. We're just about to wake it.—

MOTTU. Up! Reveille!

HUGO. Ah, what a Government!

FLOURENS' VOICE. *We'll* soon wake it! [To Hugo] Time's up! Down, down!—

CHORUS. See how he struggles! They're tearing him down!—Up, up! Hold him tight!

HUGO. God, they're tearing me to pieces!—What a curse is greatness!

(The Chorus pulls Hugo by the head, while he is held by the feet below: his body is stretched out like a piece of elastic.)

CHORUS. We've got him! He's almost out! Up, up! Hold him fast!—

VOICES (from below). We'll not let him go! Down, down!—

(When the Chorus has pulled out Hugo's body to an extravagant length he suddenly snaps to, and is dragged into the depths.)

CHORUS (after a pause of amazement). He's gone! Gone down! We haven't kept him! We pulled at him; we stretched him out; but Victor snapped together. Maybe the Devil's fetched him?—

DIEDENHOFER. 'Twas a low-bred trick on his part!—

MOTTU. *Silence*!—True Atheists shouldn't call such things in question. We soon will have the whole affair in order. For the present, sound the call for the Government! It's unheard of, that the cannonade should be so late in beginning to-day. Strike up the wakener.

CHORUS (with military precision of gesture). Government, Government, where hidest away? The enemy's troops when wilt thou slay? Where dream the three Jules? What's Gambetta about? Must we teach his legs the military trot? *En avant, Picard*! *En avant, Rochefort*! Or we'll send Flourens and Mégy to knock at your door. Are you sitting at ease in the *Rocher de Cancale*, while all Paris is gnawed by the pangs of "*Tantale*"? General Trochu, the *Galérien*, why doesn't he rumble from *Valérien*? Oh, we've plenty of pluck, and we're thirsting for blood, but a mild cannonading, it does us all good! Cannonade, cannonade, for it's getting quite late! *Gouvernement*, keep us no longer at wait! *Gouvernement, bombardement; bombardement, Gouvernement*! *Gouvernement, Gouvernement, Gouvernement—ment—ment*!

(The Government, seated at a round table, rises through a trap on the balcony.—JULES SIMON is writing; JULES FAVRE and JULES FERRY stand up. They embrace passionately, and express by pantomimic signs profound emotion.)

CHORUS (in a jumble of voices). Hurrah for the Government!—The Three Jules!—Two are embracing!—How they love each other!—Most touching!—One can't help weeping.—

JULES FERRY. Citizens. Behold the Republic of Love and mutual esteem!

CHORUS (in and out). Ah, but it's beautiful!—Come, let us weep too!

"Open the sluiceways——"

VOICES (from below, angrily). No, not yet!

CHORUS. "Let tears flow in rivers."—

VOICES (from below). We see!—Ha ha ha!

FERRY. Citizens, forgive us! Above all forgive Jules number one. He is deeply affected.

MOTTU. Citizen Favre is the very man we want to hear.—

KELLER. Far better begin cannonading!—

DOLLFUSS. *Taisez-vous! Schabskopp!*

LEFÈVRE. *Silence!* Let the Government speak!—What news?

JULES FERRY. O citizens, friends, brothers!—Have pity on Jules prémier, by whose side I gladly rank myself second.

JULES SIMON (looking up from his writing). I'm only to be the third, then?

PERRIN. You race of Julians, no dissension!

DOLLFUSS. *Pas de discorde!*

KELLER. Hold your jaw!

DIEDENHOFER. Why 's he always writing?

JULES FERRY. Patience, citizens! He is busy on Public Worship, and that easily makes him irritable. At this instant he has a most important question to settle.

MOTTU. I only hope he is drawing up the decree I spoke of!—Citizens, know that I vote for Atheism!

(JULES SIMON shakes his head and goes on writing.)

MOTTU. I won't have head-shakings. Out with the decree!—Atheism I have already introduced in my battalion; it is positively the most essential means of saving the Republic.

JULES FERRY. Citizens, I must declare myself against it; it is utterly subversive of morals.—What thinks my colleague, the Minister of Worship?—

JULES SIMON. Ferry, why will you always interrupt me in the most important business? Gabble away! I've something else to do.

MOTTU. I'm for revolution. Favre, speak up!

FERRY. But citizens, do you not see the sad state in which the great Jules is. In the famous interview with Bismarck he totally ruined his voice. And then his sobbing, and internal fury at the insolent demands of the barbarian!

CHORUS (in a savage outburst). Insolence! Most insolent of all! Oh, heard we but the cannon's bawl! Cannonade, cannonade, cannonade!—Or read us what Simon has said!

FERRY. Citizens, the Government begs you spare Jules Favre's nerves.—

DIEDENHOFER. I'm quite sorry for him.

MOTTU. No sparing! First of all I want the decree about Atheism. You shall not shuffle out of it, *sacre nom de*—pardon!—

FERRY (to Jules Simon). What thinks the Minister of Worship? Will it do?—

SIMON. Sapristi! Leave me to my writing!—For that matter, the Deity may as well remain. If he wants the crucifixes done away with—for my part, I've no special fancy for them.—

FERRY. Listen! The great Jules sobs.—He has the cramp!—He stamps!—(Aside.) Courage, courage!—(Aloud.) Citizen Mottu, I defy the subversive spirit that prompts you: did not the sainted Robespierre himself decree the existence of the Deity? So we will decree it once again.

CHORUS. Ay, ay! Citizen Mottu, hold your peace!

HUGO'S VOICE (underground). Now I *must* go up!—

VOICES (from below). Don't mix yourself in the row!—

MOTTU. But what is Worship going to tell us?—

CHORUS. Look, he's signing! He folds the paper.—

SIMON (rising, with the document). *Monsieur Perrin*—

PERRIN. Here—

SIMON. Take your orders.

(PERRIN mounts the steps, and receives a document from SIMON.)

CHORUS. See, burgher Perrin is mounting the perron: perron, Perrin, Mirliton—ton—ton! We think him much nicer than Plon—plon—plon!

PERRIN (reads). Hereby resolved by the *Ministre du culte*: the Opera once more to light shall be pulled!—

CHORUS. Bravo, bravo! Bis, bis!

PERRIN. For that you may thank my keen scent politic; and thus will we rescue the Republique!—

MOTTU. Atheism would save it sooner.

PERRIN. But Opera will save it more.

CHORUS. Bravo, bravo! Bis, bis!

FERRY (melodramatically). See!—The greatest Jules is stamping and sobbing!—(He puts his ear to Favre's mouth.) Citizens, Favre protests; he implores you to renounce the Opera; he says it is too frivolous.—Simon, what ever have you done? You might as well subscribe to Atheism!

DOLLFUSS. *C'est ce que je pense!*

SIMON. It won't be so dreadful as all that.

FERRY. Citizens, reflect! The theatres are all turned into hospitals!—

LEFÈVRE. Then you'll be amusing the invalids too.

CHORUS. That'll cure them!—

FERRY. We must economise the gas.—

CHORUS. Then burn oil! "*Des lampions! Des lampions!*"

FERRY (still prompted by Favre). But the frivolous costumes? The décolleté necks?—What will Europe say, if the Republic in her sorest trial presents herself in such a guise?—

LEFÈVRE. It will be enchanted, and save her. A hundred armies will assemble, bundle off the Prussians, and pay due homage to the Republic.

DOLLFUSS. *Pas si mal!*—

PERRIN. Citizens, I have a way out of the difficulty. We will give Robert and Tell in swallow-tail coats and kid-gloves.

SOME OF THE CHORUS. The ladies in swallow-tails too? We've no objection to that.

(FAVRE stamps his foot.)

FERRY. No, no! 'Twould be against the dignity of the sex.

PERRIN. Citizens, hear me! Save the Opera and you save the Republic! Make a sacrifice for this high end, and let the ladies appear in seemly high-necked gowns of black!—

CHORUS (annoyed). Ah, ah! *Fi donc!*—

KELLER. I didn't become a Frenchman for that.

SIMON. Do as you please, but you will never save the

Republic that way; none of the Great Powers will intervene on behalf of an Opera in black, with oil-lamps; at the outside, Switzerland and the Pope.

MOTTU. Proclaim Atheism, and Garibaldi will soon devour the whole canting Prussian army.—

LEFÈVRE. But we might as well make a trial with the black swallowtail-opera!—Rossini, Meyerbeer—after all it's something!

PERRIN. My plan is ready. Only, the Government must help me to my artists. Everyone is away with the army: tenor, barytone, bass, chorus-singers, all are fighting at Strassburg and Metz, in camp, on the ramparts; the cantatrice and ladies of the Ballet have formed a corps of Amazons, and protect Sedan. The Government must give them all leave, and send them to Paris post-haste.—

CHORUS. Quick, quick! They must be sent us!

(FAVRE sobs.)

FERRY. Citizens, how is that possible? We are invested.

CHORUS. We'll make a sortie!—Cannonade, Trochu! Trochu! Why doesn't he cannonade?—

LEFÈVRE. That short-sighted Trochu! To send our best troops away from Paris!—

CHORUS. Betrayed, betrayed!—Out with the artists. We must have Opera, and especially Ballet!—

FERRY (in despair). Who'll travel through the air?—

NADAR (creeping from under the round table). I.

(He is wrapped in a gigantic covering, which afterwards turns out to be a balloon, and which leaves nothing of him visible but his head.—Everyone is terrified: Favre falls into a faint; Perrin tumbles backwards into the orchestra; the Chorus huddles round the Altar.)

HUGO (putting his head out of the prompter's opening). 'Tis time I saved all!—Unhand me! I must!—

VOICES (from below). Don't be rash!—Follow us, and we'll lead you to the right sort of actors!—

(Hugo is drawn down again.)

CHORUS (after a pause of terror). What monster is this?

NADAR (wags his head and rolls his eyes). I am Nadar! The saviour of the Republic! If the Government will only make me a Privy Councillor, I'll travel through the air wherever it wills.—

GAMBETTA (darts up from behind the table, and clears it at one bound). Stop! Here am I!—I dreamed of you last night, Nadar, and I'm your man!—Citizens, come blow him out!—

(He draws an enormous pair of bellows from beneath the table.)

FERRY. Favre is astounded?—Simon chews his pen? ——Gambetta's a devil of a fellow!—

GAMBETTA. Now citizens, up! Put all your strength into the work!—Above all take care that Nadar doesn't begin photographing you!

CHORUS. What are we to do?

GAMBETTA. Help Nadar on to the altar of the Republic.—

(The Chorus passes Nadar down from the balcony, from hand to hand, till he is set upright on the altar. The bellows are adjusted to a capsule; the Chorus is told off into military detachments, to blow the bellows in beat with the music.)

GAMBETTA. Now, blow, blow, citizens stout, till Nadar's sails are quite blown out: the gas to his body is burning its way; but trust me, to him it's mere infant's play!

CHORUS (at work). Air! Air! Thou child of the sky! The breezes of Paris puff Nadar on high! With its light he once drew our physiognomee; in its air he now practises telegraphee.

(The balloon is quite filled out; Nadar's head, which had disappeared from the top, now peeps out at the bottom.)

NADAR. The car! The car!

GAMBETTA (commanding the Chorus). Where do you keep it?

NADAR. You keep the rope taut, lest I float away, and I'll soon make the car! The emblems of the Republic will do capitally. Here!—(He comes half out of the balloon, stretches the Jacobin's cap on the altar to an enormous length, separates the staves of the Fasces, and, with all a conjuror's swiftness, constructs a car which he fastens to the balloon with the straps.) The axe I'll take as anchor, in case of accidents.—

CHORUS. O fund of invention, inventive mind! How neatly your way out of fixes you find. Nadar, Nadar, you Freedom's star!—The Republic he's turned to a gondola: he beats great Blondin of America!—

NADAR. *Allright*!—Get in, Gambetta!—

(GAMBETTA gets in.)

CHORUS. Away you shoot! "*En route*! *En route*!"—

GAMBETTA. Citizens—

NADAR. Not yet! A little higher first!—Slack the rope!—(The balloon rises to mid-height.) That's better!—Never forget that all Europe is looking at us!—(He draws in his head, and vanishes into the balloon.)

CHORUS. Divine! Sublime! We must have that, too, at the Opera in time.—

(PERRIN makes a note of it.)

GAMBETTA (singing). "Freedom's fled from out the world; naught's left but slaves and masters!" (Speaking.) So sang erewhile a poet of the nation whose savage hordes invade us now in service of Tyranny. But: (singing) "They never shall have it, the free German Rhine!" (Speaking.) So answers an inspired singer of Gallia. And for that, o citizens, I am leaving the shackled earth and mounting to the air. Listen to my wind-speech. Citizens, put your trust in gas; through the air comes your rescue. But a little, and I draw near the Rhine, to the amazement of the Prussians and all Europe; lead the garrisons of Strassburg and Metz to brilliant victory; take Tropmann prisoner in Sedan, and—

PERRIN. Fetch the operatic company!—

CHORUS. That's the chief thing!—

GAMBETTA. Lower, Nadar!—They don't quite understand me down there.—

NADAR'S VOICE. On the contrary, they will understand

you much better if we ascend.—(He peeps out.) Let go the rope!

(The Chorus leaves hold of the rope, and the balloon mounts to the flies. Shouts of delight.)

GAMBETTA (screaming). Citizens, farewell!—I am borne on the ship of the Republic!—(To Nadar.) Where's the speaking-tube? (Nadar reaches it out.) Right! (He puts it to his mouth.) I am borne on the ship of the Republic: only as victor shall I return from the ocean of air, only on the ruins of the *ancien Régime* will I tread the earth again!—*Adieu*!—

DIEDENHOFER. What does he say?

LEFÈVRE. He'll not return without the ballet.—

CHORUS. Gambetta, Nadar! Thrice blest be your car! In aërial *équipage* we wish you both *bon voyage*! Sublime *Gouvernement,* speed well, *vole au vent*! *Gouvernement*! *Gouvernement*! *Vol-au-vent*! *Vol-au-vent*!

(Jules Favre and Ferry embrace; Simon writes.—The balloon has hovered to the back of the stage, and entangles itself with the spire of Nôtre Dame.)

GAMBETTA. We're caught!

CHORUS. They're fixed: the sexton's got them by the tail!

NADAR (looks out, and sets to work at the straps). Do go on talking!

GAMBETTA. But what about?—There's nothing to see.—

NADAR (hands him an enormous opera-glass). Look through it, and say what you see! Point it that way; there lies Strassburg. (He motions toward the statue of Strassburg.)

GAMBETTA (looking through the glass, with the speaking-tube at his mouth). Ah! . . .

CHORUS. Ah! . . .

GAMBETTA. Strassburg!—

CHORUS. Strassburg!—

GAMBETTA. All hung with flowers! Grand rejoicings! No Prussian to be seen anywhere! Our army in great glee, merry as in Paris!

CHORUS (enchanted, dances). "O Strassburg, lovely city" etc.

GAMBETTA. The army is singing the *Strasbourgeoise* and dancing. (Favre and Ferry embrace.) The Prefect and the Mayor embrace. (Jules Simon writes.) The Town-Clerk is writing a report of the victory ! (Shouts of joy.) Increasing jubilation!—

PERRIN. Those are my chorus-singers, my actors !—

CHORUS (shouting). Send the actors here! — At last! We shall get the Opera !—

NADAR (has disentangled the balloon). Take care ! (He draws his head in.)

GAMBETTA (reeling). *Gamin* ! I nearly lost my glass and trumpet!—Why do you shove so ?—

NADAR'S VOICE. Quiet ! Don't wrangle, or I'll put you out !—

(The balloon sways a little, and catches on the dome of the Pantheon.)

GAMBETTA. Bump, we're caught again !—

CHORUS. They're hanging in an airy nest: may the gods take care of all the rest !—

NADAR (setting the ropes right). Take a look, and speak up !

CHORUS. He's peeping ! Gambetta, what d' you see now ?

GAMBETTA (as before, his glass directed to the statue of Metz). Ha ! I see Metz !

CHORUS. Ah !—

GAMBETTA. All strewn with bouquets !

PERRIN. Quite the right ballet-costume !

DIEDENHOFER. "O Stadel, mein Metz ! Was bist du nett !"

CHORUS. *En avant* ! *Marchons* !—After Opera, Ballet !

GAMBETTA. Immense rejoicing of the army ! Bazaine dances with the General Staff around the Altar of the Republic.—He recognises us.—

PERRIN. Ha ! My ladies are there !—

GAMBETTA. Not a Prussian to be seen ! All routed !—

(Favre and Ferry embrace.) The Prefect and Mayor embrace; the Town-clerk writes an account of the victory!—(Immense rejoicing among the Chorus.) Greater and greater jubilation!—

PERRIN. Oh, I know my people!

CHORUS (bawling). Through the air, through the air! Send the Ballet here!—

NADAR (having set the balloon free again). Hold tight, Gambetta!—

GAMBETTA. Where are we going?

NADAR. Into the air. (He draws his head in.)

(The balloon floats to and fro for a while; then it passes over the orchestra, above the heads of the Chorus, and as far as possible into the auditorium.)

CHORUS (accompanying its course). You darling Gambetta, of joy the trumpetter! O sailor of ether, were we but together! You see them all dancing, you hear them all singing; o quick through the casemates the charmers be bringing!

GAMBETTA (to Nadar in the balloon). Where are we now?

NADAR'S VOICE. Look for yourself!—

GAMBETTA. I'm getting giddy!—

NADAR'S VOICE. Gid, then!

CHORUS. O gid, Gambetta! Gid still more! Say, the barbarous army is less than before?—

GAMBETTA (after Nadar has directed his opera-glass towards the audience). Ah!—

CHORUS. Ah!—

GAMBETTA. Quite full! A sea of heads. But no enemies!—Nothing but friends.—Everyone congratulating us.—Ha! now I see it all. Our allies!

CHORUS. What? Garibaldi before Paris already?—

GAMBETTA. Garibaldi? Stuff and nonsense! All Europe has intervened, and crowds to acclaim us!—There's Russia, Poland and the Cossacks! — There Spaniards, Portuguese and Jews!

CHORUS. And the Germans?

GAMBETTA. There sitting peaceably among the rest:

they've capitulated, and are charmed to be allowed to go to our theatres once more.—

CHORUS (in a tumult of joy). Cannonade, cannonade! When will they cannonade? *Tonnère-paraplue*!—When cannons Trochu?

(Great applause in the auditorium. Favre and Ferry embrace.)

PERRIN. Ha! I know that sound!—But I haven't got my people yet. How on earth am I to open the opera, how produce the ballet?

CHORUS. Alas, we are covered with shame! All Europe as audience came! We hear the old claquing, but the op'ra is lacking!—Perrin, Perrin! Raise the curtain, now do! Or we'll gallop the Government into a stew!

PERRIN. Citizens, I'm no magician. Ask the Government! *I'm* not in the balloon!—

FERRY. Things are becoming serious!—(Shouting through his hands.) Hei, Gambetta!—Can't you get us the comedians?—

GAMBETTA (turning toward the stage again). I see nothing but comedians.—

CHORUS. But the costume? The stage costume?

GAMBETTA (to Nadar). Nadar, what's your advice?

NADAR (peeps out). Look ahead! Steer us clear of the churches this time! Behind the wings, behind the wings! —(The balloon moves across the stage again).

CHORUS. O now they are off to the very best place; back of the wings, to see to the lace! *Cordon*! *Cordon*! *Cordon, s'il vous plaît*! Costumes, coulisses, and sweet patchoulay!

(Whilst the balloon is floating from side to side of the background, and Gambetta peeps now hither now thither, one hears a louder and louder rumbling and rattling of kettledrums underground.)

SUBTERRANEAN VOICES. Pumperumpum! Pumpum! Ratterah! "*Ça ira*! *Ça ira*! *Ça ira*!—*Aristocrats*!—

Crats! *Crats*! *Courage*! *En avant*! *Rats*! *Rats*!" Rats forward, rats forward! Pumpum ratterah!

MOTTU. *Trahison*! *Aux armes, citoyens*!—*Formez le bataillon*!

CHORUS (forming ranks). *Aux armes*! *Aux armes*!

FLOURENS' VOICE (commanding below). Forward! No hanging back!—The battering-ram to the front!—

(VICTOR HUGO, with two ram's-horns on his head, is pushed up through the prompter's box: he is packed in a rigid suit of plate-armour.)

HUGO. *Malheur*! *Malheur*!—*Trahison*! *Trahison*!

CHORUS (falling back). Victor, what are you doing, *polisson*?

HUGO. "*C'est pour vous sauver, que la France m'a armé*!" In harness of splendour, Civilisation's defender!

FLOURENS' VOICE (from below). Forward! No chattering!—Lay hold!—Ho, hey! Push away!

(Hugo is thrust out several yards at one heave, like a machine. The Chorus, which had drawn closer again, scatters in all directions. Hugo remains flat on the ground. Flourens, Mégy, and a number of Turcos dressed as Jacobins, follow him out of the opening in the altar.)

CHORUS (retreating in horror). The red republic!

FLOURENS. Not red at all! Look at us! We're the black republic.—

CHORUS. Heavens! Black enough! *Sauve qui peut*! Save the Government!

(The Chorus runs to the middle of the stage and climbs the steps to the balcony. FAVRE has fallen into a swoon, FERRY attends to him, SIMON chews his quill.)

CHORUS. Cannonade, cannonade! When *will* they cannonade?

FLOURENS (occupying the Orchestra with his troops). Mégy, come on! Help me place Victor!—(They slip Hugo on to the altar, and set him upright; the Blacks dance round it.) Now Victor, fire away!—

HUGO (motionless). Citizens, betrayed and duped, led by the nose! A windy knave has filled you with air! In armour all plastered, inspired, I am here to unveil your deceivers. Deep in the sewers, hidden we lurked; we followed the drain-pipes straight hence to the Prussians: Strassburg and Metz are in the foe's nets: through the bars, o'er the flats, none have 'scaped save the rats!—

CHORUS (in a fury). What? Rats, rats? Not a word about Opera or Ballet?—Oh that swindler Gambetta! And Nadar's no better.—Cannonade, cannonade! When *are* they going to cannonade?

FLOURENS. That I have seen to. The *Valérien* is true black. Fire away there!

(He waves a black flag toward the back of the stage. Immediately a persistent cannonade begins.)

CHORUS. The cannons, hurrah! What mercies they are!

HUGO. O citizens, pluck; come, trust to your luck!

FLOURENS. Now Mégy! Up with your Blacks! Down with the Government! (He gives the signal with a fife.) Up, from the deep!—

VOICES FROM THE DEEP. *Pip, pip, pip! pschihihi, etc.*

(Gigantic rats swarm out of the prompter's box: they file to right and left with much uproar.)

FLOURENS. On, faithful rats!—Terror attend you!—

(With Mégy as lieutenant, he leads the Blacks' attack on the balcony; the Chorus attempts to retreat on either side to the statues; but the rats rush at them, climb the statues, and frighten off the National Guard to the front of the Orchestra.)

CHORUS (facing the Altar). Victor, Victor, to thee we cry; this pest of vermin, away bid it fly!

(Persistent cannonading outside. The Blacks seize FAVRE, FERRY and SIMON.)

FERRY (through the hollow of his hands). Gambetta, help! Gambetta!

NADAR'S VOICE (from above). A plague on the cannons! I'm hit.—

(The balloon sways to the middle of the stage. Gambetta seizes the cable and swings himself to the dome of the Pantheon, where he remains sitting. The balloon collapses on to the Altar of the Republic, completely covering Hugo.—The rats gnaw up the bouquets on the statues. Chorus in despair.)

FLOURENS. Forward! Go ahead, Mégy! Down with the Government!—

(They fling the three Jules over the steps into the Orchestra, and squeeze them down the opening.)

GAMBETTA (on the Pantheon, through his speaking-trumpet). Citizens, Frenchmen, trust to me! I'm now in Tours, and swear to save you!

FLOURENS. You! Just you come down! Swindler and fool, with your lying opera-glasses!—Up, faithful Blacks! Mount guard, and don't let the three Jules sneak up again.—(Two Blacks place themselves as sentinels before the prompter's box.) What the devil's become of Victor? Nadar must have choked him. No matter!—Up! To the Government table!—(With his followers he takes possession of the balcony.)

CHORUS. O Victor, thine is a fate tragic! Choked on the Altar of the Republic!—Did you notice a smell? It's far from good; Nadar and Victor are mingling their blood!—

FLOURENS (on the balcony). Now proclaim!

MÉGY. Proclaim!

THE BLACKS. Proclaim!

CHORUS. We proclaim—

FLOURENS. Atheism!

MOTTU. Yuc!—

FLOURENS. Communism!

CHORUS (sobbing). Huc!—

FLOURENS. Black Republic!—

GAMBETTA (as before). Rats' republic!

CHORUS. No: cats' republic! Cats, cats! We're eaten up by the terrible rats!—(The rats meanwhile have been galloping about between the statues.) Gambetta! Ah, dearest Gambetta! Have you nothing to help us as yet, ah?—

GAMBETTA (turning his opera-glasses on the rats). Ha!—

CHORUS. Ha !—

GAMBETTA. Ah !—

CHORUS. Ah !—

GAMBETTA. Everything is saved ! All our trials are over !—Take down the shutters, cafés, restaurants ! Business is looking up. Plenty of victuals coming in.—

FLOURENS. Swindler !—The city is starving.

CHORUS. *Fi donc* !

DIEDENHOFER. O if we only had some of those sheep and oxen in Metz !

FLOURENS (pointing to the rats). Take and eat these ! All straight from Metz !—

LEFÈVRE. How would they taste ?

VÉFOUR. Charming with *sauce aux rats* !

CHORUS. Rats with sauces, sauces with rats ! Here, pass them, or hunger will dine off our hats !—

GAMBETTA (as before). Save the future of the country !—Nothing will save the Republic but the *garde mabile.*

FLOURENS. Windbag, hold your tongue !—Neither Mabile nor Mobile. Nothing will save you but horror and hunger !

KELLER. We've got that !—

LEFÈVRE. And the Terror too !

CHORUS. The Terror's to cure us when hunger devours ! Whoever's been playing his tricks with the hours ?—It's midday and past, and no sign of dinner ; for National Watch you may fetch the old sinner ! Véfour, Chevet, Vachette, come along ! Come serve us a rat-soup ; look sharp, ding-a-dong !—(VÉFOUR, CHEVET and VACHETTE make a quick change into cooks.) Where are the butchers ? To work, Turcos ! You're eating the rats without any *sauce* !

(The Blacks set to work catching the rats ; the rats squeak plaintively, and scamper off to the steps, the statues, into the orchestra ; the Chorus chase them back with their bayonets, the Turcos behind them.)

GAMBETTA (as before). Stop !—I see the *bal Mabile.*—Don't eat your partners !

FLOURENS. Blockhead !—Always betraying the nation,

just like Tropmann!—Catch, slay, and eat;—that's the thing, and something 'll come of it!—Up, plant the black standard!—

(Mégy hoists a black flag on the balcony. When the hubbub is at its highest, through the prompter's box a cornet [literally—valve-trumpet] is heard playing a melody by Offenbach. The two black sentries begin to dance.)

CHORUS. Hark! What is that? A parley!

FERRY'S VOICE (below). Forward, Offenbach! Courage, courage!—Up, Simon, help me push him up!

(OFFENBACH, still blowing his cornet, rises half-way.)

CHORUS. Betrayed! *Trahison*! The Prussians have sprung from their ambuscade. To our weapons! *Aux armes.* Shoot away, cannonade!—

(The commotion on the stage calms down little by little; the Turcos' hunt of the rats assumes the character of a quadrille. When the Guards attempt to hustle Offenbach, they are kept back by the two black sentries, coaxing him.)

FLOURENS. What's this? Treason! The Prussians!—Mégy, pack your traps! All's up with us!

GAMBETTA (as before). Save the Republic!—We are all lost!—

FLOURENS. Swindler, you're safe enough up there!—Where's Nadar?—We'll go aloft too.

GAMBETTA. Nadar, no! To me!—

THE THREE JULES (from below). Keep it going! Courage! Play a little louder! You'll soon inflate Nadar.—

(OFFENBACH plays more beautifully still; the balloon swells out; the Chorus hold their noses.)

CHORUS. O heav'nly, divine, o superb! Though the gas is a little acerb.—But Nadar can't resist; to the sky he must twist!—

(The balloon rises gently: in the car sits VICTOR HUGO, transfigured into the Guardian Angel of France.—The three JULES meanwhile have pushed Offenbach right up, still blowing his cornet, and carry him on their shoulders to the Altar of the Republic, where he is deposited with his legs hanging over it.)

FLOURENS. Look at the idiots, those Jules!—They've capitulated; they're positively bringing in the Prussians!—Run, run! (He and his men turn tail, and flee to the balcony.)

FERRY. False alarm!—Nothing's capitulated.—We bring you the most international individual in the world, a man who ensures us the intervention of all Europe. Whoever has him within his walls, is invincible forever and has the wide world for his friend! Know ye him not, the wonder-man, the Orpheus from the underworld, the estimable rat-catcher of Hameln?

CHORUS (all lightly dancing). Krak! Krak! Krakerakrak! This is the Jacko of Offenback! In the fort over there bid the cannonade cease, for we would not a note of the melody miss!—(The cannonading becomes quite *piano*, keeping time with the orchestra in place of the big drum.)—How sweet and agreeable, for the foot so malleable! Krak! Krak! Krakerakrak! O glorious Jack of Offenback!

(The three JULES have resumed possession of the Government table. HUGO soars over the orchestra, in the balloon.)

OFFENBACH (as Master of the Ceremonies). *Changez*!

(The rats turn into Ladies of the Ballet, in the lightest of opera-costumes. PERRIN inspects them carefully, and takes notes. Everyone is in raptures.)

CHORUS. O pleasantest of miracles, o quintessence of spectacles! No high-necked spite; and hosed so light! No more need we fear indigestion, and hunger is out of the question: little suppers so *spirituel* beat your dinners all *matériel*! Ballet, ballet, ballet we've got; and as for the foe, why, let him go rot!

FERRY. Saviour of State! Great rat-converter, come sound your melody a little perter! Orpheus from the shades has sped, the brand-new Republic with Art to wed!

GAMBETTA (as before). And nobody thinks of me, who saw it all beforehand?—

FERRY (pointing with emphasis to Gambetta). Be good, fellow-citizens! And for your reward, like Gambetta to the Pantheon you all will have soared!

FAVRE (in a sudden burst of inspiration). Ha! No longer

can I resist the spell. My voice is returning. Let me speak!—

CHORUS (passionately). Better dance, better dance!

FAVRE. Citizens, hear my voice!—

CHORUS. Sing, then, sing!

FAVRE. Speak, speak I will!—Citizens, courage, virtue and abstinence are the first of republican duties!—(He continues speaking, without anyone heeding him.)

CHORUS (one half). Sing, and above all dance!—

LEFÈVRE. Who'll lead off?

CHORUS (the other half). Offenbach, Offenbach!

(OFFENBACH excuses himself in pantomimic signs, and takes up his cornet again.)

CHORUS. We want our ballet and little *soupers*, and pithy republican spiced *couplets*!

HUGO (hovering above them in the balloon, as Guardian Angel). Ye call for the singer who hasn't a peer; whose fame strikes the clouds, as is perfectly clear.—I'll sing you the true *histoire* of the holy nation's *victoire*, of success on the Rhine and Loire, of eternally dazzling *gloire*; I'll sing it in splendid romances, in metres quite new and new stanzas: and Paris shall trip it in dances!—

(Everyone takes places for a quadrille; the Chorus of the National Guard pairs off with the Ladies of the Ballet, the Turcos turn all manner of grotesque somersaults etc.—Until the fall of the curtain JULES FAVRE continues his impassioned harangue, though one seldom hears more than a word or two, such as: "Eternal disgrace!—No! No!—Not one stone!—The demands of the barbarians!" and so on, but for the most part only sees his pathetic gesticulations.—JULES FERRY perseveres in his efforts to calm him; SIMON takes down Hugo's verses. GAMBETTA watches the proceedings through his opera-glass, and joins in the refrain of the chorus through his speaking-trumpet—but always a little behind with the bar.—OFFENBACH beats time for the orchestra, partly conducting with his cornet, partly playing the chief passages himself in shrill variations.)

CHORUS. *Dansons*! *Chantons*! *Mirliton, ton, ton*! *C'est le génie de la France qui veut qu'on chante et qu'on danse*!

HUGO (recitativo, accompanying himself on a golden lyre). "All things historical are but a—*trait*—: the purely poetical I make a—*fait*." (Arioso) As genuine *Génie de la France* I never lose my *contenance*: *victoire* and *gloire* I preserve evermore. *Civilisation, pommade, savon*; that is my dearest, my chief *passion. Chantez, dansez, allez aux soupers*! *Je veux qu'en France on s'amuse*, and from no one I take an *excuse*.— — —

OFFENBACH (giving the word of command). *Chaîne des Dames*!

CHORUS (dancing). *Dansons*! *Chantons*! *Aimons*! *Soupons*! *C'est le génie de la France qui veut qu'on chante et qu'on danse*!

HUGO. The barbarians came swarming across the Rhine—*Miriton, miriton, tontaine*!—But we've locked them away in Metz so fine—at least it was done by Marshal Bazaine! *Miriton, plon, plon*! In the fight near *Sedon* they were felled by the terrible *Mac Mahon*! And their total *armée*, General *Troché,—Troché—Trochu, Laladrons, Ledru*!—he tucked it all safe in the forts of Paris.—In the year of *mille huit cent soixante-dix* there happened all this! As genuine *Génie de la France* &c.

OFFENBACH. *Chassé croissé*!—

CHORUS. *Dansons*! *Chantons*! etc.

HUGO. Then upped we and marched them across the Rhine—*Miriton, miriton, tontaine*!—and made all their Germany yours and mine, *à la tête Mahon* and *Bazaine*, —*Schnetteretin, tin, tin*!—*Mayence* and *Berlin*, from the Danube and Spree right up to the *Rhin*. General *Monsieur* on Wilhelmshöh',—Tropfrau, Tropmann! *Tratratan, tantan*! Over three-hundred thousand man!—In the year of *mille huit cent soixante dix* etc.

OFFENBACH. *En avant deux*!—

CHORUS. *Dansons*! *Chantons*! etc.

HUGO. But *la France*, the magnanimous, she ne'er nurses animus. Now you've taken your beating, please accept our entreating: as foes you can't seize our *Paris*, but we'll give it you free as *amis*. Why knock at our forts? We open our *portes*; whatever you wished, it's all ready-dished. *Cafés, restaurants, dîners* for *gourmands*; *Garde mobile* and *bal Mabile*; *mystères de Paris* and *poudre de riz*; *chignons* and pomades, theatre, promenades; *Cirque, Hippodrôme, la colonne de Vendôme*; *concert populaire*,—what could be more fair?—And thou, *peuple de penseurs*, why turn out such *malheurs*? Be ye tumid, dégoutant, here we'll make you élégant. Your "Faust" who would find appetising, had Gounod not seen to its sizing? Don Carlos and William Tell, we've tanned both their leathers right well. What could you e'er make of Mignon, till we'd taught her to sing *Mirliton*? How you stuttered with Shakespeare and stammered, but 'twas we who first polished his Hamlet! Yet traces you've had of *génie*,—oh, we've noticed it aye in *Paris*,—so our Orpheus, fresh from below, to your stupified gaze we will show.

OFFENBACH. *Chaîne anglaise*!

HUGO. Then come quick and get yourselves *frisés, parfumés, civilisés*! The great *nation* will lend you its tone, and its terms are so foolishly easy! Send your soldiers away, while the diplomats stay! *Dîners, soupers*! We receive *Attachés*.

OFFENBACH. *Gallop*!

HUGO. As genuine *Génie de la France* &c.

CHORUS. *Dansons*! *Chantons*! &c.

(During the final dance Attachés from the various European and non-European embassies creep out of the opening in the altar; then follow the Intendants of the larger German Court-theatres, who dance with the Ladies of the Ballet in ungainly fashion, twitted by the Chorus.

REFRAIN AND BALLET.

At the close Victor Hugo illuminates himself with Bengal fire.)

REMINISCENCES OF AUBER

Erinnerungen an Auber.

The following monograph made its first appearance in the Musikalisches Wochenblatt, *November, 1871; Auber had died in Paris, during the reign of the Commune, on May 13th of the same year.*

TRANSLATOR'S NOTE.

T has been noted as characteristic of the fate of this most interesting opera-composer that his uncommonly tenacious hold on life, which at the age of eighty-nine had just borne him over his country's defeat and the hardships of the Siege of Paris, should finally have broken down beneath the horrors of the Commune. In fact he narrowly escaped the peculiar distinction of an atheistic burial, proposed to his executors by the Paris Municipal Council; from that his body was happily saved, and committed to earth with all the rites of holy Church. Herr A. Dumas then delivered a funeral oration of tender rhetorical pathos in honour of the deceased; wherein Auber, however, according to my judgment, was upheld to his nation in a very false light. And just this speech—which represented Auber as a bright angel of harmony, melting away in melodic tears at the fate of his country—has once more shewn me how little the Frenchman has succeeded in finding the phrase to characterise the most purely French of all his composers; arrived at Auber's *grave*, he deemed the occasion fully met by an empty flourish, if only its sentiment were pitched high enough.

Against this I recalled the singularly depreciatory opinion of Auber which I had encountered in the Parisian musical world of 1840. When reviewing a new opera of Halévy's, for the "Gazette musicale," I had occasion to rank French operatic music above the Italian: with entire sincerity I deplored the emasculation of taste at the Grand Opéra, where Donizetti with his slipshod sickly mannerism was at that time gaining more and more the upper hand and crowding into the background, as I tried to prove, the excellent beginnings of an individual, specifically French style in Grand Opera. I adduced the "Stumme von Portici" [*Muette de Portici*, otherwise *Masaniello*] and asked how the acclimatised operas of Italian composers, of Rossini himself, compared with that work in point of dramatic style, or even of musical invention? Well, the sentence in which I answered this question in favour of French music was suppressed by the editor; Herr Ed. Monnaie, at that time also General Inspector of all the Royal theatres in France, replied to my expostulation by saying that he could not possibly let pass a sentence in which Rossini was criticised for the benefit of Auber. It was in vain to point out to the man that I hadn't the smallest intention of criticising Rossini and his music, but simply his relation to French Grand Opera and its style; moreover, that I must appeal to his patriotic heart, which surely would feel pleased to see a German energetically upholding the merit and significance of his countryman Auber. For answer I was told that, if I wanted to enter the field of politics, there were plenty of political journals at my disposal for pitting Auber against Rossini: in a *musical* paper such a thing could not possibly be permitted. I took my rebuke, and Auber never heard into what a conflict I had been drawn for his sake.

Auber's panegyrist, to be sure, expressed himself far more patriotically than the General Inspector of Theatres and musical editor, of thirty years ago; but alas! *only* patriotically, for he remained just as far from any knowledge of the character of Auber's muse on the one side, as E. Monnaie on the other. To the Frenchman it seems impossible to orate on music without dragging in all manner of exquisite allusions to the "Swan of Pesaro," or other modern mythological wildfowl of the kind.

We Germans appear to have much better understood at once the distinctive quality of this French music, as may be seen from a comparison of our reception of the "Stumme von Portici" with that of "Tell." Whoever witnessed the first appearance of the former opera upon the German stage, must remember the quite astonishing impression it created; whilst "Tell" could never really make its way, and owes its maintenance rather to the Italianising propensities of our singers than to any lively pleasure of our public in the work itself. The "Stumme," on the contrary, took us all by surprise, as something entirely novel: an operatic subject of this vitality there had never been; the first real drama in five Acts, with all the attributes of a serious play; and furnished, to boot, with a tragical dénouement! This last circumstance in itself, as I remember, made quite a sensation. Until then the plot of an opera had always ended "well," perforce: no composer would have dared to send people home with a tragedy for their last impression. When *Spontini* was rehearsing his "Vestale" with us at Dresden he was beside himself at the idea of our letting the opera terminate, as everywhere in Germany, with the scene of Julia at the sepulchre, notwithstanding her rescue from death: he insisted on the transformation-scene, displaying the Grove of Roses with the Temple of Venus, while priests and priestesses of Amor conduct the happy couple to the altar: "*Chantez*! *Dansez*!" He would hear of nothing else. And nothing else had ever happened in an opera: the function of Art itself being "to make men gay" ("*erheitern*"), this was quite peculiarly the office of Opera. When once the General Director of the Dresden Court-theatre expressed his dissatisfaction with the mournful ending of my "Tannhäuser" he referred me to K. M. v. Weber, as having understood the thing much better and always given his operas a "satisfactory ending."—

But this "Stumme" was a grand surprise from every point of view: each of the five Acts presented a drastic picture of the most extraordinary animation, where arias and duets in the wonted Operatic sense were scarcely to be detected any more, and certainly, with the exception of a single prima-donna aria in the first Act, did not strike one at all as such; in each instance it was the ensemble of the whole Act that riveted attention and carried one away. We well may ask: How did Auber come by such an opera-text? Neither before nor since did *Scribe* turn out anything like it, albeit its immense success encouraged him to the attempt. How strained and laboured seem his texts for Meyerbeer, compared with this, how flat and ineffective the very next one for Rossini, that "Tell" itself! What auspicious influence was at work, it is difficult to make clear to oneself: in any case it must have been something quite out of the common, something wellnigh dæmonic. Certain it is, that this Auber was the only man who could have written the music for it, the right, the only music, such as Rossini with his ponderous old-fashioned Italian quadrature, which drives us to despair in his "*Opera seria*" (Semiramide, Mosé, etc.), was quite incapable of producing. For the novelty in this music to the "Stumme" was just its unaccustomed concision and drastic compactness of Form: the recitatives shot lightning at us; a veritable tempest whirled us on to the chorus-ensembles; amid the chaos of wrath we had a sudden energetic cry to keep our heads cool, or a fresh command to action; then again the shouts of riot, of murderous frenzy, and between them the affecting plaint of anguish, or a whole people lisping out its prayer. Even as the subject lacked nothing of either the utmost terror or the utmost tenderness, so Auber made his music reproduce each contrast, every blend, in contours and colours of so drastic, so vivid a distinctness as we cannot remember to have ever seen before; we might almost fancy we had actual music-paintings before us, and the idea of the Picturesque in music might easily have found substantiation here, had it not to yield to a far more apposite denomination, of the most admirable theatric Plastique.

The impression of this Whole quite revolutionised our notions at the time. We lately had known French Opera in none but the products of the "*Opéra comique.*" *Boieldieu* had just delighted and enlivened us by his "Dame blanche" ("*Weisse Dame*"); Auber himself had entertained us most agreeably with his "Maçon" ("*Maurer und Schlosser*"): the Parisian "Grand Opera" was forwarding us nothing but the stilted pathos of Spontini's "Vestale" and "Ferdinand Cortez"; taken all in all, to us it seemed more Italian than French—as indeed Rossini's "Siege of Corinth," which had recently been sent us by the selfsame institute, appeared to say that this serious lyric stage of France was always to belong to the foreigner, be his name Gluck or Piccini, or in later days Spontini or Rossini. Here reigned mere starch and chill; not a note of it thrust home to the Folk; and beside Spontini's operatic pomp the native German Opera might work its way unhindered from its scant beginnings to the height it reached in *Weber's* glorious music. Only one attempt was made to tread the realm of that "Grand Opera" itself, and that one failed; in his "Euryanthe" Weber discarded spoken dialogue, imported the Recitative, banished the popular type of song, and filled up the 'pathetic' ensemble in every direction. But the public stayed untouched, and this noble music of Weber's drew no closer to its heart than, let us say, the Spontinian Opera itself: the secret curse of stiffness and tedium lay upon the genre. *Marschner* prudently resisted the ambition of treading in his master's footsteps; fortune attended his reaching back to the more popular "romantic" opera, so-called, compounded of musical pieces and spoken scenes: the "Vampire" and "Templar" gained a solid footing on our boards.

But a sudden change of front took place, with the coming of the "Stumme." Here was a "Grand" opera, a complete five-act tragedy clad from head to foot in music: yet without a trace of stiffness, hollow pathos, high-priestly ceremony and all the classical farrago; warm to burning, entertaining to enchantment. The German musician h'med and hawed. What on earth was he to make of this music? Spectacle, noise and street-fights!—But there was many a tender touch in the thing? And it all sounded so remarkably well, unlike anything one had heard from an orchestra in the theatre before?—After all, however, it had to be dubbed Rossinian music; for whatever smacked of a tempting melody we took and thrust into Rossini's shoes. Rossini, no doubt, was the father of modern operatic melody; but what gave this music of Auber's "Stumme" so peculiar a stamp of drastic concision, Rossini himself could neither discover nor copy. As for our own composers, the bare thought of copying such music would have horrified them. Yet German Opera had positively been given its quietus: that was the other point to be considered. Marschner, above all, fell into progressive confusion: not another of his operas would hit the mark till he took it into his head at last to privily attempt a regular stretta "*à l'Italiana*," as I witnessed at the time in an opera of his, "Adolph von Nassau," otherwise meant to be root-German. For, though we finally had made vain attempts to copy this plaguing "Stumme," we had veered to the opposite pole of our invalided opera-system, to an observation of the newer Italian Opera of Donizetti & Co.; since these more pliant gentlemen had laid lighter hands on the Auberian prescription, and were particularly expert at giving the strettas of their finales quite captivating graces. But it wasn't of the slightest use: despite "Sicilian Vespers" and other nights of carnage, the German remained unequal to copying the new "Furia."

To copy the "Stumme von Portici," however, stayed forbidden to *everybody*, Italian or French, ay, even to its author. And that's the most notable thing about it, stamping this "Stumme" as a strictly isolated moment, not only in the history of French opera-music, but also in that of Auber's own career.

If we seek to explain the uniqueness of this work, or in other words its inimitability, we shall find it to be a case of a certain *excess*, possible only to the French spirit, and even to that but once.

Auber's score undoubtedly presents many excellences and telling innovations, which have since become the property of all composers, and particularly of the French: to these innovations belong above all his brilliant instrumentation, the striking colour, the sureness and audacity of his orchestral effects, among which we may instance his treatment of the strings (considered so daring in those days), and especially of the violins, to which en masse he allots the most venturesome of passages. If we class with these eventful innovations the master's drastic grouping of his chorus-ensemble, which almost for the first time he makes a real, a seriously interesting factor in the plot, in respect of the inner structure of his music we have still to mention certain quite remarkable idiosyncrasies in its harmonisation and even in the handling of the voices (*Stimmführung*), which have been retained and carried further by himself and followers as a valuable addition to the means of appropriate dramatic characterisation. In a like sense may be named the constant and subtle attention paid by the master to the progress of the play, in which he loses sight of nothing that can serve him for his orchestral preludes and postludes, thus turning into a fascinating series of suggestive musical pictures what before had consisted of mere banal commonplaces. But the extraordinary warmth, nay, wellnigh fire, that Auber poured for this once through his music, remained a peculiarity of this one work, and never could he come by it again: 'tis as though he here were standing at the zenith of his powers, of his whole nature. Only, seeing that he never gave a sign of it again, this warmth quite obviously could not have had its source in his own artistic nature. Though Auber never found a second subject so inflammable as the subject of this "Stumme," it remains more than astonishing that the fire should have died out so completely in the *artist* also, and never betrayed an even slumbering presence.

The other day a musical comic-paper retailed a conversation of the aged master's in which he said that Music had been to him a mistress down to his five-and-thirtieth year, but afterwards his wife; by which he meant to imply that a chill had since come over his relations with his art. As Auber was already considerably past the alleged period of his youthful love when he wrote the "Stumme" [1828—consequently in his forty-sixth year], it would be very characteristic if he so far underrated the pre-eminent value of this work that he deemed necessary to assign the time of its composition to the period of his cooling down. Should this last assumption prove correct, Auber's verdict upon himself would singularly harmonise with that depreciatory opinion held by his countrymen of which I made the astonishing experience adduced above. As a matter of fact, as time rolled on I have become more and more convinced that the regard which the so uncommonly prolific composer reaped in Paris in the long run is attributable solely to his works for the *Opéra comique*; whereas his trip into Grand Opera was accounted nothing but a trespassing on ground not his by right, a trespass to be pardoned in consideration of his other merits. Like all his opera-composing fellow-countrymen, indeed, Auber felt nowhere at home save on that unassuming lyric stage, the only one thoroughly congenial to Parisian taste; and there must we seek him if we wish to see him in his native element. And here, too, is shewn why this French master stayed inimitable by us Germans, nay, without any lasting influence over us even where he bore us irresistibly away.

From my own experience I may state that Auber's immediately-following operas, awaited with exceptional keenness, made a markedly disappointing impression on us in Germany. There were very pretty things in the "Braut" [*La fiancée*]; but we seemed to know them all beforehand; we were wanting big emotions. Then "Fra Diavolo" horrified us with its grotesqueness. It was succeeded by many another, among them "grand" operas again, displaying much theatrico-musical skill, manifest wit, pronounced fun: but all leaving us cold, indifferent. On the other hand we thought we found much of what had moved us in the "Stumme" cultivated almost to a higher pitch in Herold's "Zampa," which made us devote to this strange pseudo-romantic musical farce an attention bordering on the serious. Well, again it happened that the Parisians gave its author very little credit for his "Zampa," and confined their liking to his "Pré aux clercs"; a work without a tinge of romanticism, a work that wearied us to exasperation, but which was brought to its "thousandth" representation, in honour of the revival of the arts, within the last few days in half-burnt Paris. Why we not only could never warm to this genre—to which Auber also ended by limiting himself—but could do nothing with it as a model of applomb, nay, speaking strictly, of correctness in its style, was to become quite clear to me when I discovered in Parisian life itself that very element which had repelled us so instinctively in its idiosyncrasies of melody and rhythm. The singularly uniform build of all this comic-opera music, particularly when the sprightly orchestra has to animate and keep the stage-ensemble together, had long reminded us of the structure of the square dance: if we attended one of our full-dress balls where the real quintessence of an Auberian opera was played as a quadrille, we suddenly found the meaning of these curious motives and their alternation so soon as we heard each movement called aloud by its proper name: "*Pantalon*," "*En avant deux*," "*Ronde*," "*Chaîne anglaise*" and so forth. But the Quadrille itself was a weariness to us, and for that reason this whole comic-opera music wearied us also; one asked oneself how the lively French could ever find amusement in it? But there was just the rub: we did not understand these Parisian operas, because we knew not how to dance the *contredanse*; and how the latter is done, again, we never learn in Paris itself till we see the "people" dancing. Then, however, our eyes are opened: of a sudden we comprehend everything, and in particular the reason why we could have nothing to do with the Comic Opera of Paris.*

I have no memory of this "cancan"-dance being taken as material for a thorough explanation of the French, or better perhaps, the Gallico-romanic character of the inhabitants of Paris. Yet the chief feature of that character, it seems to me, might thus be given a plastic and convincing demonstration, especially if we compared it with the relation between the national dances and the characters

* Nevertheless Herr *Flotow* managed it at last, though not before the music of this Comic Opera had sunk to the uttermost triviality,—which, in its turn, throws a curious light on the *goût* of our art-adoring cavaliers.—R. WAGNER.

of other peoples; in which connection it would not be difficult to obtain a speaking likeness of the Spaniard from his "fandango," the Neapolitan from his "tarentella," the Pole from his "mazurka," and even the German from his "waltz." With regard to the Parisian "cancan" I do not feel qualified to engage in such a demonstration, and would suggest it to Herr K. Gutzkow, for example, as an entertaining task *; moreover the preliminary studies have latterly been much facilitated, as one now may make them from the parterre of our German Court-theatres, upon whose boards this dance is reproduced in great perfection.

To return to the French master of our theme, I now must advance a seemingly most hazardous assertion: namely that Auber was enabled to write a "Stumme von Portici" through his seizing by its roots that remarkable product of our civilisation, the *Parisian*, and raising it thence to its highest possible glory; just as the Revolution swung the cancan-dancing *gamin* on to the barricades, there, draped in the tricolor, to brave the murderous bullet.

I have just said that Auber's qualification proceeded from his thrusting down to the roots of the genuine folk-spirit, here accessible to him in the dance and dance-tunes of his people: no other French composer could truly boast, as he, of being a man of the people; and here lies withal the trait that so vividly distinguishes him from all his predecessors. While the fine arts, including Literature and Music, were imposed upon the French nation from above, just like a costume; while the Theatre was committed to the care of a hard-and-fast Convention, and theatrical music in consequence was placed under control of a punctilious Elegance, the French nature appeared to us in a totally different light from that in which we have learnt to know it since these Revolutions, which have laid bare to us the roots of the Paris people's life. Not until Auber—departing likewise

* As this province does not encroach on the Antique, or even on the Renaissance, he possibly might find his way without the help of Professor Lübke.—R. WAGNER.

from his standpoint of old French culture, now universally deposed—first lit upon these roots, did musical creativeness awaken in him. His talent, indeed, originally appeared particularly feeble: only very late in life did he venture forth as a composer, and suffered a succession of defeats with his earliest operas; in every respect they appeared insignificant. To us it would almost seem that this filled that period of his life in which, according to his humorous saying, he was suing music as a mistress. May this have cost him many a plunge into his inner soul, now at last he opened wide his shrewd and searching eyes; he saw his Paris people all around, and listened to the strains to which they danced. Now came to him the music he could undertake to make the whole world dance to: perhaps, after the excitement of a lover's futile wooings, it may have occurred to him as a mild dissipation (*ein kühles Vergnügen*), to which, with an ironical rub of his hands, he treated himself and "wife."

In what this "mild dissipation" consisted we must endeavour to make a little clearer to ourselves, however sorrowful the task, by explaining the character of the curious class of operatic music whose inventor Auber was. In this respect it has not been sufficiently remarked as yet, how strongly Auber's music differed from that of Boieldieu. The latter, adorning itself in the "Dame blanche" with a dainty touch of romanticism, reveals its character the plainest in "Jean de Paris." Here the Frenchman is still "gallant," and the laws of *gallantry* afford him withal the laws of both the graceful and the decorous, even for that most pleasurable art as which he always considers Music. If Art, in the commonest as in the loftiest sense, may be regarded as a *play*, then the Frenchman both in life and art took his laws of gallantry into his playing with chivalric love, that love with the point-of-honour on which the gaming gallant stakes his life. Gallant music found in the chansons of the "troubadour," as in the tunes of French court-dances, a rhythmic-melodic element most suitable for cultivation, and no one knew better how to make the most of it than its last professor, Boieldieu. But when the custom of gallantry faded out of French life and became a fretful spectre with a prudish halo of hypocrisy, there established itself a brand-new law to which everything, and Art above all, had henceforth to submit. This law is: *Amusement.* Now reigned the "bourgeois," who, after his plaguing worries of the day, meant to "amuse" himself in the evening; the joys of Gallantry, even when specially arranged to suit him, merely bored him; the wellspring had to be sought for, not above, but underneath him. And there it flowed, the spring which erst "the Gods had graciously kept veiled in night and mystery" and the Parisians had arched over with élégance and esprit. Even this "cancan" possesses an artistic element: even *it* is a playing at love, but only with the most material, the grossest of love's acts. I remember having seen a fairly intelligent writer in Paris fall quite into a temper at the Frenchman's treating his materialistic national dance with so much prudery, whilst our Grand Opera-ballets set the dances of all other nations before us with the greatest fidelity. Unfortunately he omitted to notice that even in the most impassioned Spanish dance the wooing of love alone is symbolised, whereas in the Parisian cancan the immediate act of procreation is symbolically consummated. How any artistic element can enter into the thing, seems difficult to comprehend; yet it lies in the fact that the incidents of this dance, as well, are after all mere play: after the most loathsome kicks and bounds with which the Parisian celebrates the symbolic sacrifice to Venus, he steps back from the dance, conducts his partner to her seat with wellnigh old-French gallantry, and refreshes her with orgeat [barley-water], just as though it were the most respectable of balls. Thus even this dance was to be come at—artistically, and Auber's muse has carried out the experiment with astonishing ability.

Now, if Auber characterised the lengthy period of this carrying-out as the period of his life and work in which he came into a cooler relation with his once beloved, Music, we need have no difficulty in understanding that remark as well: for the beloved obviously rejected him when he wooed her by the laws of gallantry, but now that he had cut the story short by wedding her according to the Parisian laws of "*mariage de raison*," she simply was bound to obey him. And in what consists the obedience of the Parisian wife, one also learns from modern customs of the world's-metropolis. With his "*amour*" the Frenchman can never dispense; but he satisfies its needs in manner of the cancan. It is a favourite and ever varied subject of French pieces, how a decent but neglected wife gets a lost maiden of the people to teach her her allurements, and in particular the cancan, and how she proceeds to reproduce them to the life for her husband's benefit, whereupon he feels irresistibly drawn to his own wife. If we may take it, then, that Auber entered somewhat this relation with his formerly beloved and now wedded Music, we may style the curious offspring of this marriage a kind of formally-legitimate bastards. They are almost metaphysical creations, and one scarcely marks in them at all the nature of their mother, Music. Strange as this sounds, we can hardly count as music proper that tardy progeny which confronts us in the great majority of Auber's operas. In fact, Auber did not reckon himself in the ranks of Music at all. With the stupidity only credible in the case of a French Government, he was made Director of the Conservatoire: there he sat in the box of honour while a Beethovenian symphony was played in the hall below, and turned to his guest with smiling puzzlement: "Can you make anything of it? *Je n'y comprends mot*!"—I find that capital. Much in the same way did Rossini treat his Parisian worshippers when they greeted him as high-priest of music. Here comes to light a greatness of the man's whole nature, a candour rarer everyday and owned by those alone who feel sure and whole in what they do, even though it belong not to a lofty sphere, and therefore can quietly waive aside the best-intentioned misconceptions.

This wholeness and straightforwardness was Auber's in a

high degree. Nothing moved him to 'pathos'; he pointed to the ouvrier in the blouse: *voilà mon publique.*" In the year 1860 I often met him at the Café Tortoni, over an ice: he would always look in about midnight after one of the Grand Opéra's three-hundredth or four-hundredth performances, which he regularly attended in his box—generally asleep, as I was told. Ever inclined to be friendly and sociable, he asked after the progress of my "Tannhäuser" affairs, then making some noise in Paris: his special point of interest was to hear whether there would be anything to see in it. When I related to him a little of the subject of my opera, he cheerily rubbed his hands: "*ah, il y aura du spectacle*; *ça aura du succès, soyez tranquille*!" Of his latest work, *la Circassienne*, an uncommonly childish piece of patchwork scarcely credible as coming from its grey-haired author, he would not let me speak: "*ah, laissons les farces en paix*!" On the contrary he rubbed his hands with utmost glee, his eyes sparkled in his wizened face, when I told him of the zeal with which, as Musikdirektor at Magdeburg, I had once performed his opera "Lestocq." In truth I had taken quite exceptional pains with this opera, really charming of its kind: as I made it my object to give due effect in it to everything that might recall the spirit of the "Stumme," I had levied a large body of military singers for the Russian battalion which is called upon the scene to support a revolution, and thus increased it to respectable proportions, terrifying the Director of our theatre, but arriving at a quite immense effect. With us the opera had a great success too, and, I believe, deservedly: that among the feebler and feebler platitudes and grotesques of Adam & Co. it did not maintain its footing in Germany, to me was not astonishing; but that in Paris it could not hold its ground against the "*Pré aux clercs*" and other hoarded treasures of the kind, I understood less easily, and bewailed the fact to Auber. Roguishly he smiled again: "*que voulez-vous? C'est le genre*!"—His ultimate opinion of my "Tannhäuser" I never heard, but should imagine he "didn't understand a word of it"!—

Even to-day, when I recall the physiognomy of this wonderful old man who could outstrip the youngest in many a thing, as I have been assured, I can only ask myself again and again: How was it possible that he wrote the "Muette de Portici"? Upon no side of his nature did he exhibit a sign of actual *force*, still less of fire; rather a certain toughness and wellnigh terrifying power of endurance, aided and protected by a blandly cynical frigidity. This frigidity was in any case the main feature of the mass of his eternally uniform opera-music, making it lose at last all influence upon us Germans: but it is a main feature of all French theatric art, from Racine to Scribe, ay, and I believe of all French products in every other department of the arts. With the genius of Art, which ever refuses to bless him with a full exchange of love, the Frenchman seems obliged to "arrange" himself, much as Auber had to arrange himself with Music. The relationship stays cold, and whence it may derive a show of warmth we believe we have pointed out in the source of the Frenchman's passion for the Auberian muse: a latent lewdness, in the elegance of whose disguise consists the singular art of deceiving all the world about the basis of obscenity. Hence the surprising, the almost classical polish (*fast stylistisch erscheinende Glätte*), through whose glamour none but the sympathetic Parisian initiate can pierce to the substratum that alone has interest for him in the long run. Shamelessly to bring this latter to the glare of day, was reserved for Auber's followers: he must have thought his whole artistic toil in vain, when he saw Jacques Offenbach disporting himself on the filth so gracefully concealed before. "*Fi donc*!" he well might say; till the German Court-theatres came and snapped the morsel for themselves. Oh! there's warmth enough in it now; the warmth of the dungheap: on it might wallow all the swine in Europe. But the marvellously chill old man, who now had held out for nine-and-eighty years, shut fast his eyes; in his last death-struggle there may have risen before them his "Muette de Portici," which now seemed coming to performance in the streets of Paris, with naked réalism but the strangest variations.

However, we still have to explain to ourselves how this singular artist, according to our judgment of him, won that inspiration without which no work like the "Stumme" could possibly have been composed. I fancy we may seek this phenomenon's explanation in that "*Fi donc*!" which we had good reason for attributing to the master above. The peculiar spirit of Parisian Culture has woken in the Frenchman a certain touchy sense of honour, which feels wounded to the quick when brusquely reminded of what it keeps so cleverly concealed; one has frequently found it difficult for a Frenchman to remember of his own accord a promise given: but he turns furious when we remind him of it; the most amiable will then let trifles end in bloodshed. Thus the Frenchman is ready enough to mock at his own vices and foibles, but he loses his senses if others tell him of them. Now, the political catastrophes of France, each of them consummated by the spirit of the Paris populace, have repeatedly shewn us that this spirit cannot bear, and furiously rebels against, a Government that takes a pessimistic view of the nation's acknowledged evil qualities and publicly gives token of its scorn. Then, as comes out plainest in the July Revolution of 1830, it has not been merely or mainly the rabble, but the delicately cultured who have flung themselves upon the barricades at the head of an otherwise torpid bourgeoisie; here, less in a warlike than a positively murderous frenzy the wealthy banker, the witty littérateur, the artist, and the actor from the Grand Opéra as well, have rubbed shoulders with the genuine cancan-dancer of the people: personal bravery was the motto, and just as the gallant cavalier once staked his life upon his questioned honour, so here a whole populace shewed itself aflame to dispute its Government's right to chide it.

The Paris July-Revolution aroused precisely the same

sympathetic stir in other nations as the "Stumme von Portici" had already caused at the theatres; precisely the same terror was spread by both among the adherents of the various Legitimates. This opera, whose very representations had brought émeutes about, was recognised as the obvious theatrical precursor of the July Revolution, and seldom has an artistic product stood in closer connection with a world-event.

I have called the "Stumme" an *excess* of its author's; the July Revolution was very soon regarded as an excess of the Paris folk-spirit by French politicians, nay, taken strictly, by the whole populace itself. When I arrived in Paris at the end of the 'thirties, the July Revolution had been dropped from people's thoughts, nay, it annoyed them to be reminded of it: the "Stumme" was given now and again as stopgap, but in so slovenly a fashion that I was strongly advised to stay away from it. If I wanted Auber to amuse me, so I was told, I must go and hear the "*Domino noir*" or the "*Diamants de la couronne.*" In this and similar undervaluations of their so pre-eminently national opera-composer there seemed expressed a national self-disgust which had seized French taste and driven it to the sexless operatic muse of Italy, as if to drown all consciousness of self in the shapeless surfeit of an opium-eater's dream.—In the February Revolution Auber had no hand; in advanced old age, however, he greeted the Emperor Louis Napoleon with a "*premier jour de bonheur*" [an opera produced in 1868], and returned the sovereign's smiling compliment, presumably with his good-humouredly ironic washing of the hands, by calling that night his "second day of happiness."

With us Germans things went otherwise: the "Stumme von Portici" alone retained an actual hold on life. In it we recognised the modern French spirit under its most attractive aspect; to rightly estimate this work, and lay to heart its many lessons, might prove the best apology for our more serious judgment having allowed itself to be suborned and led astray, to its own great detriment, about the substance and meaning of those Parisian revolutions. One lesson to be derived from an unprejudiced inspection of that work of Auber's might haply guide us to certain weighty conclusions, still very remote from our art-criticism of nowadays, concerning the true factors of a dramatico-musical artwork. Here we should have to return once more to the question whose answer we have hitherto confined to mere general, socio-psychological grounds, namely: how came it that this so feeble talent, regarded purely as musician, succeeded in writing a score of such undeniable merit, viewed even from the purely musical side? That the author's Phantasy was kindled here to fever-heat, as never before or after, does not fully explain the excellence of his musical conception; and that explanation will seem robbed of all its force, if we ask ourselves how Auber would have managed with a Symphony, for instance, or a Mass?—Starting from this one point, it seems to me, the conclusions to which I now allude might easily lead to the most unexpected amendment of our wonted views of one central fact (*Kernpunkt*) in both musical endowment and musical conception; that is to say, so soon as ever we extended our inquiry to all the French composers, with Méhul and Cherubini, ay, and pre-eminently to Gluck, and then figured to ourselves what we should know of the music of these masters if the Dramatic Muse had not inspired them. If we try to imagine the music of Mozart himself with his dramatic masterpieces cut away, and if we reflect that a composer so steeped in music as Weber would barely exist for us without his operas, among musicians of the highest rank there remain only Bach and Beethoven to illustrate a genesis of music without immediate fertilisation by the drama. That a profound and searching inquiry into this very parthenogenesis (*Aus-sich-wachsen*) of music conducts us once more to the drama, and to the great, the veritable Drama, I have submitted elsewhere at sufficient length; here let its mention merely serve to mark a boundary-line between the creations of the German and the French spirit,—a line which, however fundamental it must seem, has been much oftener overstepped already than may appear to many a know-all.

Certain it is, that we Germans have nothing to be ashamed of in the great impression made by Auber's masterpiece upon us; rather may we pity the French, on whom the like impression was most transient. And so I believe I wasn't wrong when, thirty years ago, I took up arms for Auber against the Paris art-critics. The idea cannot have been far from my mind, that upon the path laid open by this "Stumme" the French Grand Opéra might have advanced to a truly national goal, whereas I now have had to seek the reasons why my wish for the prospering of that institute could not be consummated. In any such inquiry, alas! we reach the fact that every nation has some radically evil trait: a survey of the doings of our present German Theatre brings us to the mournful knowledge of this plaguespot in our national character; the discovery of a kindred plaguespot in the French affords us the additional sad interest of teaching us, to our despair, that even from over there, whence everything of influence comes to us, no ray of hope is left for us.

For to-day let this be our sorrowful farewell to Auber and his "Stumme," as to which I reserve a more exhaustive judgment for a future opportunity.—

Beethoven.

(1870.)

Originally published by E. W. Fritzsch, Leipzig, in the autumn of 1870, the essay on Beethoven reached a second edition before the end of the same year.

TRANSLATOR'S NOTE.

PREFACE.

S the author of the accompanying work felt a longing to contribute his quota to the celebration of the hundredth birthday of our great BEETHOVEN,* and as no other opportunity worthy of that event was offered him, he has chosen a literary exposition of his thoughts, such as they are, on the import of Beethoven's music. The form of treatment came to him through the fiction that he had been called to deliver a speech at an ideal feast in honour of the great musician; as that speech, however, was not to be delivered in reality, he might give it the advantage of a greater compass than would have been permissible in the case of an address to an actual audience. Hereby it became possible for him to conduct the reader through a more searching inquiry into the nature of Music, and thus to submit to the consideration of men of serious culture a contribution to the Philosophy of Music; as which the following treatise may be regarded on the one hand, whilst the fiction that it is being read to a German audience upon a given day of this so uncommonly significant year, on the other, made natural a warm allusion to the stirring events of the time. The author having been enabled both to draft and execute

* Born December 17, 1770.—TR.

his work under the immediate stimulus of these events, may it also enjoy the advantage of bringing the German heart, in its present state of higher tension, into closer touch with the depths of the German Spirit than could ever be effected in the national life of everyday.

IFFICULT as it must always appear to the thinker, to satisfactorily define the true relation of a great artist to his nation, that difficulty is enormously increased when the subject is neither a poet nor a modeller (*Bildner*), but a musician.

In judging the poet and plastic artist it certainly has ever been kept in eye that their mode of grasping the world's occurrences or forms is governed in the first place by the particularity of the nation to which they belong. If the tongue in which he writes has a prominent share in determining the thoughts the poet utters, no less strikingly does the nature of his Folk and country betray itself in the plastic artist's forms and colours. But neither through language, nor through any form wherein his country or his people greets the eye, does the musician reveal his origin. It therefore has been generally assumed that Tone-speech belongs to the whole human race alike, that Melody is an absolute tongue, in power whereof the musician speaks to every heart. Upon closer examination, to be sure, we recognise that it is very possible to talk of a German, as distinguished from an Italian music; and for this difference one may even assign a national physiologic ground, to wit the Italian's great advantage in point of voice, giving just as definite a direction to the development of his music as the German's lack in this regard has driven him to his special province of the art of tone. Yet as this difference does not touch the essence of Tone-speech at all, but every melody, be it of German or Italian origin, is equally intelligible, that 'moment' may surely be neglected as a mere external, and cannot be conceived as exerting an influence to be compared with that of his native tongue in the case of the poet, or the physiognomic aspect of his country in that of the plastic artist: for even in the latter cases we may regard those outward differences as favours granted or withheld by Nature, without our allowing them any bearing upon the artist's spiritual organism.

The idiosyncrasy that marks the musician as belonging to his nation must in any case be seated deeper than that whereby we recognise Goethe and Schiller as Germans, Rubens and Rembrandt as Netherlanders, even though we must take it that both have sprung, at bottom, from the selfsame cause. To follow up that cause, might be every whit as attractive as to explore the depths of Music's nature. On the other hand it may prove easier to obtain a glimpse of what has hitherto eluded the grasp of Dialectics, if we set ourselves the more definite task of inquiring into the connexion of the great musician, whose hundredth anniversary we are now about to celebrate, with the German nation which has lately undergone such earnest trials of its worth.

Were we first to examine this connexion from the outer side, it might be none too easy to avoid deception by appearances. If it proves so difficult to account for a poet that we have been treated by a famous German literary-historian * to the most idiotic statements as to the evolution of Shakespeare's genius, we need not be surprised to find still greater aberrations when a musician like *Beethoven* is taken for subject in a similar strain. Into Goethe's and Schiller's evolution it has been granted us to look with greater sureness, for they have left us certain definite data in their conscious communications: but even these reveal the course of nothing but their æsthetic culture, which more accompanied than led their artistic work; as to the latter's material basis (*realen Unterlagen*), and in particular the choice of their poetic 'stuffs,' we merely learn in fact that accident surprisingly preponderated over purpose; an actual tendence in step with the march of outer world- or national history is the very last thing we discover there. Even as to the part played by purely personal life-impressions in the choice and moulding of these poets' stuffs we

* Gervinus.—TR.

can only argue with the greatest caution, lest it escape us that any such influence never shewed itself directly, but so indirectly that its operation on their true poetic fashioning is quite beyond all positive proof. One only thing we know for certain from our researches in this quarter, that an evolution observable in this wise could pertain to none but German poets, to the great poets of that noble period of German rebirth.

But what conclusion is there to draw from the surviving letters of *Beethoven* and our uncommonly scanty store of information anent the outer, to say nothing of the inner life of our great musician, as to their relation with his tone-creations and the evolutionary course displayed therein? If we possessed the most microscopic data of all conscious incidents in this connection, they could yield us nothing more definite than is contained in the story of the master having originally sketched the "*Sinfonia eroica*" in homage to young General Bonaparte and written his name on the title-page, but afterwards crossed out that name when he heard of Bonaparte's having made himself Emperor. Never has any of our poets defined the tendence of one of his most important works with such precision: and what do we gain for our judgment of one of the most wondrous of all tone-works from this distinct enunciation? Can we make it explain a single bar of that score? Must it not appear sheer madness, even to seriously engage in the attempt?

I believe that the most positive fact we shall ever ascertain about Beethoven the man, in the very best event, will stand in the same relation to Beethoven the musician as General Bonaparte to the "*Sinfonia eroica.*" Viewed from this side of consciousness, the great musician must always remain a complete enigma to us. At all to solve this enigma, we undoubtedly must strike an altogether different path from that on which it is possible, up to a certain point at least, to follow the creative work of Goethe and Schiller: and that point itself becomes a vanishing one exactly at the spot where creation passes from a conscious to an unconscious act, i.e. where the poet no longer chooses the æsthetic Form, but it is imposed upon him by his inner vision (*Anschauung*) of the Idea itself. Precisely in this beholding of the Idea, however, resides the fundamental difference between poet and musician; and to arrive at a little clearness on this point we first must proceed to a deeper examination of the problem touched on.—

The said diversity comes out quite plainly in the plastic artist, when compared with the musician; betwixt them stands the poet, inclining toward the plastic artist in his conscious fashioning (*Gestalten*), approaching the musician on the mystic ground of his unconsciousness. With *Goethe* the conscious leaning toward plastic art was so strong that at a momentous epoch of his life he actually deemed himself intended for its practice, and, in a certain sense, his whole life through he preferred to regard his poetic labours as a kind of effort to make up for a missed career as painter: on the side of consciousness he was a thorough student of the visual world.* Schiller, on the contrary, was far more strongly attracted to an exploration of the subsoil of inner consciousness that lies entirely aloof from vision (*Anschauung*), to that "thing in itself" of the Kantian philosophy, whose study so engrossed him in the main period of his higher evolution. The point of lasting contact of these two great minds lay precisely where the poet, journeying from either extreme, alights on his self-consciousness. They met, too, in their presage of the *essence of Music*; only, with Schiller it was accompanied by a deeper insight than with Goethe, who, in keeping with his whole tendence, regarded more the pleasing, plastic symmetry of art-music, that element which gives the art of Tone an analogy with Architecture. Schiller took a deeper grasp of the problem, giving it as his opinion—to which he obtained the assent of Goethe—that the Epos leans toward Plastic art, the Drama, on the contrary, toward Music. And quite in harmony with our foregoing

* "Er war mit seinem Bewusstsein ein durchaus der anschaulichen Welt zugewendeter schöne Geist."

judgment of both these poets, Schiller was actually the happier in drama proper, whilst Goethe shewed an unmistakable preference for the epic style of treatment.

But it was *Schopenhauer* who first defined the position of Music among the fine arts with philosophic clearness, ascribing to it a totally different nature from that of either plastic or poetic art. He starts from wonder at Music's speaking a language immediately intelligible by everyone, since it needs no whit of intermediation through abstract concepts (*Begriffe*); which completely distinguishes it from Poetry, in the first place, whose sole material consists of concepts, employed by it to visualise the *Idea*.* For according to this philosopher's so luminous definition it is the Ideas of the world and of its essential phenomena, in the sense of Plato, that constitute the 'object' of the fine arts; whereas, however, the Poet interprets these Ideas to the visual consciousness (*dem anschauenden Bewusstsein*) through an employment of strictly rationalistic concepts in a manner quite peculiar to his art, Schopenhauer believes he must recognise *in Music itself an Idea of the world*, since he who could entirely translate it into abstract concepts would have found withal a philosophy to explain the world itself.

* "Zur Veranschaulichung der *Idee*." The word "*Anschauung*"—derived from "*Schauen*," "to look"—presents the English translator with one of his greatest difficulties, as I once before have pointed out: from its original meaning, "the act of looking at," it has passed to the metaphorical "view" and even to "intuition," which latter word, in ordinary parlance, expresses the very reverse of a physical inspection; in this essay, however, Wagner adopts the Schopenhauerian meaning of the term, i.e. a simple outward operation of the senses, without any analysis or synthesis by the reasoning faculty on the one hand, and without any disturbance of the emotions on the other. The present participle "*anschauend*" and the adjective "*anschaulich*" may be rendered, for lack of a better term, as "visual," since vision is the principal sense by which we take cognisance of the outer world: an old proverb tells us that "seeing is believing," while the opposite mode of knowledge, that by which we take cognisance of the inner world, is suggested in the words of the most esoteric of the Evangelists, "blessed are they that have not seen, and yet have believed." As Wagner in *Opera and Drama* has used the expression "the *eye* of hearing," it is easy to understand the difference between what he here calls "art-music," the music of mere sound-patterns, and that veritable music which passes through "the *ear* of hearing" to the seat of the emotions. —Tr.

Though Schopenhauer propounds this theory of Music as a paradox, since it cannot strictly be set forth in logical terms, he also furnishes us with the only serviceable material for a further demonstration of the justice of his profound hypothesis; a demonstration which he himself did not pursue more closely, perhaps for simple reason that as layman he was not conversant enough with music, and moreover was unable to base his knowledge thereof sufficiently definitely on an understanding of the very musician whose works have first laid open to the world that deepest mystery of Music; for *Beethoven*, of all others, is not to be judged exhaustively until that pregnant paradox of Schopenhauer's has been solved and made right clear to philosophic apprehension.—

In making use of this material supplied us by the philosopher I fancy I shall do best to begin with a remark in which Schopenhauer declines to accept the Idea derived from a knowledge of "relations" as the essence of the Thing-in-itself, but regards it merely as expressing the objective character of things, and therefore as still concerned with their phenomenal appearance. "And we should not understand this character itself"—so Schopenhauer goes on to say—"were not the inner essence of things confessed to us elsewise, dimly at least and in our Feeling. For that essence cannot be gathered from the Ideas, nor understood through any mere *objective* knowledge; wherefore it would ever remain a mystery, had we not access to it from quite another side. Only inasmuch as every observer [lit. knower, or perceiver—*Erkenner*] is an Individual withal, and thereby part of Nature, stands there open to him in his own self-consciousness the adit to Nature's innermost; and there forthwith, and most immediately, it makes itself known to him as *Will*." *

If we couple with this what Schopenhauer postulates as the condition for entry of an Idea into our consciousness, namely "a temporary preponderance of intellect over will, or to put it physiologically, a strong excitation of the

* "*Die Welt als Wille und Vorstellung*" II. 415.—R. W.

sensory faculty of the brain (*der anschauenden Gehirnthätigkeit*) without the smallest excitation of the passions or desires," we have only further to pay close heed to the elucidation which directly follows it, namely that our consciousness has two sides: in part it is a consciousness of *one's own self*, which is the will; in part a consciousness of *other things*, and chiefly then a *visual* knowledge of the outer world, the apprehension of objects. "The more the one side of the aggregate consciousness comes to the front, the more does the other retreat." *

After well weighing these extracts from Schopenhauer's principal work it must be obvious to us that musical conception, as it has nothing in common with the seizure of an Idea (for the latter is absolutely bound to physical perception of the world), can have its origin nowhere but upon that side of consciousness which Schopenhauer defines as facing inwards. Though this side may temporarily retire completely, to make way for entry of the purely apprehending 'subject' on its function (i.e. the seizure of Ideas), on the other hand it transpires that only from this inward-facing side of consciousness can the intellect derive its ability to seize the Character of things. If this consciousness, however, is the consciousness of one's own self, i.e. of the Will, we must take it that its repression is indispensable indeed for purity of the outward-facing consciousness, but that the nature of the Thing-in-itself—inconceivable by that physical [or "visual"] mode of knowledge—would only be revealed to this inward-facing consciousness when it had attained the faculty of seeing within as clearly as that other side of consciousness is able in its seizure of Ideas to see without.

For a further pursuit of this path Schopenhauer has also given us the best of guides, through his profound hypothesis † concerning the physiologic phenomenon of Clair-

* Ibid. 418.—R. Wagner.—In the edition of 1879 the corresponding pages are 417 and 419-20.—Tr.

† In the original we have the words "durch seine hiermit verbundene tiefsinnige Hypothese" &c.,—literally "through his profound hypothesis linked herewith," or perhaps "allied hereto." This "dream" hypothesis

voyance, and the Dream-theory he has based thereon. For as in that phenomenon the inward-facing consciousness attains the actual power of sight where our waking daylight consciousness feels nothing but a vague impression of the midnight background of our will's emotions, so from out this night *Tone* bursts upon the world of waking, a direct utterance of the Will. As dreams must have brought to everyone's experience, beside the world envisaged by the functions of the waking brain there dwells a second, distinct as is itself, no less a world displayed to vision; since this second world can in no case be an object lying outside us, it therefore must be brought to our cognisance by an *inward* function of the brain; and this form of the brain's perception Schopenhauer here calls the Dream-organ. Now a no less positive experience is this: besides the world that presents itself to sight, in waking as in dreams, we are conscious of the existence of a second world, perceptible only through the ear, manifesting itself through sound; literally a *sound-world* beside the *light-world*, a world of which we may say that it bears the same relation to the visible world as dreaming to waking: for it is quite as plain to us as is the other, though we must recognise it as being entirely different. As the world of dreams can only come to vision through a special operation of the brain, so Music enters our consciousness through a kindred operation; only, the latter differs exactly as much from the operation consequent on *sight*, as that Dream-organ from the function of the waking brain under the stimulus of outer impressions.

As the Dream-organ cannot be roused into action by outer impressions, against which the brain is now fast

does not appear in the "*Welt als W. u. V.*," however, but in a lengthy essay on "Ghost-seeing" in Vol. I. of the "*Parerga und Paralipomena*," written after the publication of the larger work; so that the "connection" must be regarded in a purely subjective light, that is to say, as Wagner's own discovery. In fact our author, partly by re-arranging the "material supplied [elsewhere] by the philosopher," partly by his independent observations, has carried Schopenhauer's Theory of Music infinitely farther than its originator could ever have dreamt.—Tr.

locked, this must take place through happenings in the inner organism that our waking consciousness merely feels as vague sensations. But it is this inner life through which we are directly allied with the whole of Nature, and thus are brought into a relation with the Essence of things that eludes the forms of outer knowledge, Time and Space; whereby Schopenhauer so convincingly explains the genesis of prophetic or telepathic (*das Fernste wahrnehmbar machenden*), fatidical dreams, ay, in rare and extreme cases the occurrence of somnambulistic clairvoyance. From the most terrifying of such dreams we wake with a *scream*, the immediate expression of the anguished will, which thus makes definite entrance into the Sound-world first of all, to manifest itself without. Now if we take the Scream in all the diminutions of its vehemence, down to the gentler cry of longing, as the root-element of every human message to the ear; and if we cannot but find in it the most immediate utterance of the will, through which the latter turns the swiftest and the surest toward Without, then we have less cause to wonder at its immediate intelligibility than at an *art* arising from this element: for it is evident, upon the other hand, that neither artistic beholding nor artistic fashioning can result from aught but a diversion of the consciousness from the agitations of the will.

To explain this wonder, let us first recall our philosopher's profound remark adduced above, that we should never understand even the Ideas that by their very nature are only seizable through will-freed, i.e. objective contemplation, had we not another approach to the Essence-of-things which lies beneath them, namely our direct consciousness of our own self. By this consciousness alone are we enabled to understand withal the inner nature of things outside us, inasmuch as we recognise in them the selfsame basic essence that our self-consciousness declares to be our very own. Our each illusion hereanent had sprung from the mere *sight* of a world around us, a world that in the show of daylight we took for something quite apart from us*: first through (intellectual) perception of the Ideas, and thus upon a circuitous path, do we reach an initial stage of undeception, in which we no longer see things parcelled off in time and space, but apprehend their generic character; and this character speaks out the plainest to us from the works of Plastic art, whose true province it therefore is to take the illusive surface (*Schein*) of the light-shewn world and, in virtue of a most ingenious playing with that semblance, lay bare the Idea concealed beneath. In daily life the mere sight of an object leaves us cold and unconcerned, and only when we become aware of that object's bearings on our will, does it call forth an emotion; in harmony wherewith it very properly ranks as the first æsthetic principle of Plastic art, that its imagings shall entirely avoid such references to our individual will, and prepare for our sight that calm which alone makes possible a pure Beholding of the object according to its own character. Yet the effector of this æsthetic, will-freed contemplation, into which we momentarily plunge, here remains nothing but the *show* of things. And it is this principle of tranquillisation by sheer pleasure in the semblance, that has been extended from Plastic art to all the arts, and made a postulate for every manner of æsthetic pleasing. Whence, too, has come our term for *beauty* (*Schönheit*); the root of which word in our German language is plainly connected with Show (*Schein*) as object, with Seeing (*Schauen*) as subject.—

But that consciousness which alone enabled us to grasp the Idea transmitted by the Show we looked on, must feel compelled at last to cry with Faust: "A spectacle superb! But still, alas! a spectacle. Where seize I thee, o Nature infinite?"

This cry is answered in the most positive manner by *Music*. Here the world outside us speaks to us in terms intelligible beyond compare, since its sounding message to our ear is of the selfsame nature as the cry sent forth to it

* Cf. "In lichten Tages Schein, wie war Isolde mein?" and in fact the whole love-scene in *Tristan und Isolde*, act ii.—Tr.

from the depths of our own inner heart. The Object of the tone perceived is brought into immediate rapport with the Subject of the tone emitted: without any reasoning go-between we understand the cry for help, the wail, the shout of joy, and straightway answer it in its own tongue. If the scream, the moan, the murmured happiness in our own mouth is the most direct utterance of the will's emotion, so when brought us by our ear we understand it past denial as utterance of the same emotion; no illusion is possible here, as in the daylight Show, to make us deem the essence of the world outside us not wholly identical with our own; and thus that gulf which seems to sight is closed forthwith.

Now if we see an art arise from this immediate consciousness of the oneness of our inner essence with that of the outer world, our most obvious inference is that this art must be subject to æsthetic laws quite distinct from those of every other. All Æsthetes hitherto have rebelled against the notion of deducing a veritable art from what appears to them a purely pathologic element, and have consequently refused to Music any recognition until its products shew themselves in a light as cold as that peculiar to the fashionings of plastic art. Yet that its very rudiment (*ihr blosses Element*) is felt, not seen, by our deepest consciousness as a world's Idea, we have learnt to recognise forthwith through Schopenhauer's eventful aid, and we understand that Idea as a direct revelation of the oneness of the Will; starting with the oneness of all human being, our consciousness is thereby shewn beyond dispute our unity with Nature, whom equally we recognise through Sound.*

Difficult as is the task of eliciting Music's nature as an art, we believe we may best accomplish it by considering the inspired musician's modus operandi. In many respects this must radically differ from that of other artists. As to the latter we have had to acknowledge that it must be preceded by a will-freed, pure beholding of the object, an act

* Cf. Vol. II.—*Opera and Drama*—page 219.—Tr.

of like nature with the effect to be produced by the artwork itself in the mind of the spectator. Such an object, however, to be raised to an Idea by means of pure Beholding, does not present itself to the musician at all; for his music is itself a world's-Idea, an Idea in which the world immediately displays its essence, whereas in those other arts this essence has to pass through the medium of the understanding (*das Erkenntniss*) before it can *become* displayed. We can but take it that the *individual will*, silenced in the plastic artist through pure beholding, awakes in the musician as the *universal Will*, and—above and beyond all power of vision—now recognises itself as such in full self-consciousness. Hence the great difference in the mental state of the concipient musician and the designing artist; hence the radically diverse effects of music and of painting: here profoundest stilling, there utmost excitation of the will. In other words we here have the will in the Individual as such, the will imprisoned by the fancy (*Wahn*) of its difference from the essence of things outside, and unable to lift itself above its barriers save in the purely disinterested beholding of objects; whilst there, in the musician's case, the will feels *one* forthwith, above all bounds of individuality: for Hearing has opened it the gate through which the world thrusts home to it, it to the world. This prodigious breaking-down the floodgates of Appearance must necessarily call forth in the inspired musician a state of ecstasy wherewith no other can compare: in it the will perceives itself the almighty Will of all things: it has not mutely to yield place to contemplation, but proclaims itself aloud as conscious World-Idea. One state surpasses his, and one alone,—the Saint's, and chiefly through its permanence and imperturbability; whereas the clairvoyant ecstasy of the musician has to alternate with a perpetually recurrent state of individual consciousness, which we must account the more distressful the higher has his inspiration carried him above all bounds of individuality. And this suffering again, allotted him as penalty for the state of inspiration in which he so unutterably entrances us, might make us hold the musician in higher reverence than other artists, ay, wellnigh give him claim to rank as holy. For his art, in truth, compares with the communion of all the other arts as *Religion* with the *Church.*

We have seen that in the other arts the Will is longing to become pure Knowledge (*gänzlich Erkenntniss zu werden verlangt*), but that this is possible only in so far as it stays stock-still in its deepest inner chamber: 'tis as if it were awaiting tidings of redemption from there outside; content they it not, it sets itself in that state of clairvoyance; and here, beyond the bounds of time and space, it knows itself the world's both One and All. What it here has seen, no tongue can impart*: as the dream of deepest sleep can only be conveyed to the waking consciousness through translation into the language of a second, an allegoric dream which immediately precedes our wakening, so for the direct vision of its self the Will creates a second organ of transmission,—an organ whose one side faces toward that inner vision, whilst the other thrusts into the reappearing outer world with the sole direct and sympathetic message, that of Tone. The Will cries out; and in the countercry it knows itself once more: thus cry and countercry become for it a comforting, at last an entrancing play with its own self.

Sleepless one night in Venice, I stepped upon the balcony of my window overlooking the Grand Canal: like a deep dream the fairy city of lagoons lay stretched in shade before me. From out the breathless silence rose the strident cry of a gondolier just woken on his barque; again and again his voice went forth into the night, till from remotest distance its fellow-cry came answering down the midnight length of the Canal: I recognised the drear melodic phrase to which the well-known lines of Tasso were also wedded in his day, but which in itself is certainly as old as Venice's canals and people. After many a solemn pause the ringing dialogue took quicker life, and seemed

* Cf. *Tristan und Isolde*, act iii.: "Die Sonne sah ich nicht, nicht sah ich Land noch Leute: doch was ich sah, das kann ich dir nicht sagen."—Tr.

at last to melt in unison; till finally the sounds from far and near died softly back to new-won slumber. Whate'er could sun-steeped, colour-swarming Venice of the daylight tell me of itself, that that sounding dream of night had not brought infinitely deeper, closer, to my consciousness?—Another time I wandered through the lofty solitude of an upland vale in Uri. In broad daylight from a hanging pasture-land came shouting the shrill jodel of a cowherd, sent forth across the broadening valley; from the other side anon there answered it, athwart the monstrous silence, a like exultant herd-call: the echo of the towering mountain walls here mingled in; the brooding valley leapt into the merry lists of sound.—So wakes the child from the night of the mother-womb, and answer it the mother's crooning kisses; so understands the yearning youth the woodbird's mate-call, so speaks to the musing man the moan of beasts, the whistling wind, the howling hurricane, till over him there comes that dreamlike state in which the ear reveals to him the inmost essence of all his eye had held suspended in the cheat of scattered show, and tells him that his inmost being is one therewith, that only in *this* wise can the Essence of things without be learnt in truth.

The dreamlike nature of the state into which we thus are plunged through sympathetic hearing—and wherein there dawns on us that other world, that world from whence the musician speaks to us—we recognise at once from an experience at the door of every man: namely that our eyesight is paralysed to such a degree by the effect of music upon us, that with eyes wide open we no longer intensively see. We experience this in every concert-room while listening to any tone-piece that really touches us, where the most hideous and distracting things are passing before our eye, things that assuredly would quite divert us from the music, and even move us to laughter, if we actively saw them; I mean, besides the highly trivial aspect of the audience itself, the mechanical movements of the band, the whole peculiar working apparatus of an orchestral production. That this spectacle —which preoccupies the man untouched by the music—at last ceases to disturb the spellbound listener, plainly shews us that we no longer are really conscious of it, but, for all our open eyes, have fallen into a state essentially akin to that of hypnotic clairvoyance. And in truth it is in this state alone that we immediately belong to the musician's world. From out that world, which nothing else can picture, the musician casts the meshwork of his tones to net us, so to speak; or, with his wonder-drops of sound he dews our brain as if by magic, and robs it of the power of seeing aught save our own inner world.

To gain a glimpse of his procedure, we again can do no better than return to its analogy with that inner process whereby—according to Schopenhauer's so luminous assumption—the dream of deepest sleep, entirely remote from the waking cerebral consciousness, as it were translates itself into the lighter, allegoric dream which immediately precedes our wakening. We have seen that the musician's kindred glossary extends from the scream of horror to the suave play of soothing murmurs. In the employment of the ample range that lies between, the musician is controlled, as it were, by an urgent impulse to impart the vision of his inmost dream; like the second, allegoric dream, he therefore approaches the notions (*Vorstellungen*) of the waking brain—those notions whereby it is at last enabled to preserve a record, chiefly for itself, of the inner vision. The extreme limit of this approach, however, is marked by the notions of *Time*: those of Space he leaves behind an impenetrable veil, whose lifting needs must make his dream invisible forthwith. Whilst *harmony*, belonging to neither Space nor Time, remains the most inalienable element of Music, through the *rhythmic* sequence of his tones in point of time the musician reaches forth a plastic hand, so to speak, to strike a compact with the waking world of semblances; just as the allegoric dream so far makes contact with the Individual's wonted notions that the waking consciousness, albeit at once detecting the great difference of even this dream-picture from the outer incidents of actual life, yet is able to retain its image. So the musician makes contact with the plastic world through the *rhythmic* ordering of his tones, and that in virtue of a resemblance to the laws whereby the motion of visible bodies is brought to our intelligence. Human Gesture, which seeks to make itself intelligible in Dance through an expressive regularity of changeful motion, thus seems to play the same part toward Music as bodies, in their turn, toward Light: without refraction and reflection, Light would not shine; and so we may say that without rhythm, Music would not be observable. But, at this very point of contact between Plastique and Harmony, the nature of Music is plainly shewn to be entirely distinct from that of Plastic art in particular; whereas the latter fixes Gesture in respect of space, but leaves its motion to be supplied by our reflective thought, Music speaks out Gesture's inmost essence in a language so direct that, once we are saturated with the music, our eyesight is positively incapacitated for intensive observation of the gesture, so that finally we understand it without our really seeing it. Thus, though Music draws her nearest affinities in the phenomenal world into her dream-realm, as we have called it, this is only in order to turn our visual faculties inwards through a wondrous transformation, so to speak, enabling them to grasp the Essence-of-things in its most immediate manifestment, as it were to read the vision which the musician had himself beheld in deepest sleep.—

As for Music's standing toward the plastic forms of the phenomenal world, and toward abstractions derived from things themselves, nothing can possibly be more lucid than what we read under this heading in Schopenhauer's work; so that it would be quite superfluous for us to dwell thereon, and we may turn to our principal object, namely an inquiry into the nature of the Musician himself.

However, we first must dwell on a crucial point in the æsthetic judgment (*Urtheil*) of Music as an art. For we find that from the forms wherein Music seems to join hands with the outer world of Appearance there has been deduced an utterly preposterous demand upon the character of her utterances. As already mentioned, axioms founded simply on a scrutiny of Plastic art have been transferred to Music. That such a solecism could have been committed, we have at any rate to attribute to the aforesaid "nearest approach" of Music to the visual side of the world and its phenomena. In this direction indeed the art of Music has taken a development which has exposed her to so great a misapprehension of her veritable character that folk have claimed from her a function similar to that of plastic works of art, namely the susciting of our *pleasure in beautiful forms.* As this was synchronous with a progressive decline in the judgment of plastic art itself, it may easily be imagined how deeply Music was thus degraded ; at bottom, she was asked to wholly repress her ownest nature for mere sake of turning her outmost side to our delectation.

Music, who speaks to us solely through quickening into articulate life the most universal concept of the inherently speechless Feeling, in all imaginable gradations, can once and for all be judged by nothing but the category of the *sublime* ; for, as soon as she engrosses us, she transports us to the highest ecstasy of consciousness of our infinitude.*

* "Die Musik, welche einzig dadurch zu uns spricht, dass sie den allerallgemeinsten Begriff des an sich dunklen Gefühles in den erdenklichsten Abstufungen mit bestimmtester Deutlichkeit uns belebt, kann an und für sich einzig nach der Kategorie des *Erhabenen* beurtheilt werden, da sie, sobald sie uns erfüllt, die höchste Extase des Bewusstseins der Schrankenlosigkeit erregt."—A very difficult sentence to render justice to, even in a partial paraphrase, without appealing to Schopenhauer's convincing theory of the Sublime (*Welt als W. u. V.* I. § 39). As an element of that theory is formed by the recognition that in the Sublime, whether in Nature or Art, we are brought into direct contact with the *universal* Will, our author's argument as to the nature of Music is really far more strongly supported by his present paragraph, to the ordinary mind, than by Schopenhauer's assumption of a "dream-organ" ; which latter, however, Wagner explicitly has adopted by mere way of "analogy"—a purpose it admirably serves, though it has given offence to those who have been misled by the oft-repeated *illustration* into considering it a main factor in the *exposition*, whereas each several reference to "dreams" might be omitted without in the slightest degree affecting the philosophic basis of Richard Wagner's remarkable contribution to a much-needed Science of Music.—Tr.

On the other hand what enters only *as a sequel* to our plunging into contemplation of a work of plastic art, namely the (temporary) liberation of the intellect from service to the individual will through our discarding all relations of the object contemplated to that will—the required effect of *beauty* on the mind,—is brought about by Music at her very *first entry*; inasmuch as she withdraws us at once from any concern with the relation of things outside us, and—as pure Form set free from Matter—shuts us off from the outer world, as it were, to let us gaze into the inmost Essence of ourselves and all things. Consequently our verdict on any piece of music should be based upon a knowledge of those laws whereby the effect of Beauty, the very first effect of Music's mere appearance, advances the most directly to a revelation of her truest character through the agency of the Sublime. It would be the stamp of an absolutely empty piece of music, on the contrary, that it never got beyond a mere prismatic toying with the effect of its first entry, and consequently kept us bound to the relations presented by Music's outermost side to the world of vision.

Upon this side alone, indeed, has Music been given any lasting development; and that by a systematising of her rhythmic structure (*Periodenbau*) which on the one hand has brought her into comparison with Architecture, on the other has made her so much a matter of superficies (*ihr eine Ueberschaulichkeit gegeben hat*) as to expose her to the said false judgment by analogy with Plastic art. Here, in her outermost restriction to banal forms and conventions, she seemed e.g. to Goethe so admirably suited for a standard of poetical proportion (*zur Normirung dichterischer Konzeptionen*). To be able in these conventional forms so to toy with Music's stupendous powers that her own peculiar function, the making known the inner essence of all things, should be avoided like a deluge, for long was deemed by æsthetes the true and only acceptable issue of maturing the art of Tone. But to have pierced through these forms to the innermost essence of Music in such a way that from that inner side he could cast the light of the Clairvoyant on the outer world, and shew us these forms themselves again in nothing but their inner meaning,—this was the work of our great *Beethoven*, whom we therefore have to regard as the true archetype of the Musician.—

If, retaining our oft-adduced analogy of the allegoric dream, we mean to think of Music as incited by an inner vision (*Schau*) and endeavouring to convey that vision to the world without, we must subsume a special organ for the purpose, analogous to the Dream-organ in the other case, a cerebral attribute in power whereof the musician first perceives the inner In-itself close-sealed to earthly knowledge (*das aller Erkenntniss verschlossene innere An-sich*): a kind of eye, when it faces inwards, that becomes an ear when directed outwards. For the most speaking likeness of that inmost (dream-) image of the world perceived thereby, we have only to listen to one of those famous church-pieces of *Palestrina's*. Here Rhythm is nowhere traceable save through the play of the harmonic sequences; as a symmetrical succession in time, apart from them, it does not exist at all. Here, then, Succession (*Zeitfolge*) is still so rigidly bound to that timeless, spaceless essence, Harmony, that we cannot as yet employ the laws of Time to aid us in the understanding of such music. The sole idea of Succession in such a piece is expressed by wellnigh nothing but the gentlest fluctuations of one ground-colour, which presents us with the most varied modulations within the range of its affinity, without our being able to trace a line in all its changes. As this colour itself does not appear in Space, we here are given an image almost as timeless as it is spaceless, an altogether spiritual revelation; and the reason why it moves us so indicibly is that, more plainly than all other things, it brings to our consciousness the inmost essence of Religion free from all dogmatic fictions.

Let us turn from this to a piece of dance-music, to an orchestral symphonic movement modelled on the dance-motive, or finally to a downright operatic *pièce*: we find our fancy chained forthwith by a regular order in the recurrence of rhythmic periods, the *plastic* element that forms the chief factor in Melody's insistence.* Music developed along these lines has very properly been given the name of "secular," in opposition to that "spiritual." Elsewhere I have expressed myself plainly enough upon the principle of this development,† and here will merely touch upon its already-noted aspect of the allegoric dream; whence it would seem that the musician's "eye," now woken to the phenomena of the outer world, attaches itself to such of them whose inner essence it can understand forthwith. The outer laws which he thus derives from the gestures of life, and finally from its every element of motion, become the laws of Rhythm in virtue whereof he constructs his periods of contrast and return. The more these periods are instinct with the true spirit of Music, the less will they be architectonic emblems diverting our attention from the music's pure effect. On the contrary, wherever that aforesaid inner Spirit of Music—sufficiently described above—tones down its surest manifestment for sake of this columnar ordering of rhythmic parts, there nothing will arrest us but that outward symmetry, and we shall necessarily reduce our claims on Music herself to a prime demand for regularity.—Music here quits her state of lofty innocence; she loses her power of redeeming from the curse of Appearance: no longer is she the prophetess of the Essence of things, but herself becomes entangled in the illusive show of things outside us. For to *this* music one wants to *see* something as well, and that something to-be-seen becomes the chief concern: as "Opera" proves right plainly, where spectacle, ballet and so forth make out the

* "Eindringlichkeit"—literally "penetrative quality," for which there really is no better equivalent than "catchiness."—Tr.

† To specify, I have done this in brief and general terms in an essay entitled "Zukunftsmusik," published at Leipzig about twelve years ago, without, however, finding any manner of attention; it has been included in the seventh volume of these *Ges. Schr. u. Dicht.* [Vol. III[a] of the present series], and may here be recommended to fresh notice.—R. WAGNER.

lure, the main attraction, and visibly enough proclaim the degeneracy of the music there employed.—

We will now illustrate the above by an inquiry into the *evolution of Beethoven's genius*; and here, to abandon generalities, we have first to consider the practical maturing of the master's own peculiar style.—

The qualification, the predestination of a musician for his art, can only be shewn in the effect produced upon him by the music going on around him. In what manner his faculty of inner vision, that clairvoyance of the deepest world-dream, has been aroused thereby, we do not learn till he has fully reached the goal of his self-development; up to then he obeys the laws of reaction of outward impressions, and for him, as musician, these latter are chiefly derived from the tone-works of masters of his time. Here we find Beethoven roused the least by works of Opera, whereas he was more alive to impressions from the church-music of his age. The métier of pianoforte-player however, which he had to adopt in order "to be something" in the profession, brought him into lasting and most familiar contact with the pianoforte-compositions of the masters of his period. In this department the "*sonata*" had become the model form. We might say that Beethoven was and remained a Sonata-composer, for in the great majority and the most eminent of his instrumental works the Sonata-form was the veil through which he looked into the realm of tones, or—to put it another way—through which he spoke to us from out that realm; whilst other forms, and notably those of 'mixed' vocal music, despite the most extraordinary achievements with them, were merely touched by him in passing, as if tentatively.

The laws of the Sonata-form had been established for all time by Emanuel Bach, Haydn and Mozart; they were the product of a compromise between the German and

Italian spirits of music. Its external character was conferred on it by its employment: with the Sonata the pianoforte-player made his bow to the public, which he was to regale with his dexterity as such, and at like time to entertain agreeably as musician. Here we no longer had Sebastian Bach, who gathered his congregation in the church before the organ, or thither called the connoisseurs to a contest twixt himself and colleagues; a wide gulf divided the wondrous master of the Fugue from the cherishers of the Sonata. By them the art of Fugue was learnt as a means of fortifying their musical study, but employed in the sonata by way of nothing but artifice: the rugged strictness of pure Counterpoint yielded to pleasure in a set Eurhythmy; to fill whose ready-made mould with the nearest approach to Italian euphony, appeared to answer every claim on music. In Haydn's instrumental works we seem to see the genie (*Dämon*) of Music playing with its fetters, with the childishness of a greybeard born. Not incorrectly have the earlier works of Beethoven been attributed to Haydn's example; nay, even at a riper period of its evolution, his genius has been rated more akin to that of Haydn than to that of Mozart. Into the peculiar nature of this kinship, however, we gain a striking insight from Beethoven's personal attitude toward Haydn, whom he absolutely refused to recognise as his teacher, even allowing his young arrogance to indulge in positively insulting remarks about him. It seems that he felt the same relation to Haydn as the born adult to the man in second childhood. Far above and beyond the formal resemblance to his teacher, the genie of his inner music, indomitable by those fettering forms, was driving him to a demonstration of his force; and that, like every outward act of this prodigy of a musician, could only take the shape of inconciliable brusqueness.—Of his interview with Mozart [1787] we are informed that the petulant youth sprang up from the clavier after playing a sonata by the master's desire, and, to shew himself in his true colours, requested permission to improvise; which being granted, he produced so marked an impression on Mozart that the latter told his friends: "from *this* one the world will get something worth hearing." That would be about the time when Mozart's own genius, till then held back from following its inner bent by the untold tyranny of a musician's wretchedly toilsome career, was consciously ripening toward its full expansion. We know how the master faced his all too early death with the bitter consciousness that at last he would have been able to shew the world what music there was in him.

Young Beethoven, on the contrary, we see daring the world from the first with that defiant temper which kept him in almost savage independence his whole life through: a stupendous sense-of-self, supported by the proudest spirit, armed him at every hour against the frivolous demands addressed to Music by a world of pleasure. Against the importunities of an etiolated taste, he had a treasure of inestimable price to guard. In those same forms, in which Music was expected to merely shew herself a pleasing art, he had to proclaim the divinations of the inmost world of Tone. Thus he is at all times like a man possessed; for to him in truth applies what Schopenhauer has said of the Musician in general: he speaks the highest wisdom in a tongue his reason (*Vernunft*) does not understand.*

The "Vernunft" of his art he found in that spirit which had built the formal framework of its outer scaffolding. And what a scant Vernunft it was that spoke to him from that architectonic poise of periods, when he saw how even the greatest masters of his youth bestirred themselves with banal repetition of flourishes and phrases, with mathematical distribution of loud and soft, with regulation introductions of just so many solemn bars, and the inevitable passage through the gate of just so many half-closes to the saving uproar of the final cadence! 'Twas the Vernunft that had formed the operatic aria, dictated the stringing-together of operatic numbers, the logic that made Haydn chain his genie to an everlasting counting of his rosary-

* *Welt als W. u. V.*, I. § 52.—Tr.

beads. For Religion had vanished from the Church with Palestrina's music, and the artificial formalism of Jesuit observance had counterformed Religion and Music alike. So the thoughtful visitor finds venerable Rome disguised beneath the Jesuit architecture of the last two centuries; so glorious Italian painting turned to slops and sugar; so, and under the selfsame lead, arose French "classic" poetry, in whose spirit-slaying laws we may trace a speaking likeness to the laws of construction of the operatic Aria and the Sonata.

We know that it was the "German spirit," so terribly dreaded and hated "across the mountains," that stepped into the field of Art, as everywhere else, to heal this artfully induced corruption of the European race. As in other realms we have hailed our Lessing, Goethe, Schiller and the rest, as our rescuers from that corruption, to-day we have to shew that in this musician Beethoven, who spoke the purest speech of every nation, the German spirit redeemed the spirit of mankind from deep disgrace. For inasmuch as Music had been degraded to a merely pleasing art, and by dint of her ownest essence he raised her to the height of her sublime vocation, he has set open for us the understanding of that art which explains the world to everyone as surely as the profoundest philosophy could ever explain it to the abstract thinker. *And herein lies the unique relation of great Beethoven to the German people*, which we now will try to follow through the special features of his life and work, so far as known to us.—

Nothing can yield us a more instructive answer as to the relation borne by the Artist's modus operandi to the synthetic operations of the Reason, than a correct apprehension of the course pursued by Beethoven in the unfolding of his musical genius. For it to have been a logical procedure, he must consciously have changed, or even overthrown the outward forms of music; but we never light upon a trace of that. Assuredly there never was an artist who pondered less upon his art. The aforesaid brusque impetuosity of his nature shews us how he felt as an actual personal injury, almost as direct as every other shackle of convention, the ban imposed upon his genius by those forms. Yet his rebellion consisted in nothing but the exuberant unfolding of his inner genius, unrestrainable by those outward forms themselves. Never did he radically alter an existing form of instrumental music; in his last sonatas, quartets, symphonies and so forth, we may demonstrate beyond dispute a structure such as of the first. But compare these works with one another; compare e.g. the Eighth Symphony in F with the Second in D, and marvel at the wholly new world that fronts us in wellnigh the identical form!

Here is shewn once more the idiosyncrasy of German nature, that profoundly inward gift which stamps its mark on every form by moulding it afresh from within, and thus is saved from the necessity of outward overthrow. Thus is the German no revolutionary, but a reformer; and thus he wins at last a wealth of forms for the manifesting of his inner nature, as never another nation. In the Frenchman this deep internal spring seems silted up: wherefore, when troubled by the outer form of matters in his State or art, he fancies he must dash it into atoms, as though the new, the pleasanter form would thereafter leap into existence of itself. Thus, strange as it may sound, his mutiny is really directed against his own nature, which never displays an inch more depth than already in that troubling Form. On the contrary it has not harmed the German spirit's evolution, that our poetic literature of the Middle Ages drew its nurture from the adaptation of French chivalric poems: the inner depth of a Wolfram von Eschenbach shaped eternal types of poesy from that selfsame 'stuff' whose primal form is stored for us as nothing but a curiosity.* So, too, did we adopt the classic Form of Greek and Roman culture, followed their mode of speech, their metres, and knew to make our own the antique view of things (*Anschauung*); but always giving voice therein to our own inmost spirit. Thus we took over

* Chrêtien de Troyes' twelfth-century poem, *Perceval le Galois.*—Tr.

Music, with all its forms, from the Italians; and what we poured into them, we have before us in the unfathomable works of Beethoven.

To attempt to explain those works themselves, were an act of folly. As we follow their order of succession, with ever growing distinctness must we perceive in them the permeation of the musical form by the Genius of Music. 'Tis as though the works of his forerunners were a painted transparency seen by daylight, a quite inferior type of art, obviously beneath comparison in drawing or colour with the works of the painter proper, and therefore looked down upon by all true connoisseurs as a pseudo-artwork: erected for the embellishment of feasts, at princely banquets, to entertain luxurious company and so forth,* the virtuoso placed the candle of his art-dexterity in front of it, instead of at its back, to light it up. But Beethoven comes, and sets this painting in the hush of Night, between the world of semblance and the deep interior world of all things' essence, from whence he brings behind the picture the light of the Clairvoyant: and lo! it shimmers into wondrous life, a second world now stands before us, a world whereof the grandest masterpiece of Raphael himself could give us no foreboding.

Here the might of the musician is conceivable as nothing but Magic. It certainly is an enchanted state into which we fall while listening to a true Beethovenian masterwork, when in every particle of the piece—which our sober senses would tell us was merely the technical means of exhibiting a given form—we discern a supernatural life (*geisterhafte Lebendigkeit*), an agency now soothing now appalling, a

* Cf. Schopenhauer's *Welt als W. u. V.* vol. I. § 38: "Light has become the symbol of all good and salutary things . . . colours directly rouse in us a lively pleasure, which reaches the highest pitch when they are transparent," and, on the other hand, Goethe's *Wilhelm Meister*, Book III. cap. vi. (Carlyle's translation): "These virtues were to advance together, to recite the Prince's praises, and finally to encircle his bust with garlands of flowers and laurels; behind which a transparency might be inserted, representing the princely Hat, and his name illuminated on it. . . . But how can it flatter any reasonable man to see himself set up in effigy, and his name glimmering on oiled paper?" —Tr.

pulse, a thrill, a throb of joy, of yearning, fearing, grief and ecstasy, whilst it all appears to take its motion from the depths of our own inner being. For in Beethoven's music the factor of so great moment for the history of Art is this: each technical accidentia of art, each convention employed by the artist for sake of making himself intelligible to the world outside him, itself is raised to the supreme importance of a direct outpouring of his spirit. As I have remarked elsewhere, we here have no subsidiaries, no more foiling to the melody, but the whole is melody, every voice in the accompaniment, each rhythmic note, ay, e'en the pauses.

Since it is quite impossible to discuss the essential substance of Beethoven's music without promptly falling into the tone of rhapsody, and since we have already sought by the philosopher's aid to gain some clearer knowledge of the true essence of Music in general (and consequently of Beethovenian music in particular), if we are to abstain from the impossible we still must rivet our attention to the personal Beethoven, the focus of all the rays of light that issue from his wonder-world.—

So let us ask whence Beethoven derived this force, or rather—as the mystery of Nature's gifts must needs remain close-veiled to us, and the very existence of this force we can but unquestioningly infer from its effect—let us seek to ascertain by what peculiarity of personal character, and through what moral bent, the great master was enabled to concentrate that force upon this one stupendous effect that constitutes his deed for Art. We have seen that we must here dismiss all assumption of a reasoning process (*Vernunfterkenntniss*) that haply might have guided the development of his artistic bent. No: we shall have to abide by that virile force of character to whose influence over the unfolding of the master's inner genius we have already had to allude.

That reference itself brought Beethoven into comparison with Haydn and Mozart. Upon considering the outer lives of these last two, again, we find Mozart standing midway between Haydn and Beethoven. *Haydn* was and remained a prince's musical officer, with the duty of catering for the entertainment of his pomp-struck master. Temporary respites, such as his visits to London, effected little alteration in the practice of his art; for there, too, he was always the musician recommended to, and paid by noble lords. Docile and devout, the peace of his kind and cheerful temper stayed unruffled till advanced old age; only the eye, that looks upon us from his portrait, is suffused with a gentle melancholy.—The life of *Mozart*, on the other hand, was one continuous struggle for a peacefully assured existence, against the most unequal odds. Caressed as a child by the half of Europe, as youth he finds all satisfaction of his sharpened longings made doubly difficult, and from manhood on he miserably sickens toward an early grave. To him the musical service of a royal master became unbearable forthwith: he seeks to support himself on the plaudits of the larger public, gives concerts and "academies"; the fugitive wage is squandered on the joys of life. If Haydn's *prince* demanded constant change of entertainment, Mozart no less had to plan something new from day to day to tempt the public; hastiness in conception and execution, given an acquired routine, will mostly explain the character of their works. His truly noble masterworks Haydn did not write until already an old man, in enjoyment of a competence insured by foreign fame. Mozart never arrived at comfort: his loveliest works were sketched between the elation of one hour and the anguish of the next. Thus again and again his hopes are set on a handsome royal pension, as guarantee of a mode of life more favourable to artistic production. What his Kaiser withholds is offered him by a King of Prussia: he remains true to "his Kaiser," and perishes in destitution.

Had *Beethoven* reflected on the lives of his two great predecessors, and taken cold Reason for the chooser of his own, it could not have guided him more safely than in fact was done by the naïve dictates of his inborn character. It is amazing to see how everything here was determined by the potent instinct of Nature. Quite plainly is this expressed in Beethoven's abhorrence of a life like Haydn's. One glance at the youthful Beethoven, indeed, must have sufficed to turn any Prince from the thought of making *this* one his Kapellmeister. Still more strongly does his complexion come out in those features which preserved him from a fate such as that of Mozart. Thrown like him upon a world where the Useful alone can pay itself, the Beautiful only gets paid when it flatters the senses, but the Sublime must go without all manner of return, Beethoven found himself debarred in advance from propitiating the world with beauty. That beauty and effeminacy must rank as one and the same to him, his physiognomy declared at once with overpowering distinctness. The world of Appearance had but a poor approach to him. The well-nigh unearthly poignance of his eye saw nothing in the outer world but plaguing perturbations of his inner world, and to hold them at arm's length made out his almost only rapport with that world. Thus paroxysm (*Krampf*) becomes the expression of his visage: the paroxysm of defiance holds this nose, this mouth at strain, a strain that never can relax to smiles, but only to gargantuan laughter. Though it has been an axiom of physiology that, for high mental gifts, a large brain must be set in a thin and delicate brain-pan—as if to facilitate immediate recognition of things outside us,—yet upon examination of the dead man's remains some years ago it transpired that, in keeping with an exceptional strength of the whole bony skeleton, the skull was of quite unusual density and thickness. Thus Nature shielded a brain of exceeding tenderness, that it might solely look within, and chronicle the visions of a lofty heart in quiet undisturbed.* What this fearsomely rugged strength surrounded and preserved, was an inner world of such tenuous delicacy that, given defenceless to the rough fingering of the outer world, it must straightway

* "So schützte die Natur in ihm ein Gehirn von übermässiger Zartheit, damit es nur nach innen blicken, und die Weltschau eines grossen Herzes in ungestörter Ruhe üben könnte."—

have melted into air,—like that radiant spirit of light and love, Mozart.

Now say, how such a being would look out upon the world from so close-barred a dwelling!—Assuredly the inner promptings (*Willensaffekte*) of such a man could never, or but impalpably, affect his conception of the outer world; they were at once too ardent and too delicate, to cleave to any of the semblances his eye but grazed in timid haste, and finally with that suspicion of the ever-unappeased. Here nothing drew him with those fleeting fetters of illusion which still could tempt Mozart to sally from his inner world in quest of outer enjoyment. A childlike pleasure in the distractions of a lively capital could scarce so much as appeal to Beethoven, for the promptings of his will were far too strong to find the smallest satisfaction in such superficial pastimes. Whilst this encouraged his bent towards solitude, the latter coincided with his destiny to independence. A marvellously certain instinct led him here, and became the mainspring of each utterance of his character. No reasoning could have directed him more plainly, than this peremptory dictate of his instinct. What induced Spinoza to support himself by glass-cutting; what filled our Schopenhauer with that care to keep his little heritage intact—determining his whole outer life, and accounting for otherwise inexplicable traits in his character—namely the recognition that the sincerity of philosophic research is always seriously imperilled by a dependence on the necessity of earning money by scientific labours: that selfsame thing determined Beethoven in his defiance of the world, his love of solitude, the wellnigh boorish tastes displayed in his choice of a mode of living.

Beethoven too, to be sure, had to earn his living by his musical labours. But, as smiling comfort had no charms for him, he had the less need either to engage in rapid, superficial work, or to make concessions to a taste that naught but sweets could capture. The more he thus lost touch with the outer world, the clearer-sighted did he turn his gaze upon his world within. And the more familiar he becomes with the administration of his inner riches, the more consciously does he propound his outward requirements, actually requesting his patrons no longer to pay him for his works, but to ensure his being able to work entirely for himself, without one thought for all the world. And so it happened, for the first time in the life of any musician, that a few benevolent persons of high station pledged themselves to maintain Beethoven in the desired state of independence. Arrived at a similar crisis in his life, Mozart, too soon worn out, had gone to ground. This great boon conferred on Beethoven, albeit not continued without break and undiminished, yet formed the base of that peculiar harmony which shewed itself henceforward in the master's still so strangely-fashioned life. He felt himself victor, and knew that he belonged to the world but as a freeman. As for it, it must take him as it found him. To his high-born patrons he behaved as a despot, and nothing could be got from him save what and when he pleased.

But never and in nothing had he pleasure, save in what henceforth engrossed him: the play of the magician with the figures of his inner world. For the outer now had faded out completely, not because its sight was reft from him by blindness, but since *deafness* held it finally far off his ear. The ear had been the only organ through which the outer world could still disturb him: to his eye it was long since dead. What *saw* the spellbound dreamer when he wandered through Vienna's bustling streets, with open eyes fixed hard on distance, and animated solely by the waking of his inner tone-world?—The advent and exacerbation of his aural malady distressed him terribly, and moved him to deep melancholy: about his total deafness, and especially the loss of all ability to listen to performances of music, we hear no serious complaint from him; merely the intercourse of life was rendered difficult, an intercourse that in itself had never any charm for him, and which he now avoided more and more emphatically.

A musician sans ears!—Can one conceive an eyeless painter?

But the blinded *Seer* we know. Tiresias to whom the world of Appearance has closed itself, and whose inner eye beholds instead the ground of all appearances: his fellow is the deaf musician who now, untroubled by life's uproar, but listens to his inner harmonies, now from his depths but speaks to that world—for it has nothing more to tell him. So is genius freed from all outside it, at home forever with and in itself. Whoso could then have seen Beethoven with the vision of Tiresias, what a wonder must have opened to him: a world walking among men,—the In-itself of the world as a living, moving man!—

And now the musician's eye grew bright within. Now did he gaze upon Appearance, and, illumined by his inner light, it cast a wondrous reflex back upon his inner soul. Now speaks but the essence of things to him, and shews them in the tranquil light of Beauty. Now does he understand the woods, the brook, the fields, the clear blue sky, the merry throng, the loving pair, the song of birds, the flocking clouds, the raging of the storm, the happiness of rhythmic rest. And all his seeing and his fashioning is steeped in that marvellous serenity (*Heiterkeit*) which Music first acquired through him. Even the cry, so immanent in every sound of Nature, is lulled to smiling: the world regains its childhood's innocence.* "To-day shalt thou be with me in Paradise"—who has not heard these words of the Redeemer, when listening to the "Pastoral Symphony"?

Now thrives apace that power of shaping the unfathomable, the never-seen, the ne'er experienced, which yet becomes a most immediate experience, of most transparent comprehensibility. The joy of wielding this new power turns next to humour: all grief of Being breaks before this vast enjoyment of the play therewith; the world-creator Brahma

* "Die Welt gewinnt ihre Kindesunschuld wieder." Cf. *Tannhäuser*, act i.: "Ha, jetzt erkenne ich sie wieder, die schöne Welt, der ich entrückt! Der Himmel blickt auf mich hernieder, die Fluren prangen reich geschmückt," and *Parsifal*, act iii.: "Das dankt denn alle Kreatur, was all' da blüht und bald erstirbt, da die entsündigte Natur heut' ihren Unschulds-Tag erwirbt." —Tr.

is laughing at himself,* as he sees how hugely he had duped himself; guiltlessness re-won disports it with the sting of guilt atoned; freed conscience banters with its torment overpassed.

Never has any art in the world created aught so radiant (*etwas so Heiteres*) as these Symphonies in A and F, with all their so closely allied tone-works from this godlike period of the master's total deafness. The effect upon the hearer is precisely that deliverance from all earthly guilt, as the after-effect is the feeling of a forfeited paradise wherewith we return to the world of semblances. Thus do these glorious works preach penitence and a contrite heart with all the depth of a divine revelation.

Here the only æsthetic term to use, is the *Sublime*: for here the operation of the Radiant at once transcends all pleasure in the Beautiful, and leaves it far behind. Each challenge of self-vaunting Reason is hushed forthwith by the Magic mastering our whole nature; knowledge pleads confession of its error,† and the transport of that avowal bids our deepest soul to shout for joy, however earnestly the spellbound features of the listener betray his marvel at the impotence of all our seeing and our thinking to plumb this truest of all worlds.—

What of the human being of this world-rapt genius could there be left for observation of the world? What could the eye of earthly man behold in him when now it faced him? Nothing, surely, but the misunderstandable, just as he himself had no communion with our world save that of misunderstanding: our world as to which the naïve greatness of his heart set him in constant contradiction with himself, only to be harmonised again upon the loftiest footing of his art. Whenever his reason tried to comprehend the world, his mind was set at rest by the

* Cf. Wotan in *Siegfried*; "my jovial god who craves his own undoing" (*Letter to A. Röckel*, Jan. 1854).—Tr.

† "Die Erkenntniss flieht mit dem Bekenntniss ihres Irrthumes." Cf. *Parsifal*, act. ii.: "Bekenntniss wird Schuld und Reue enden, Erkenntniss in Sinn die Thorheit wenden."—Tr.

teachings of Optimism, such as the maudlin (*schwärmerisch*) Humanistic tenets of last century had raised into a commonplace of the bourgeoisely religious world. Each mental doubt his own experiences of Life advanced against the correctness of this doctrine, he combated with hard-and-fast religious maxims. His Inmost told him: Love is god; and so he wrote down: God is love. In the works of our poets, only what laid emphatic stress upon this dogma could meet with his approval; though "Faust" had a powerful and lasting fascination for him, his special reverence was paid to Klopstock and many a shallower preacher of Humanity. His moral principles were of the strictest bourgeois stripe; a frivolous tone would make him foam. Certainly he thus offered to the most observant company no single sign of breadth of intellect, and, for all Bettina's gushings over Beethoven, Goethe may well have had a heart-ache in his conversations with him. But just as, caring naught for luxury, he frugally kept watch on his finances, nay, often with a miser's parsimony, so in his rigorously religious morals is expressed that surest instinct in power whereof he guarded his noblest of possessions, the freedom of his genius, against the subjugating influence of the world around him.

He lived in Vienna, knew no place but Vienna: that says enough.

The Austrian, brought up in the school of the Roman Jesuits after the uprooting of every vestige of German Protestantism, had even lost the proper accent for his speech; like the classic names of the antique world, it was taught him now in nothing but an un-German latinisation. German spirit, German character and customs, were explained to him from class-books of Spanish and Italian origin; on the soil of a falsified history, a falsified science, a falsified religion, a populace by nature prone to mirth and gaiety had been nursed into a scepticism which—as every fibre of the true, the free, the sterling, was to be plucked out with all despatch—could only take the form of rank frivolity.

'Twas the same spirit that had imposed on the only art

still practised in Austria, on Music, that development and truly humbling tendence which we have already passed in review. We have seen how Beethoven warded off this tendence by the strength of his own nature, and now we see an equal force at work in him to vehemently ward off a frivolous tendency of life and mind. A catholic baptised and bred, the whole spirit of German protestantism breathed in this bent of his. And as artist, again, it led him to the path whereon he was to meet the only comrade in his art to whom he could pay obeisance, the only musician he could take to his heart as revealer of the deepest secret of his nature. If Haydn passed as teacher of the youth, for the mightily unfolding art-life of the man our great *Sebastian Bach* became his leader.

Bach's wonder-work became his bible; in it he read, and clean forgot that world of clangour, heard no longer. There stood inscribed the answer to the riddle of his deepest dream, that answer the poor Leipzig Cantor erst had penned as everlasting symbol of the new, the other world. The same mysteriously inwoven lines and wondrous scrolls wherein the secret of the world of light and all its shapes had dawned upon great *Albrecht Dürer*, the spell-book of the necromantist who bids the macrocosmic light to shine upon the microcosm. What none save the eye of the German spirit could look on, none but *its* ear perceive; what drove that spirit's inmost conscience to irresistibly protest against all bonds imposed upon it from without: that Beethoven deciphered in his holiest of books, and—himself became a holy one.—

But how could *this* "holy one" (*gerade dieser Heilige*) conform his life to his hallowedness? For it was given him indeed "to speak the deepest wisdom," but "in a tongue his reason did not understand." Must not his commune with the world resemble nothing but that state of the awakened out of deepest sleep, the toilsome effort to recall the blissful vision of his inner soul? A similar state may be imagined in the case of the religious saint when, driven by the most inevitable life-need, he turns to some measure of rapprochement with the practices of common life: saving that in that Want itself this saint distinctly recognises the penance for a mortal's life of sin, and in his patient bearing of it he makes his very burden the inspired means of his redemption; whereas that hallowed seer simply grasps the penance' meaning as a torture, and drags his portion of all Being's guilt as nothing but a sufferer.* And so the optimist's error avenges itself by heightening both that suffering and his resentment. Each sign of callousness that meets him, every trace of rigour or self-seeking that he ever and again observes, revolts him as an incomprehensible perversion of that original Goodness of man to which he cleaves with a religious faith. Thus he is perpetually hurled from the paradise of his inner harmony to the hell of an existence filled with fearful discords, and only as artist can he finally resolve them into harmony.

If we would set before ourselves the picture of a day from our "holy one's" life, we scarce could gain a better than from one of those marvellous tone-pieces themselves; though, not to deceive ourselves, we must follow the course we adopted when referring the genesis of Music as an art to the phenomenon of the Dream, that is to say, employing it as a mere analogy, and not identifying one thing with the other. In illustration of such a veritable day from Beethoven's inmost life I will choose the great *C-sharp minor Quartet*†: and what we scarce could do while listening to it, as we then are forced to leave behind all cut-and-dry comparisons and give ourselves entirely to the direct revelation from another world, we may find attainable in a measure when conjuring up this tone-poem in our memory. Even thus, however, I must leave the reader's phantasy to supply the living details of the picture,

* "Nur dass dieser in der Noth des Lebens selbst deutlich die Sühne für ein sündiges Dasein erkennt, und in deren geduldiger Ertragung sogar mit Begeisterung das Mittel der Erlösung ergreift, wogegen jener heilige Seher den Sinn der Busse einfach als Qual auffasst, und seine Daseins-Schuld eben nur als Leidender abträgt."—

† Cf. Vol. IV., p. 323.—Tr.

and therefore simply offer the assistance of a skeleton outline.

The lengthy opening Adagio, surely the saddest thing ever said in notes, I would term the awaking on the dawn of a day "that in its whole long course shall ne'er fulfil one wish, not *one* wish!" * Yet it is alike a penitential prayer, a communing with God in firm belief of the Eternal Goodness.—The inward eye then traces the consoling vision (*Allegro* 6/8), perceptible by it alone, in which that longing becomes a sweet but plaintive playing with itself: the image of the inmost dream takes waking form as a loveliest remembrance. And now (with the short transitional *Allegro moderato*) 'tis as if the master, grown conscious of his art, were settling to work at his magic; its re-summoned force he practises (*Andante* 2/4) on the raising of one graceful figure, the blessed witness of inherent innocence, to find a ceaseless rapture in that figure's never-ending, never-heard-of transformation by the prismatic changes of the everlasting light he casts thereon.—Then we seem to see him, profoundly gladdened by himself, direct his radiant glances to the outer world (*Presto* 2/2): once more it stands before him as in the Pastoral Symphony, all shining with his inner joy; 'tis as though he heard the native accents of the appearances that move before him in a rhythmic dance, now blithe now blunt (*derb*). He looks on Life, and seems to ponder (short *Adagio* 3/4) how to set about the tune for Life itself to dance to: a brief but gloomy brooding, as if the master were plunged in his soul's profoundest dream. One glance has shewn him the inner essence of the world again: he wakes, and strikes the strings into a dance the like whereof the world had never heard (*Allegro finale*). 'Tis the dance of the whole world itself: wild joy, the wail of pain, love's transport, utmost bliss, grief, frenzy, riot, suffering; the lightning flickers, thunders growl: and above it the stupendous fiddler who bans and bends it all, who leads it haughtily from whirlwind into whirlpool, to the brink of the

* Goethe's *Faust*.—Tr.

abyss*;—he smiles at himself, for to him this sorcery was the merest play.—And night beckons him. His day is done.—

It is impossible to keep Beethoven the man before us for an instant, without at once re-calling Beethoven the wonderful musician to explain him.

We have seen how the instinctive tendence of his life ran parallel with the tendence to emancipate his art; as he himself could be no lackey in the pay of Luxury, so should his music, too, be freed from every token of subjection to a frivolous taste. And of how his optimistic creed went hand-in-hand with an instinctive tendence to enlarge the province of his art we have evidence, of the sublimest naïvety, in his *Ninth Symphony with Choruses*; into whose genesis we now must look, to make clear the marvellous connexion of these two root-tendencies in the nature of our "saint."—

The same bent that led Beethoven's reasoning faculty to frame for itself the *good* human being, guided him in the construction of this "good man's" *melody*. Melody having lost its innocence at the hand of our art-musicians, he wished to restore to it this purest innocence. One has only to recall the Italian Opera-melody of last century, to recognise in that singular scarecrow the abject servant of the Mode and its ends: through Fashion and its uses Music had been brought so low that wanton taste demanded of it only something new, and new again, because the melody of yesterday was past all listening-to to-day. But Melody was also the sheet-anchor of our Instrumental-music, whose employment for the ends of a by no means noble social life we have already mooted above.

Here *Haydn* had soon laid hands on the blunt but cheery folk-dance, whose strains he often quite recognisably borrowed from the dances of Hungarian peasants in his immediate neighbourhood; but he thus remained in a lower sphere with a strong impress of narrow provincialism. From what sphere, then, was this Nature-melody to be

* Cf. Lenau's *Faust* as cited in Liszt's *Mephisto-Walzer*.—Tr.

derived, to bear a nobler, an eternal character? For even that peasant-dance-tune of Haydn's had its chief attraction as a piquant curiosity, in nowise as a purely-human type of art for every age. Yet it was impossible to find that type in the higher spheres of our society, for that was just where reigned the patched and powdered melody of the opera-singer and ballet-dancer, a nest of every vice. So Beethoven went Haydn's way; only, he no longer served up the folk-dance tune at a prince's banquet, but, in an ideal sense, he played it for the Folk itself to dance to. Now it is a Scotch, now a Russian, now an old-French folk-tune, in which he recognised the dreamt nobility of innocence, and at whose feet he laid his whole art in homage. But one Hungarian peasant-dance (in the final movement of his Symphony in A) he played for the whole of Nature, so played that who could see her dancing to it in orbital gyrations must deem he saw a planet brought to birth before his very eyes.

But his aim was to find the archetype of innocence, the ideal "good man" of his belief,* to wed him with his "God is love." One might almost think the master had already seized the clue in his "*Sinfonia eroica*": the unusually simple theme of its last movement, a theme he worked again elsewhere, seems meant as a scaffold for this purpose; but the wealth of exquisite melos he built upon it still pertains too much to the sentimental Mozartian cantabile, so characteristically developed and expanded by himself, to rank as attainment of the aforesaid aim.—The clue is plainer in the jubilant closing section of the C-minor Symphony, where the naïvety of the simple march-tune, moving almost exclusively on tonic and dominant in the nature-scale of horns and trumpets, appeals to us the more as the whole symphony now seems to have been nothing but a straining of our attention for it; like the bank of clouds, now torn by storm, now stirred by gentlest breezes, from whence the sun at last breaks forth in splendour.

* Cf. *Parsifal*, act i.: "Wer ist gut?"—Tr.

At like time (and this apparent digression has an important bearing on our subject) the C-minor Symphony appeals to us as one of those rarer conceptions of the master's in which a stress of bitter passion, the fundamental note of the commencement, mounts rung by rung through consolation, exaltation, till it breaks into the joy of conscious victory. Here lyric pathos already verges on the definitely dramatic, in an ideal sense; and though it might be doubted whether the purity of Musical Conception would not ultimately suffer by the pursuance of this path, through its leading to the dragging-in of fancies altogether foreign to the spirit of Music, yet it cannot be denied that the master was in nowise prompted by a truant fit of æsthetic speculation, but simply and solely by an ideal instinct sprung from Music's ownest realm.* As shewn when we started on this last inquiry, that instinct coincided with the struggle to rescue from every plausible objection raised by his experience of life the conscious belief in human nature's original goodness, or haply to regain it. Those conceptions of the master's which breathe wellnigh throughout the spirit of sublimest gladness (*Heiterkeit*) belong pre-eminently, as we have seen, to the period of that blessed seclusion which seems upon arrival of his total deafness to have wholly rapt him from this world of pain. From the sadder mood that reappears in certain of his most important works we perhaps have no need to infer a downfall of that inner gladness, since we undoubtedly

* "Hier betritt das lyrische Pathos fast schon den Boden einer idealen Dramatik im bestimmteren Sinne, und, wie es zweifelhaft dünken dürfte, ob auf diesem Wege die musikalische Konzeption nicht bereits in ihrer Reinheit getrübt werden möchte, weil sie zur Herbeiziehung von Vorstellungen verleiten müsste, welche an sich dem Geiste der Musik durchaus fremd erscheinen, so ist andererseits wiederum nicht zu verkennen, dass der Meister keineswegs durch eine abirrende ästhetische Spekulation, sondern lediglich durch einen dem eigensten Gebiete der Musik entkeimten, durchaus idealen Instinkt hierin geleitet wurde."—A somewhat difficult sentence to translate, as our author in this essay has studiously avoided all direct reference to post-Beethovenian composers, and yet the key to the present generalisation would appear to lie in the remarks upon Berlioz contained in his *Letter on Liszt's Symphonic Poems*, Vol. III.—Tr.

should make a grave mistake if we thought the Artist could ever conceive save in a state of profound cheerfulness of soul. The mood expressed in the conception must therefore belong to that world's-Idea itself which the artist seizes and interprets in his artwork. But, as we have taken for granted that in Music the Idea of the whole World reveals itself, the inspired musician must necessarily be included in that Idea, and what he utters is therefore not his personal opinion of the world, but the World itself with all its changing moods of grief and joy, of weal and woe. The conscious doubt of *Beethoven the man* was included in this World, as well; and thus his doubt is speaking for itself, in nowise as an object of his reflection, when he brings the world to such expression as in his Ninth Symphony, for instance, whose first movement certainly shews us the Idea of the world in its most terrible of lights. Elsewhere, however, this very work affords us unmistakable evidence of the purposely ordaining will of its creator; we are brought face to face with it when he stops the frenzy of despair that overwhelms each fresh appeasement, and, with the anguished cry of one awaking from a nightmare, he speaks that actual Word whose ideal sense is none other than: "Man, despite all, *is* good!"

It has always been a stumbling-block, not only to Criticism, but to the ingenuous Feeling, to see the master here falling of a sudden out of Music, in a manner, as if stepping outside the magic circle he himself had drawn, and appealing to a mental faculty entirely distinct from that of musical conception. In truth this unprecedented stroke of art resembles nothing but the sudden waking from a dream, and we feel its comforting effect upon the tortured dreamer; for never had a musician led us through the torment of the world so relentlessly and without end. So it was with a veritable leap of despair that the divinely naïve master, inspired by nothing save his magic, set foot on that new world of Light from out whose soil the long-sought godlike-sweet and guileless-human melody bloomed forth to greet him with its purity.

Thus with even what we have styled the ordaining will that led him to this melody, we find the master still abiding in the realm of Music, the world's Idea; for it is not the meaning of the Word, that really takes us with this entry of the human voice, but the human character of that voice. Neither is it the thought expressed in Schiller's verses, that occupies our minds thereafter, but the familiar sound of the choral chant; in which we ourselves feel bidden to join and thus take part in an ideal Divine Service, as the congregation really did at entry of the Chorale in S. Bach's great Passions. In fact it is obvious, especially with the chief-melody proper, that Schiller's words have been built in perforce and with no great skill;* for this melody had first unrolled its breadth before us as an entity *per se*, entrusted to the instruments alone, and there had thrilled us with the nameless joy of a paradise regained.

Never has the highest art produced a thing more artistically simple than this strain, whose childlike innocence as though breathes into us a holy awe when first we hear the theme in unaccented whispers from the bass instruments of the string-orchestra in unison. It then becomes the *cantus firmus*, the Chorale of the new communion, round which, as round S. Bach's own church-chorales, the harmonic voices group themselves in counterpoint. There is nothing to equal the sweet intensity of life this primal strain of spotless innocence acquires from every new-arising voice; till each adornment, every added gem of passion, unites with it and in it, like the breathing world around a final proclamation of divinest love.†—

Surveying the historical advance which the art of Music made through Beethoven, we may define it as the winning

* "Ganz ersichtlich ist es, dass namentlich der eigentlichen Hauptmelodie die Worte Schiller's, sogar mit wenigem Geschicke, nothdürftig erst untergelegt sind."—

† "Nichts gleicht der holden Innigkeit, zu welcher jede neu hinzutretende Stimme diese Urweise reinster Unschuld belebt, bis jeder Schmuck, jede Pracht der gesteigerten Empfindung an ihr und in ihr sich vereinigt, wie die athmende Welt um ein endlich geoffenbartes Dogma reinster Liebe."—

of a faculty withheld from her before: in virtue of that acquisition she mounted far beyond the region of the æsthetically Beautiful, into the sphere of the absolutely Sublime; and here she is freed from all the hampering of traditional or conventional forms, through her filling their every nook and cranny with the life of her ownest spirit. And to the heart of every human being this gain reveals itself at once through the character conferred by Beethoven on music's chiefest Form, on *Melody*, which has now rewon the utmost natural simplicity, the fount whereat in every age, for every need, it may renew itself and thrive to richest, amplest multiplicity. And this we may sum in a single term, intelligible to everyone: Melody has been emancipated by Beethoven from all influence of the Mode, of shifting taste, and raised to an eternal purely-human type. Beethoven's music will be understood throughout all time, whereas the music of his predecessors will for the most part stay un-understandable save by aid of art-historical Reflection.—

But, on the path whereon Beethoven arrived at this memorable ennoblement of Melody, there is yet another advance to note: to wit, the new meaning gained by *Vocal music* in its relation to purely Instrumental music.

This meaning was previously unknown to 'mixed' vocal-and-instrumental music. The latter we first meet in compositions for the church, and need have no scruple in calling it vocal music spoilt, inasmuch as the orchestra is here employed as mere accompaniment or reinforcement to the singing voices. The church-compositions of great S. Bach are only to be understood as works for a vocal choir, saving that this choir itself is already handled with the freedom and mobility of an instrumental orchestra,—which naturally suggested the latter's introduction for reinforcement and support. Then, concurrently with the greater and greater decline of the spirit of church-music, we find added to this mixture the Italian operatic song with orchestral accompaniment, in fashions varying with the times. It was reserved for Beethoven's genius to employ the resulting compound purely in the sense of an Orchestra of increased resources. In his great *Missa solemnis* we have a strictly Symphonic work, of the truest Beethovenian spirit. Here the vocal parts are handled quite in that sense of human instruments which Schopenhauer very rightly wished to see alone assigned to them: when presented as a musical artwork, the text to which these great church-compositions are set is never seized by us according to the letter, but simply serves as material for the singing; and it has no disturbing effect on our musical impressions for simple reason that it starts no train of inductive thought (*Vernunftvorstellungen*), but affects us solely through well-known symbolic formulæ of faith, as indeed is conditioned by its churchly character.

Moreover the experience that a piece of music loses nothing of its character even when the most diverse texts are laid beneath it, shews the relation of Music to *Poetry* to be a sheer illusion: for it transpires that in vocal music it is not the poetic thought one seizes—which in choral singing, in particular, one does not even get intelligibly articulated—but at most the mood that thought aroused in the musician when it moved him to music.* The union of Music and Poetry must therefore always end in such a subordination of the latter that we can only wonder above all at our great German poets returning again and again to the problem, to say nothing of the attempt. They evidently were instigated by the effect of music in *Opera*: and here, at any rate, appeared to lie the only field whereon the problem might be solved at last. Now, whether our poets' hopes were directed more to music's formal symmetry of structure, or more to its profoundly stirring effect on the feelings, they obviously could have only proposed to use the mighty aids it seemed to offer to give their poetic aim alike a more precise expression and a

* "Denn es bestätigt sich, dass, wenn zu einer Musik gesungen wird, nicht der poetische Gedanke, den man namentlich bei Chorgesängen nicht einmal verständlich artikulirt vernimmt, sondern höchstens Das von ihm aufgefasst wird, was er im Musiker als Musik und zu Musik anregte."—

more searching operation. They may have thought that Music would gladly render them this service if, in lieu of the trivial operatic subject and opera-text, they brought her a poetic conception to be taken seriously. What continually held them back from serious attempts in this direction may have been a vague, but legitimate doubt whether Poetry would be noticed at all, as such, in its co-operation with Music. Upon careful consideration it cannot have escaped them that in Opera, beyond the music, only the scenic goings-on, but not the explanatory poetic thought, engrossed attention; that Opera, in fact, merely arrested *hearing* and *sight* in turn. That a perfect æsthetic satisfaction was not to be gained for either the one receptive faculty or the other, is fully accounted for by the circumstance noted above, namely that opera-music did not attune us to that devotional state (*Andacht*)—the only one in keeping with Music—in which vision is so far reduced in power that the eye no longer sees objects with the wonted intensity; on the contrary, as found before, we here were but superficially affected, more excited than filled by the music, and consequently desired to *see* something too,—by no means to *think*, however, for our whole faculty of thought was stolen from us by just that shuttlecock desire for entertainment, thrown hither and thither in its distracting battle with tedium.

Now the foregoing considerations have made us sufficiently familiar with Beethoven's specific nature, to understand at once the master's attitude toward *Opera* when he categorically refused to ever set an opera-text of frivolous tendency. Ballets, processions, fireworks, amorous intrigues etc., to make music for such as these he declined with horror. His music required a whole, a high-souled, passionate plot, to search it through and through. What poet could have offered him the needful hand? One solitary trial brought him into contact with a dramatic situation that at least had nothing of the hated frivolity about it, and moreover quite harmonised with the master's leading dogma of Humanity through its glorification of wifely troth. And yet this opera-subject embraced so much that was foreign to Music and unassimilable, that in truth the great Overture to *Leonora* alone makes really plain to us how Beethoven would have the drama understood. Who can ever hear that thrilling tone-piece without being filled with the conviction that Music includes within itself the most consummate *Drama*? What is the dramatic action of the librettist's opera "Leonora" but an almost repulsive watering of the drama we have lived through in its overture, a kind of tedious commentary by Gervinus on a scene of Shakespeare's?

But the feeling that here occurs to everyone can only be made a matter of clear knowledge by our returning to the philosopher's explanation of Music itself.

Seeing that Music does not portray the Ideas inherent in the world's phenomena, but is itself an Idea of the World, and a comprehensive one, it naturally includes the Drama in itself; as Drama, again, expresses the only world's-Idea proportionate (*adäquat*) to Music. Drama towers above the bounds of Poetry in exactly the same manner as Music above those of every other art, and especially of plastic art, through its effect residing solely in the Sublime. As a drama does not depict human characters, but lets them display their immediate selves, so a piece of music gives us in its motive the character of all the world's appearances according to their inmost essence (*An-sich*). Not only are the movement, interchange and evolution of these motives analogous to nothing but the Drama, but a drama representing the [world's] Idea can be understood with perfect clearness through nothing but those moving, evolving and alternating motives of Music's. We consequently should not go far astray, if we defined Music as man's qualification *a priori* for fashioning the Drama. Just as we construct for ourselves the world of semblances through application of the laws of Time and Space existing *a priori* in our brain, so this conscious representment of the world's Idea in Drama would thus be foreordained by those inner laws of Music, operating in the dramatist equally unconsciously with the laws of Causality we bring into employment for apperception of the phenomenal world.

It was a presage of precisely this, that occurred to our great German poets; and perhaps in that guess they gave voice withal to the hidden reason of the impossibility of explaining *Shakespeare* by other methods. This prodigy of a dramatist in fact was comprehensible by no analogy with any poet you please; for which reason, also, all æsthetic judgment of him has remained as yet unbased. His dramas seem to be so direct a transcript of the world, that the *artist's* intervention in their portrayal of the Idea is absolutely untraceable, and certainly not demonstrable by criticism. So, marvelled at as products of a superhuman genius, they became to our great poets a study for discovery of the laws of their creation wellnigh in the same manner as the wonders of Nature herself.

With that extraordinary sincerity of his every touch, the height to which Shakespeare towered above the Poet proper often comes out ruggedly enough; in the scene where Brutus and Cassius fall a-quarrelling (*Julius Cæsar*), for instance, we find the poet positively treated as a "jigging fool." Nowhere do we meet the "poet" Shakespeare, save in the inmost heart of the characters that move before us in his dramas.—Shakespeare therefore remained entirely beyond comparison, until in *Beethoven* the German genius brought forth a being only to be explained through his analogy.—If we take the whole impression left by Shakespeare's world of shapes upon our inner feeling, with the extraordinary relief of every character that moves therein, and uphold to it the sum-total of Beethoven's world of motives, with their ineluctable incisiveness and definition, we cannot but see that the one of these worlds completely covers the other, so that each is contained in each, no matter how remote may seem their orbits.

To make this operation easier, let us cite the instance where Beethoven and Shakespeare join hands over the same subject, the *Overture to Coriolanus*. If we recall to mind the impression made upon us by the figure of Coriolanus in Shakespeare's drama, and from all the details of the complicated plot first single that which lingered with us through its bearing on the principal character, we shall see one solitary shape loom forth: the defiant Coriolanus in conflict with his inmost voice, that voice which only speaks the more unsilenceably when issuing from his mother's mouth; and of the dramatic development there will remain but that voice's victory over pride, the breaking of the stubbornness of a nature strong beyond all bounds. For his drama Beethoven chooses nothing but these two chief-motives, which make us feel more surely than all abstract exposition the inmost essence of that pair of characters. Then if we devoutly follow the movement developing solely from the opposition of these two motives in strict accordance with their musical character, and allow in turn the purely-musical detail to work upon us—the lights and shades, the meetings and partings of these two motives,—we shall at like time be following the course of a drama whose own peculiar method of expression embraces all that held our interest, the complex plot and clash of minor characters, in the acted work of the playwright. What gripped us there as an action set immediately before us, almost lived through by ourselves, we here receive as inmost kernel of that action; there set forth by characters with all the might of nature-forces, it here is just as sharply limned by the musician's motives, identical in inmost essence with the motives at work in those characters. Merely in the one sphere *those*, in the other *these*, laws of movement and dimension take effect.

We have called Music the revelation of the inner vision of the Essence of the world, and Shakespeare we might term a Beethoven who goes on dreaming though awake. What holds their spheres asunder, are the formal conditions of the laws of apperception obtaining in each. The perfect art-form would therefore have to take its rise from the point where those respective laws could meet. Now, what makes Shakespeare at once so incomparable and so inexplicable, is this: those Forms which bound the plays of great Calderon himself to prim conventionality, and made them strictly artist's-works, he saturated with such life that they seem dissolved away by Nature: no longer do we think we see fictitious men, but real live men before us; and yet they stand so wondrous far from us, that we cannot but deem material contact with them as impossible as if we were looking at ghosts.—Seeing, then, that Beethoven is the very counterpart of Shakespeare even in his attitude towards the formal laws of his art, his fulfilling abrogation of them, we perhaps may gain the clearest notion of that point where their two spheres would touch, or melt into each other, if we take our philosopher once more for guide, and proceed to the goal of his Dream-theory, his hypothesis of ghostly apparitions.

Here our business would lie less with the metaphysical, than the physiologic explanation of so-called "second sight." We have already cited our philosopher's theory that the Dream-organ is situate in that portion of the brain which responds to impressions received from the operations of the inner organism in profound sleep, and responds in a manner analogous to the effect produced by waking impressions from the outer world on the portion of the brain immediately connected with the organs of sense, now completely at rest. We have also seen that the dream-message received by this inner organ can be transmitted [to the waking consciousness] only through a second type of dream, a dream that directly precedes our wakening, and which can render in none but an allegoric form the contents of the first; and the reason was, that, even in the preparatory stage of the brain's awaking to external objects, the forms of perception pertaining to the phenomenal world, such as Space and Time, must already be brought into play, and thus construct an image akin to the experiences of daily life.—Further, we have compared the work of the Musician to the clairvoyante's hypnotic vision (*dem Gesichte der hellsehend gewordenen Somnambule*), as the direct transcript of the inmost dream [*Wahrtraum*—lit.

"true-dream"] beheld by her and now imparted, in her most active state of clairvoyance, to those outside; and we have found the channel for this message by following the genesis and evolution of the world of Sound.—Still pursuing our analogy, with this physiologic phenomenon of hypnotic clairvoyance let us couple its fellow, that of ghost-seeing, and borrow from Schopenhauer, again, his hypothesis that it is a state of clairvoyance occurring in the waking brain; that is to say, it results from a temporary reduction in the waking power of sight, whose clouded eyes are now made use of by the inner impulse to impart to the form of consciousness most near to waking the message of the inmost veridical dream.* This shape, projected before the eye from within, belongs in nowise to the material world of Appearance; yet it appears to the ghost-seer with all the signs and tokens of actual life. With this projection of the inner image before the waking eye—an act the inner will can accomplish only in rare and extraordinary cases—let us now compare the work of Shakespeare; and we shall find him to be the ghost-seer and spirit-raiser, who from the depths of his own inner consciousness conjures the shapes of men from every age, and sets them before his waking eye and ours in such a fashion that they seem to really live.

As soon as we have fully grasped the consequences of this analogy we may term Beethoven, whom we have likened to the clairvoyant, the hidden motor (*den wirkenden Untergrund*) of Shakespeare the ghost-seer: what brings forth Beethoven's melodies, projects the spirit-shapes of Shakespeare; and both will blend into one being, if we let the musician enter not only the world of Sound, but at like

* "Zu diesem, hier analogisch angezogenen, physiologischen Phänomene der somnambulen Hellsichtigkeit halten wir nun das andere des Geistersehens, und verwenden hierbei wiederum die hypothetische Erklärung Schopenhauer's, wonach dieses ein bei wachem Gehirne eintretendes Hellsehen sei; nämlich, es gehe dieses in Folge einer Depotenzirung des wachen Gesichtes vor sich, dessen jetzt umflortes Sehen der innere Drang zu einer Mittheilung an das dem Wachen unmittelbar nahe Bewusstsein benutze, um ihm die im innersten Wahrtraume erschienene Gestalt deutlich vor sich zu zeigen."—

time that of Light. This would be analogous to the physiologic occurrence that on one side becomes the cause of ghost-seeing, on the other produces somnambulistic clairvoyance; in respect of which it is to be conjectured that an inner stimulus travels through the brain in a similar but inverse fashion to the outer impressions received when awake, and, ultimately arriving at the organs of sense, makes them regard as an external object what has really thrust its way from within. But we have already recorded the indisputable fact that, while we are lost in the hearing of music, our sight is so far paralysed that it no longer perceives objects with any degree of intensity; so this would be the state induced by the innermost Dream-world, the blinding of the eye that it might see the spirit-shape.

This hypothetical explanation of a physiologic phenomenon, otherwise inexplicable, we may apply to the solution of our present artistic problem from various sides and arrive at a like result. For instance, Shakespeare's spirit-shapes would be brought to sound through the full awaking of the inner organ of Music: or Beethoven's motives would inspire the palsied sight to see those shapes distinctly, and embodied in those spirit-shapes they now would move before our eyes turned clairvoyant. In either case, identical in essence, the prodigious force here framing appearances from within outwards, against the ordinary laws of Nature, must be engendered by the deepest Want (*Noth*). And that Want presumably would be the same as finds vent, in the common course of life, in the scream of the suddenly-awakened from an obsessing vision of profoundest sleep *; saving that here, in the extraordinary, the stupendous event which shapes the life of manhood's genius, that Want awakens to a new, a world laid open by such awaking only, a world of clearest knowledge and highest capability.

This awaking out of deepest Want we witness in that redoubtable leap from instrumental into vocal music—so offensive to ordinary æsthetic criticism—which has led us from our discussion of Beethoven's Ninth Symphony to

* Cf. Kundry's awakening in *Parsifal*, acts ii. and iii.—Tr.

the above prolonged digression. What we here experience is a certain overcharge, a vast compulsion to unload without, only to be compared with the stress to waken from an agonising dream; and the important issue for the Art-genius of mankind, is that this special stress called forth an artistic deed whereby that genius gained a novel power, the qualification for begetting the highest Artwork.

As to that Artwork itself, we can only conclude that it will be *the most perfect Drama*, and thus stand high above the work of Poetry. This we may conclude after having recognised the identity of the Shakespearian and the Beethovenian Drama, whilst we may assume, on the other hand, that it will bear the same relation to "Opera" as a play of Shakespeare's to a literature-drama, a Beethovenian symphony to an opera's music.

That Beethoven returns in the course of his Ninth Symphony to the 'choral cantata with orchestra,' must not mislead our judgment of that eventful leap from instrumental into vocal music; we have already gauged the import of this choral portion of the symphony, and found it pertaining to the strictest field of Music: beyond that said ennoblement of Melody, we have in it no formal innovation; it is a Cantata with words, to which the music bears no closer relation than to any other vocal text. For we know that it is not the verses of a text-writer, and were he a Goethe or Schiller, that can determine Music. *Drama* alone can do that; and not the dramatic poem, but the drama that moves before our very eyes, the visible counterpart of Music, where word and speech belong no more to the poet's thought, but solely to the action.

It is not the *work* of Beethoven, then, but the unparalleled artistic *deed* contained therein, that we must stamp on our minds as climax of the musician's genius, when we declare that an artwork founded and modelled throughout on this deed must afford withal the perfect *art-form*: that form wherein, for Drama as for Music in especial, each vestige of conventionality would be entirely upheaved. And this Form would also be the only one to throughly fit the German Spirit, so powerfully individualised in our great Beethoven: the new, the Purely-human art-form made by it, and yet originally immanent in it; the form for which, when likened with the antique world, the new still goes a-lacking.

Whoever allows himself to be influenced by the views I have here expressed in regard of Beethovenian music, will certainly not escape being called fantastic and extravagant; and this reproach will be levelled at him not merely by our educated and uneducated musicians of the day—who for the most part have seen that dream-vision of Music's under no other guise than Bottom's dream in the Midsummer's-night—but in particular by our literary poets and even our plastic artists, so far as they ever trouble their heads with questions that seem to lie entirely beyond their sphere. We must make up our minds to tranquilly bear that reproach however, even should it take the form of a high and mighty, nay, a deliberately insulting snub; for to us it is manifest, firstly that these people are downright incapable of seeing what we see, and secondly that any glimmer they may get thereof is only just sufficient to shew them their own unproductiveness: that they should recoil in horror from the sight, we need no pains to understand.

If we review the general character of our current public art and literature, we are struck by a notable change, which dates from about a generation back. Here every-one not only looks quite hopeful, but in a certain sense quite sure that the great period of the German Rebirth, with its Goethe and Schiller, is falling into disesteem—of course well-tempered. A generation ago it was somewhat otherwise: then the character of our age proclaimed itself, without disguise, as essentially critical; folk called the spirit of the time a "paper" one, and believed that even plastic art must renounce all idea of originality and content itself with a merely reproductive use and combination of existing types. We cannot but think that people then saw more clearly, and expressed themselves more honestly, than is the case to-day. Whoever is still of that earlier opinion, despite the confident demeanour of our literary writers, literary painters, builders and other artists conversant with the spirit of the times, with him we may hope to come to readier terms if we try to set in its proper light the unparalleled importance won by Music for the [future] evolution of our Culture; in conclusion we therefore will rise from our plunge into the inner world, with which the preceding inquiry has chiefly concerned us, and take a glance at the outer world in which we live and under whose pressure that inner essence has acquired at last the force to react without.

Not to get lost in a maze of "culture-history," we will take one characteristic feature of the public mind in the immediate present.—

With the victorious advance of the German arms to the centre of French civilisation, a feeling of shame at our dependence on that civilisation has suddenly appeared among us, and steps into publicity as an appeal to lay aside the Parisian mode of dress. So! at last the sense of patriotism rebels against what, not only the nation's æsthetic sense of seemliness has borne so long without a murmur, but our public mind has striven for in hottest haste. What, in fact, could a glance at our public life have told the modeller? It simply furnished our comic papers with food for caricature, on the one hand, while on the other our poets continued undeterred their compliments to the "German woman."—Upon an illustration of this singularly complicated situation we surely need not waste our breath.—But some might haply regard it as a passing evil: they might be expecting that the blood of our sons, our brothers and husbands, shed for the German Spirit's sublimest thought on the deadliest battlefields in history, at least must redden the cheeks of our daughters, sisters and wives, and a sudden noblest Want must wake in them the pride that no longer could stoop to present themselves to their males as the most ridiculous of caricatures. For the honour of all German women we too will gladly believe that such a proper feeling is at work in them; and yet each man must have smiled when he read the first appeals to them to clothe themselves in a novel style. Who cannot have felt that the thing would end in a new, and presumably a very unbecoming masquerade? For 'tis no mere accidental whim of our public life, that we stand under rule of the Mode; just as it is in character with the whole history of modern civilisation, that the whims of Parisian taste dictate to us the laws of Mode. In truth it is French taste, i.e. the spirit of Paris and Versailles, that for two hundred years has been the sole productive ferment in European culture; while the spirit of no single nation could evolve an art-type any more, the spirit of the French at least laid down the outward form of society, and to to-day the cut of clothes.

However paltry these affairs may seem, they are original to the French spirit: they express it quite as definitely and vividly as the Italians of the Renaissance, the Greeks, the Egyptians and Assyrians expressed their spirit in their art-types; and nothing yields us clearer evidence of the French being the ruling race of to-day's Civilisation, than the fact that our fancy promptly falls into the ridiculous if we try to imagine ourselves emancipated from their Mode. At once we recognise that a "German Mode," set up as rival to the French, would be something too absurd; and since our feeling nevertheless revolts against that reign, we can only conclude that we are stricken with a veritable curse, from which nothing but a profoundly radical new-birth can ever redeem us. Our whole root-nature, to wit, would have so thoroughly to change, that the very term *the Mode* would lose all meaning for the outward fashion of our life.

In what this new-birth must consist, we should have to argue with the greatest caution, after first discovering the causes of the deep decline of public art-taste. And as we have already found the employment of analogies of some service for elucidating the otherwise difficult subject of our main inquiry, let us once more betake ourselves to a seemingly distant field of observation, but a field whereon we at any rate may hope to win an addition to our knowledge of the plastic aspect of our public life.—

If we would conjure up a paradise of the human spirit's productivity, we must transfer ourselves to the days before the invention of *Writing* and its preservation on parchment or paper. We cannot but hold that here was born the whole of that Culture which now maintains a halting life as mere object of study or useful adaptation. Here *Poesis* was nothing other than the actual invention of Myths, i.e. of ideal occurrences in which the various characteristics of the life of man were mirrored with an objective reality like to that of ghostly apparitions. This faculty we see innate in every Folk of noble blood, down to the point when the use of written letters reached it. From then it loses its poetic force; Speech, theretofore in a living flux of natural evolution, now falls into the crystallising stage and stiffens; Poetry becomes the art of decking out the ancient myths, no longer to be new-invented, and ends in Rhetoric and Dialectics.—Let us picture next the leap from Writing into Printing. From the rare hand-written tome the father of the household read before his guests: now everyone reads dumbly to himself the printed book, and for the readers writes the scribbler. To obtain an inkling of the storm of madness that followed in the wake of printed letters, we must resummon the religious sects of the Reformation era, with their polemical tracts and disputations. One may presume that only Luther's glorious hymn saved whole the spirit of the Reformation, and that because it touched the heart and thereby healed the lexicomania (*Buchstaben-Krankheit*) of the brain. Yet the genius of a race might come to terms with the book-printer, however painful it might find the intercourse; but with the invention of the Newspaper, the full unfolding of the flower of Journalism, this good angel of the Folk could not but fly away from life. For now reigns nothing but Opinions, and "public" ones at that; they're to be had for pay, like the public strumpets: who buys a paper, has procured not only the printed sheet, but its opinion; he needs no more to think, or yet to ponder; there stands all ready-thought for him in black on white what folk are to think of God and the world. And so the Paris fashion-journal tells the "German wife" how she must dress; for the Frenchman has earned a perfect right to dictate to us in things like that, as he has soared to the undisputed position of the colour-illustrator of our Journal-paper world.

If by side of this metamorphosis of the poetic world into a journalistic-literary world we set the transformation of the world of Form and Colour, we shall find a precisely similar result.

Who could have the presumption to say he was able to form a true idea of the grandeur, the divine sublimity of the Plastic world of ancient Greece? Each glance at a single fragment of its ruins makes us feel with awe that we here are standing in presence of a Life for whose judgment we have not even the first beginning of a scale. That world had earned the right to teach us by its very ruins how the remainder of man's earthly life might yet be fashioned into something bearable. We may thank the great *Italians* for having revived for us that lesson, and nobly put it into practice for the newer world. This people, gifted with such abundant Phantasy, we see consume itself away in passionate adoption of that lesson; after one marvellous century it melts from history like a dream, and History erroneously takes up a kindred-seeming nation, as if to see what she could make of that for form and colour of the world. A crafty statesman and prince of the Church endeavoured to inoculate Italian art and culture into the *French* folk-spirit, after Protestantism had been completely rooted out therefrom: it had seen the fall of its noblest heads; and what the Paris Feast of St Bartholomew had spared, had finally been carefully burnt down to the lowest stump. The remnant of the nation was treated "artistically"; but as it had never had, or had lost all Phantasy, productiveness would nowhere shew itself, and particularly not in the creating of a work of Art. The attempt to make the Frenchman himself an artificial being was more successful; the artistic idea (*künstlerische Vorstellung*) that failed to find a home in his imagination, could be turned into an artificial exhibition (*künstliche Darstellung*) of the whole man in and to himself. Indeed this even might pass as Antique, if one only granted that man must be an artist in his person before he thought of producing artworks. If a "gallant" worshipped King but set the good example of a highly elegant demeanour in every act and situation, 'twas easy to descend the climax through the courtier lords, and at last induce the whole nation to put on the gallant manner; with whose growth into a second nature the Frenchman might end by fancying himself superior to the Italians of the Renaissance, inasmuch as these had merely brought forth artworks, whilst he had become a work of art himself.

One may describe the Frenchman as the product of a special art of expressing, behaving and clothing himself. His law for this is "*Taste*,"—a word transferred from the humblest function of the senses to a tendence of the mind; and with this taste he savours himself, precisely as he has dressed himself, as a highly flavoured sauce. Beyond cavil, he has turned the thing into a virtuosity: "modern" is he out-and-out, and if he thus exhibits himself for all the civilised world to copy, it's not *his* fault that he is copied inexpertly; rather is it a constant source of flattery to him, that he alone should be original in a thing which others feel compelled to copy.—And then the man is wholly "journal"; plastic art, no less than music, is an object for his "feuilleton." As a thorough modern, he has trimmed the former just as much to his liking as the cut of his clothes, in which he is governed purely by the principle of Novelty, i.e. perpetual change. Here the furniture is the chief affair; for it the architect constructs the house. The tendence displayed herein in earlier times, down to the great Revolution, was still original; in the sense that it fitted the character of the ruling classes of society as admirably as the dress their bodies, the coiffure their heads. Since then, this tendence has fallen in exact degree as the superior classes have timidly withdrawn from the leadership of *ton*, and left the Mode's initiative to the emerging broader strata of the populace (we are speaking of Paris throughout). And here the so-called "*demi-monde*," with its entreteneurs, has taken the lead: the Paris dame seeks to attract her husband by copying its dress and manners; for on this side, again, things are still so original that dress and manners belong to and complete each other. This side, however, abjures all influence over plastic art; which consequently has fallen into the hands of the fancy dealer, under the shape of quincaillerie and hangings, wellnigh as in the first beginnings of the arts among nomadic races. With the constant demand for novelty, and seeing that itself can never produce a thing really new, the Mode is left with no resource but a constant changing of extremes: indeed it is to this tendence that our oddly-counselled plastic artists tack themselves at last, to bring noble forms of art—naturally not of their own invention—once more to daylight with the rest. Antique and Roccoco, Gothic and Renaissance, take turn and turn about; the factories put forth Laocoon-groups, Chinese porcelain, copies of Raphael and Murillo, Etrurian vases, Medieval curtain-stuffs, meubles à la Pompadour, stuccos à la Louis XIV.; the architect frames the whole in Florentine style, and sets an Ariadne-group atop.

Thus "modern art" becomes a new principle in Æsthetics too: its originality consists in its total want of originality, and its priceless gain in the exchange of every style; all which have now been brought within range of the commonest observation, and can be adapted to the taste of every man.—Also, it is credited with a new humanitarian principle, the Democratising of artistic taste. They tell us to have every hope of the education of the people; for art and its products, you see, are no longer reserved for the privileged classes, but the smallest citizen has now the opportunity of placing the noblest types of art before his eyes upon his chimney-piece, whilst the beggar himself may peep at them in the art-shop windows. One certainly should rest content; for, everything being already laid in a heap at our feet, it would really be impossible to conceive how even the most gifted brain could manage to invent a novel style in either plastic art or literature.—

Yes, we may fully concur with that opinion; for here we have an outcome of history as consequent as our civilisation itself. 'Twere thinkable that these consequences might be blotted out, namely in the foundering of our civilisation; an event to be conceived if all History went by the board as result, let us say, of social Communism imposing itself on the modern world in the guise of a practical religion. At any rate our civilisation has come to the end of true productiveness in respect of its Plastic form, and we shall do well to accustom ourselves no longer to expect anything at all resembling the unapproachable model bequeathed us by the antique world in that domain, and haply to accept this strange result of modern civilisation—so very comforting to many persons—with the same conviction as makes us now regard the suggestion of a new German mode of dress for us men, and especially for our women, as a vain attempt to kick against the spirit of our civilisation.

Far as our *eye* can roam, the *Mode* commands us.—

But coevally with this world of Mode another world has risen for us. As Christianity stepped forth amid the Roman civilisation of the universe, so *Music* breaks forth from the chaos of modern civilisation. Both say aloud: "our kingdom is not of this world." And that means: we come from within, ye from without; we spring from the Essence of things, ye from their Show.

Let anyone experience for himself how the whole modern world of Appearance, which hems him in on every side to his despair, melts suddenly to naught if he but hears the first few bars of one of those godlike symphonies. How were it possible in a modern concert-room (where Turks and Zouaves would assuredly feel at home!) to listen to music with even a modicum of devotion, if our visual surroundings did not vanish from our optic range in manner said above? And, taken in the most earnest sense, it is this effect that Music has on our whole modern civilisation; she effaces it, as the light of day the lamp-light.—

'Tis hard to form an adequate notion of the way in which Music from of old has exerted her own peculiar might in face of the material world. To us it would seem that the music of the Hellenes steeped the world of semblances itself, and blended with its laws of sense. The numbers of Pythagoras are surely only to be understood aright through Music; by the laws of Eurhythmy the architect built, by those of Harmony the sculptor seized the human figure; the laws of Melody made the poet a singer, and from out the choral chant the Drama was projected on the stage. Everywhere we see the inner law, only conceivable as sprung from the spirit of Music, prescribe the outer law that regulates the world of sight: the genuine ancient Doric State which Plato tried to rescue for philosophy, nay, the order of war, the fight itself, the laws of Music led as surely as the dance.—But that paradise was lost: the fount of motion of a world ran dry. Like a ball once thrown, the world span round the curve of its trajectory, but no longer was it driven by a moving soul; and so its very motion must grow faint at last, until the world-soul had been waked again.

It was the spirit of Christianity that rewoke to life the soul of Music. And Music lit the eye of the Italian painter, inspiring it to penetrate the veil of things and reach their soul, the Christian spirit, fast decaying in the Church. Almost all these great painters were musicians, and when we lose ourselves in contemplation of their saints and martyrs, it is the spirit of Music that makes us forget we here are *seeing*.—But there came the reign of Mode: as the spirit of the Church fell victim to the artificial nurture of the Jesuits, so plastic art and music each became a soulless artifice.

Now, in our great Beethoven we have followed the wondrous process of emancipating Melody from the tyranny of Mode; and we have seen that, while making unrivalledly individual use of all the material which his glorious forerunners had toilsomely recovered from the influence of this Mode, he restored to Melody its everlasting type, to Music her immortal soul. With a godlike naïvety all his own, our master also stamps upon his victory the seal of that full consciousness wherewith he won it. In the poem of Schiller's which he chose for the marvellous closing section of his Ninth Symphony he recognised the joy of Nature liberated from the rule of "Mode." But observe the remarkable reading given by him to the poet's words:

"Deine Zauber binden wieder	"Thy blest magic binds together
Was die Mode streng getheilt."	What the Mode had sprung apart."

As we have seen before, Beethoven simply laid the words beneath his melody as a vocal text, a poem whose general character was in accord with the spirit of this melody. What is customarily meant by correct declamation, especially in the dramatic sense, he leaves almost entirely out of count; so—as with the singing of the whole first three strophes of the poem—he lets that verse: "Was die Mode streng getheilt" pass by us without any particular stress on the words. Then however, as the strain of dithyrambic inspiration reaches a climax never heard before, he gives to the words of this verse at last their full dramatic value, and repeating them in a *unisono* of wellnigh frantic menace, he finds the "streng" inadequate to signalise his wrath. Remarkably enough, this milder epithet for the operation of the Mode is also due to a toning-down on the part of the poet, who in the first edition of his Ode to Joy had printed:

"Was der Mode *Schwert* getheilt."	"What the fashion's *sword* had cleft."

But this "sword," again, to Beethoven did not appear to say the right thing; allotted to the Mode, it seemed to him too noble and heroic. So of his own sovereign power he substituted "*frech*," and now we sing:

"Was die Mode frech getheilt."	"What the Mode had *dared* to part." *

Could anything be more speaking than this vehement, this passionate artistic act? We might be looking on a *Luther* in his rage against the Pope!—

As for our present Civilisation, especially insofar as it influences the artistic man, we certainly may assume that nothing but the spirit of our Music, that music which Beethoven set free from bondage to the Mode, can dower it with a soul again. And the task of giving to the new, more soulful civilisation that haply may arise herefrom, the new Religion to inform it—this task must obviously be reserved for the German Spirit alone, that spirit which we ourselves shall never rightly understand till we cast aside each spurious tendency ascribed thereto.

Yet how hard of gain is true self-knowledge, above all for an entire nation, we now have learnt to our genuine horror from the case of our once so powerful neighbours the French; and we thence may derive a serious call to self-examination, for which we happily have but to pursue the earnest efforts of our own great poets, with whom, both consciously and unconsciously, this self-examination was the root-endeavour.

To them it must needs have seemed questionable, how

* In Härtel's otherwise so admirable Complete Edition of Beethoven's Works a member of what I have elsewhere styled the "Musical Temperance Union," entrusted with the "critical" supervision, has effaced this speaking feature from pages 260 *et seq.* of the score of the Ninth Symphony, and on his own authority has substituted for the "frech" of Schott's Original Edition the decorous, the moral-moderate "streng." Pure chance disclosed to me this falsification, whose motive is calculated to fill us with grave anxiety as to the ultimate fate of the works of our great Beethoven if they are to be subjected to a revision progressing along such lines.—R. WAGNER.

the uncouth and heavy-footed German nature could take rank at all advantageously beside the light and supple Form of our neighbours of Romanic descent. As the German spirit possessed, however, an undeniable advantage in the depth and inwardness of its conception of the world and all that moves therein, with them it was a constant question how this advantage could best be employed in the refining of the national character, and thence exert a beneficial influence on the mind and character of neighbouring peoples; whereas it was manifest that influences of this kind had taken hitherto the opposite route, and wrought on us more harm than good.

Now if we rightly judge the two poetic schemes that ran through the life of our greatest poet like two main arteries, we gain an excellent clue to the problem which presented itself to this freest of German men from the very commencement of his unparalleled career as poet.—We know that "Faust" and "Wilhelm Meister" were both conceived in the same period of the first exuberant blossoming of Goethe's poetic genius. The fervour of the deep idea that filled his mind first urged him to the execution of the earliest parts of "Faust": as if terrified by the vastness of his own conception, he turned from the mighty project to the more tranquillising treatment of the problem in "Wilhelm Meister." In full maturity of man's estate he completed this light-flowing novel. His hero is a German burgher's son who goes out in quest of sweet and stable Form, and journeying across the stage, through the heart of aristocratic society, is finally conducted to a life of usefulness as citizen of the world; to him is appointed a genie whom he understands but superficially: much in the same way as Goethe then understood Music, is "Mignon" understood by Wilhelm Meister. The poet lets us feel distinctly that an appalling crime has been committed against "Mignon"; yet he helps his hero over such a feeling, to lead him to a sphere set free from heat of passion and tragical intensity, a sphere of beauteous culture. He takes him to a gallery, to shew him pictures. Music is made for Mignon's death, and Robert Schumann actually composed it later.—It appears that Schiller was aghast at the last book of "Wilhelm Meister"; yet he surely knew no way of helping his great friend out of his strange aberration; especially as he could but assume that Goethe, who had created Mignon and therewith called a wonderful new world to life for us, must have inwardly fallen into a profound distraction, beyond all power of his friend to wake him from. Only Goethe himself, could wake himself; and—he awoke: in advanced old age he finished his *Faust*. Whatever had distracted him, he here assembles in one archetype of beauty: *Helena*, the full antique ideal, he conjures from the shadow-realm and marries to his Faust. But the shade will not stay banned; it melts into a radiant cloud, and floats away while Faust looks on in brooding but painless melancholy. *Gretchen* alone could redeem him: from the world of the blest that early sacrifice, still dwelling in his inmost heart unheeded, extends to him her hand. And if as sequel to the analogies we have drawn from likenesses between philosophy and physiology we now may venture to give the profoundest work of poetry an application to ourselves, the "Alles Vergängliche ist nur ein Gleichniss" ("All things terrestrial are but a likeness") we will interpret as the spirit of Plastic art, which Goethe so long and ardently had striven for; whilst "Das ewig Weibliche zieht uns dahin" ("The Eternal-womanly beckons us hence") we will read as the spirit of Music, which mounted from the poet's deepest consciousness, and, soaring over him, led his footsteps on the pathway of redemption.—

And by this path, commencing in the inmost of experiences, must the German Spirit lead its Folk, if it is to bless the nations in due measure with its calling. Scoff at us, who will, for attributing to German music this unbounded significance; we shall as little let ourselves be led astray thereby, as the German nation allowed itself to be misled when its enemies presumed to insult it on the ground of a too well reasoned doubt of its unanimity and staunchness. This also our great poet knew, when he sought a consolation for the Germans appearing so empty and foolish to him in their badly-copied airs and manners; his consolation was: "*The German is brave.*" And that is something!—

So let the German Folk be brave in peace as well; let it cherish its native worth, and cast the false show from it: let it never seek to pass for what it is not, but recognise the quality in which it is unique! To it the art of pleasing is denied; in lieu thereof its veritable deeds and thoughts are heartfelt and sublime. And beside its valour's victories in this wondrous 1870 no loftier trophy can be set, than the memory of our great *Beethoven*, who was born to the German Folk one hundred years ago. Whither our arms are urging now, to the primal seat of "shameless Mode" (*der "frechen Mode"*), there had *his* genius begun already the noblest conquest: what our thinkers, our poets, in toilsome transposition, had only touched as with a half-heard word, the Beethovenian Symphony had stirred to its deepest core: the new religion, the world-redeeming gospel of sublimest innocence, was there already understood as by ourselves.

So let us celebrate the great path-breaker in the wilderness of a paradise debased! But let us celebrate him worthily,—and no less worthily than the victories of German valour: for the benefactor of a world may claim still higher rank than the world-conqueror!

THE DESTINY OF OPERA.

Über die
Bestimmung der Oper.

This essay was published in the Spring of 1871 (E. W. Fritzsch, Leipzig), with the subsidiary title "An Academic Lecture by Richard Wagner." The author had in 1869 been elected a member of the Royal Academy of the Arts in Berlin, and "The Destiny of Opera" was intended as the thesis for his installation, which followed on April 28, 1871.

TRANSLATOR'S NOTE.

PREFACE.

N preparing the following essay for an Academic lecture, the author experienced the difficulty of having to enlarge once more on a subject he many years ago had treated exhaustively, as he believes, in a special book entitled *Oper und Drama*. As the requisite brevity of its present treatment would only allow of the main idea being sketched in outline, whoever might haply feel roused to more serious interest in the subject must needs be referred to that earlier book of mine. It then would scarcely escape his notice that, albeit a complete agreement holds between the older, lengthier, and the present conciser treatment of the subject itself—namely the character and importance ascribed by the author to the Musically-conceived drama—yet in many respects this recent setting offers new points of view, from whence regarded certain details necessarily assume another aspect; and that, perhaps, may make this newer treatment interesting even to those already familiar with the older one.

Certainly I have been given ample time to digest the topic started by myself, and I could have wished to have been diverted from the process by practical proof of the justice of my views being made more easy to me. The obtaining of single stage-performances, correct in my sense of the term, could not suffice me so long as they were not withdrawn completely from the sphere of modern operatic doings; for the ruling theatrical element of our day, with all its outward and inward attributes, entirely inartistic, un-German, both morally and mentally pernicious, invariably gathers again like a choking mist over any spot where the most arduous exertions may have given one for once an outlook on the sunlight. May the present writing therefore be not taken as an ambitious contribution to the field of Theory proper, but merely as a last attempt from that side to awaken interest and furtherance for the author's efforts on the realm of artistic Practice. It will then be understood why, prompted by this wish alone, he has constantly endeavoured to place his subject in new lights; for he was bound to keep on trying to propound the problem, that occupied his mind, in such a way that it finally might strike the minds of those alone qualified to give it serious attention. That this result has hitherto been so hard of attainment that he could but regard himself as a lonely wanderer soliloquising to a croaking accompaniment of the frogs in our stage-reporters' swamp, has simply shewn him how low had sunk the sphere to which he found himself and problem banned: but this sphere alone contains the elements capable of producing a higher Artwork, and thus the object of the following treatise, too, can only be to direct to those elements the gaze of those who at present stand entirely outside this sphere.

 WELL-MEANT cry of earnest friends of the Theatre lays the blame of its downfall on the Opera. The charge is founded on the unmistakable decline of interest in the spoken Play, as also on the degeneration of dramatic performances in general.

The correctness of this accusation must needs seem obvious. Merely, one might ask how it came to pass that the foundations of Opera were laid with the first beginnings of the modern Theatre, and why the most distinguished minds have repeatedly dwelt on the potentialities in a genre of dramatic art whose one-sided development has taken the shape of current Opera? In such an inquiry we might easily be led into regarding our greatest poets as, in a certain sense, the pioneers of Opera. Though such an allegation must be accepted with great reserve, on the other hand the issue of our great German poets' labours for the theatre, and their effect on the whole spirit of our dramatic representations, can but cause us earnestly to ponder how it was that Opera could have acquired so overpowering a control over theatric taste in general, in face of just the influence of those great poetic works themselves. And here we perhaps may gain an answer if we limit ourselves at first to the actual result, upon the character of stage-doings in the stricter province of the *Play*, of the effect of the Goethe-and-Schiller Drama upon the spirit in which our actors approach their work.

That result we recognise at once as due to a disproportion between the capacity of our actors and the nature of the tasks proposed them. A full account of this misrelation belongs to the history of German Acting, and has already been undertaken in praiseworthy fashion.*

* Ed. Devrient's "*Geschichte der deutschen Schauspielkunst.*"—Tr.

Referring to that account, on the one hand, and on the other reserving the deeper æsthetic problem at bottom of the evil for the later course of our inquiry, our present concern is that our poets had to couch their idealising tendence in a dramatic form to which the natural parts and training of our actors could not adapt themselves. It needed the rarest talents, such as of a Sophie Schröder, to completely solve a task pitched far too high for our players; accustomed solely to their native element of German burgher life, the sudden demand could not but set them in the most ruinous bewilderment. To that disproportion we owe the rise and eventual rampancy of "false pathos." This had been preceded, at an earlier epoch of the German stage, by the grotesque affectation peculiar to the "English comedians" so-called: a grotesquery applied by them to the rough-and-ready representation of old-English and even Shakespearian pieces, and to be met to this day at the degenerate English national theatre. In healthy opposition there had since arisen the so-called "true-to-nature," which found its suitable field of expression in the "Burgher" drama. Though Lessing himself, as also Goethe in his youth, wrote poems for this Burgher drama, we must note that it always derived its chief supply from pieces written by the foremost actors of this period. Now, the narrow sphere and scant poetic value of these products impelled our great poets to extend and elevate dramatic style; and though their original purpose was to continue the cultivation of the "true-to-nature," it was not long before the Ideal tendence shewed itself,—to be realised, as for expression, by *poetic pathos*. Those at all acquainted with this branch of our art-history, know how our great poets were disturbed in their endeavours to instil the new style into the players; however, it is much to be doubted whether in any event they would finally have proved successful, as they had previously been obliged to content themselves with a mere artificial semblance of success, which persistently developed into just that so-called "false pathos." In harmony with the German's modest talent for play-acting, this remained the sole but doubtful profit, as regards the character of performance of dramas of an Ideal trend, of that else so gigantic influence of our poets on the Theatre.

Now, what took the outward form of this "false pathos" became in turn the tendence of all the dramatic conceptions of our lesser stage-poets, whose matter from first to last was every whit as hollow as that pathos itself: we need but recall the products of a Houwald, Müllner, and the string of similar playwrights who have made for the Pathetic to the present day. The only adducible reaction against this tendence would be the constantly reviving Burgher play or prose-comedy of our time, had the French "Sensational piece" ("*Effektstück*") not overwhelmed us with its influence in this direction also. Hereby has the last trace of purity of type been wiped from our stage; and all that our Play has retained from the dramas of Goethe and Schiller themselves, is the now open secret of the employment of "false pathos," to wit "*Effect.*"

As everything written for, and acted at the theatre is nowadays inspired by nothing but this tendence to "Effect," so that whatever ignores it is promptly condemned to neglect, we need feel no surprise at seeing it systematically applied to the performance of pieces by Goethe and Schiller; for, in a certain sense, we here have the original model that has been misconstrued to this tendence. The need of "poetic pathos" made our poets deliberately adopt a *rhetorical mode of diction*, with the aim of working on the Feeling; and, as it was impossible for our unpoetic actors to either understand or carry out the ideal aim, this diction led to that intrinsically senseless, but melodramatically telling style of declamation whose practical object was just the said "Effect," i.e. a stunning of the spectator's senses, to be documented by the outburst of "applause." This "applause" and its unfailing provoker, the "exit"-tirade, became the soul of every tendence of our modern theatre: the "brilliant exits" in the rôles of our classical plays have been counted up, and the latters' value rated by their number—exactly as with an Italian operatic part. Surely we cannot scold our applause-dry priests of Thalia and Melpomene for casting envious glances at the Opera, where these "exits" are far more plentiful, and the storms of applause are raised with much greater certainty, than in even the most effective play; and since our playwrights live on the Effect of the rôles of our actors, 'tis easy to understand why the opera-composer appears to them a very hateful rival, for he can bring all this about by simply arranging for a good loud scream at the close of any vocal phrase you please.

In truth the outer reason, as also the most obvious character of the complaint we noted at starting, turns out to be thus and not otherwise. That I am far from thinking I have herewith shewn its deeper ground, I sufficiently hinted above: but, before we touch the inner core, I deem it more advisable to first weigh well its outer tokens, open to the experience of everyone. Let us therefore remember that in the character of all theatrical performances there inheres a tendency whose worst consequence comes out as the striving for "*effect*," and, though just as rampant in the spoken Play, in Opera it has the fullest opportunity of satiation. At bottom of the common actor's cry against the Opera there probably lies nothing but jealousy of its greater wealth of means of effect: but we must admit that the earnest actor has far more show of reason for annoyance, when he compares the seeming easiness and frivolity of these means of effect with the certainly much severer pains he has to take, to do some justice to the characters he represents. For, even from the standpoint of its outward effect on the public, the Play may boast of at least this merit:—that the plot itself, with the incidents that hold the plot together and the motives that explain it, must be intelligible, to rivet the spectator's interest; and that a piece composed of nothing but declamatory phrases, without an underlying plot intelligibly set forth and thereby centering the interest, is here as yet unthinkable. Opera, on the contrary, may be taxed with simply stringing together a number of means of exciting a purely physical sense, whilst a mere agreeable contrast in their order of sequence suffices to mask the absence of any understandable or reasonable plot.

Plainly, a very serious point in the indictment. Yet even of this we may have our doubts, on closer scrutiny. That the so-called text of an opera must be interesting, composers have felt so clearly in every age, and particularly of late, that to obtain a good "book" has been one of their most earnest endeavours. An attractive, or if possible a rousing plot, has always been essential for an opera to make its mark, especially in our time; so that it would be difficult to argue wholly away the dramatic tendence in the flimsy structure of an operatic text. In fact this side of the procedure has been so little unpretentious, that there is hardly a play of Shakespeare's, and there soon will be none of Schiller's and Goethe's, which Opera has not deemed just good enough for adaptation. Precisely this abuse, however, could only irritate our actors and playwrights still more, and this time with great justice; they might well protest: "Why should we take any pains in future to acquit ourselves of true dramatic tasks, when the public runs from us to where the selfsame themes, most frivolously distorted, are employed for mere multiplication of the vulgarest effects?" To this we at any rate might reply by asking how it would have been possible to set Herr Gounod's opera "Faust" before the German public, if our acting-stage had been able to make it really understand the "Faust" of Goethe? No: 'tis not to be disputed that the public has turned away from our actors' singular efforts to make something of the monologue of our own "Faust," to Herr Gounod's aria with the theme on the pleasures of youth, and here applauds whilst it there refused to move a hand.

Perhaps no instance could shew us more plainly and distressingly, to what a pass our Theatre has come. Yet even now we cannot admit the perfect equity of laying the whole blame of this undeniable downfall on the vogue enjoyed by Opera; rather, that very vogue should open our eyes alike to the failings of our Play and the impossibility of fulfilling within its bounds, and with the only expressional means at its command, the *ideal* scope of Drama. Precisely here, where the highest ideal is faced with its utmost trivialising, as in the above example, the horror of the thing must force us to look deeper into the nature of our problem. We still might shirk the obligation, if we merely meant to take a great depravation of public taste for granted, and to seek its causes in the wider field of our public life. But for ourselves, having reached that horrifying experience from just this standpoint, it is hopeless to contemplate an improvement of public art-taste, in particular, by the lengthy route of a regeneration of our public spirit itself; we deem wiser to take the direct path of an inquiry into the purely æsthetic problem lying at bottom, and thus to arrive at an answer which perchance may give us hopes of the possibility of an influence being exerted on the public spirit from this opposite side.

We therefore will formulate a thesis, whose working-out may haply guide us to that end. As follows:—

We grant that Opera has made palpable the downfall of the Theatre: though it may be doubted whether it really brought about that downfall, yet its present supremacy shews clearly that by it alone can our Theatre be raised again; but this restoration can never truly prosper till it conducts our Theatre to that Ideal to which it is so innately predisposed, that neglect and misapprehension thereof have done far greater harm to the German stage than to the French, since the latter had no idealistic aspirations and therefore could devote itself to the development of realistic correctness in a narrower sphere.—

An intelligent history of stage "pathos" would make plain what the idealistic trend in modern drama has ever aimed at. Here it would be instructive to note how the Italians, who sat at the feet of the Antique for wellnigh all their art-tendences, left the spoken drama almost quite in embryo; they promptly attempted a reconstruction of the antique drama on a basis of musical Lyrics, and, straying ever farther to one side, produced the Opera. While this was taking place in Italy under the omnipotent influence of the cultured upper circles of the nation, among the Spaniards and English the Folk-spirit itself was evolving the modern Play, after the antiquarian bent of lettered poets had proved incapable of any vital influence on the nation. Only by starting from this realistic sphere, wherein Lope de Vega had shewn such exuberant fertility, did Calderon lead the Spanish drama to that idealising tendence, which brought him so close to the Italians that many of his pieces we can but characterise as wellnigh operatic. Perhaps the English drama also would not have held aloof from a similar tendence, had not the inscrutable genius of a Shakespeare enabled the loftiest figures of history and legend to tread the boards of the realistic Folk-play with such a truth to nature that they passed beyond the reach of any rule erewhile misborrowed from the antique Form. Perhaps their awe at Shakespeare's unfathomable inimitability had no less share than their recognition of the true meaning of the Antique and its forms, in determining our great poets' dramatic labours. They pondered too the eminent advantages of Opera, though it finally passed their understanding how this Opera was to be dealt with from their standpoint. Schiller, transported by Gluck's "Iphigenia in Tauris," nevertheless could not discover a modus vivendi with the Opera; and Goethe appears to have plainly seen that the task was reserved for the musical genius, when he regarded the news of Mozart's death as effacing all the splendid prospects of a Musically-conceived Drama opened up to him by "Don Giovanni."

Through this attitude of Goethe and Schiller we are afforded a deep insight into the nature of the *poet* pure and simple. If on the one hand Shakespeare and his method to them seemed incomprehensible, and on the other they felt compelled to leave to the *musician*—whose method was equally incomprehensible—the unique task of breathing ideal life into the figures of the Drama, the question arises: how did they stand as poets toward the genuine Drama, and whether, solely as such, they could feel themselves equipped for Drama at all? A doubt of this seems to have invaded more and more these so profoundly truthful men, and the constant change of Form in their projects shews, of itself, that they felt as if engaged in one continual series of experiments. Were we to try to probe that doubt, we might find in it the confession of a certain insufficiency in the poetic nature (*das Bekenntniss einer Unzulänglichkeit des dichterischen Wesens*); for Poetry, taken by itself, is only to be conceived as an *abstractum*, and first becomes a *concretum* through the matter of its fashionings. If neither the Plastic artist nor the Musician is thinkable without a trace of the poetic spirit, the question simply is how that latent force, which in them brings forth the work of art, can lead to the same result in the Poet's shapings as a conscious agent?

Without embarking on an inquiry into the mystery just mooted, we yet must call to mind the distinction between the modern culture-poet and the naïve poet of the ancient world. The latter was in the first place an inventor of Myths, then their word-of-mouth narrator in the Epos, and finally their personal performer in the living Drama. Plato was the first to adopt all three poetic forms for his "dialogues," so filled with dramatic life and so rich in myth-invention; and these scenes of his may be regarded as the foundation—nay, in the poet-philosopher's glorious "Symposium," the model unapproached—of strictly literary poetry, which always leans to the didactic. Here the forms of naïve poetry are merely employed to set philosophic theses in a quasi-popular light, and conscious *tendence* takes the place of the directly-witnessed scene from life. To extend this "Tendence" to the acted drama, must have appeared to our great culture-poets the surest mode of elevating the existing popular play; and in this they may have been misled by certain features of the Antique Drama. The Tragedy of the Greeks having evolved from a compromise between the Apollinian and the Dionysian elements, upon the basis of a system of Lyrics wellnigh past our understanding, the didactic hymn of the old-Hellenian priests could combine with the newer Dionysian dithyramb to produce that enthralling effect in which this artwork stands unrivalled. Now the fact of the Apollinian element in Greek Tragedy, regarded as a literary monument, having attracted to itself the principal notice in every age, and particularly of philosophers and didacts, may reasonably have betrayed our later poets—who also chiefly viewed these tragedies as literary products—into the opinion that in this didactic tendence lay the secret of the antique drama's dignity, and consequently into the belief that the existing popular drama was only to be raised and idealised by stamping it therewith. Their true artistic instinct saved them from sacrificing living Drama to Tendence bald and bare: but what was to put soul into this Drama, to lift it on the cothurnus of ideality, they deemed could only be the purposed elevation of its tendence; and that the more, as their sole disposable material, namely Word-speech, the vehicle of notions (*Begriffe*), seemed to exclude the feasibility, or even the advisability, of an ennoblement and heightening of expression on any side but this. The lofty *sentence* alone could match the higher *tendence*; and to impress the hearer's physical sense, unquestionably excited by the drama, recourse must be had to so-called *poetic diction*. But this diction lured the exponents of their pieces into that "false pathos," whose recognition must needs have given our great poets many a pang when they compared it with their deep delight in Gluck's "Iphigenia" and Mozart's "Don Juan."

What so profoundly moved them in these last, must surely have been that here they found the drama transported by its music to the sphere of the Ideal, a sphere where the simplest feature of the plot was at once transfigured, and motive and emotion, fused in one direct expression, appealed to them with noblest stress. Here hushed all desire to seize a Tendence, for the Idea had realised itself before them as the sovereign call of Fellow-feeling. "Error attends man's ev'ry quest," or "Life is not the highest good," was here no longer to be clothed in words, for the inmost secret of the wisest apothegm itself stood bared to them in limpid Melody. Whilst that had said "it means," this said "it is!" Here had the highest pathos come to be the very soul of Drama; as from a shining world of dreams, Life's picture stepped before us here with sympathetic verity.

But what a riddle must this artwork have seemed to our poets!—where was the Poet's place therein? Certainly not where their own strength lay, in the poetic thought and diction, of which these "texts" were absolutely destitute. There being, then, no possible question of the Poet, it was the Musician alone to whom this artwork appeared to belong. Yet, judged by their artistic standard, it fell hard to accord this latter a rank at all commensurate with the stupendous force he set in motion. In Music they saw a plainly irrational art, a thing half wild half foolish, not for a moment to be approached from the side of true artistic culture. And in Opera, forsooth, a paltry, incoherent pile of forms, without the smallest evidence of a sense for architectonics; whilst the last thing its capriciously assorted items could be said to aim at, was the consistence of a true dramatic plan. So that, admitting it was the dramatic groundwork that in Gluck's "Iphigenia" had held that jumble of forms together for once, and made of it a thrilling whole, there arose the question: Who would ever care to step into the shoes of its librettist, and write the threadbare text for the arias of even a Gluck, unless he were prepared to give up all pretence to rank as "poet"? The incomprehensible in the thing, was the supreme ideality of an effect whose artistic factors were not discoverable by analogy with any other art soever. And the incomprehensibility increased when one passed from this particular work of Gluck's, instinct with the nobility of a tragic subject taken bodily from the antique, and found that under certain circumstances, no matter how absurd or trivial its shape, one could not deny to Opera a power unrivalled even in the most ideal sense. These circumstances arose forthwith, whenever a great dramatic artist filled a rôle in such an opera. We need but instance the impersonation, surely unforgettable by many yet alive, once given us by Frau Schröder-Devrient of "Romeo" in Bellini's opera. Every fibre of the musician rebels against allowing the least artistic merit to the sickly, utterly threadbare music here hung upon an opera-poem of indigent grotesqueness; but ask anyone who witnessed it, what impression he received from the "Romeo" of Frau Schröder-Devrient as compared with the Romeo of our very best play-actor in even the great Briton's piece? And this effect by no means lay in any vocal virtuosity, as with the common run of our prime donne's successes, for in this case that was scant and totally unsupported by any richness of the voice itself: the effect was simply due to the dramatic power of the rendering. But that, again, could never possibly have succeeded with the selfsame Schröder-Devrient in quite the finest spoken play; and thus the whole achievement must have issued from the element of music, transfiguring and idealising even in this most meagre form.

Such an experience as this last, however, might set us on the high road to discover and estimate the veritable factor in the creation of the Dramatic Artwork.—As the Poet's share in it was so infinitesimal, Goethe believed he must ascribe the whole authorship of Opera to the Musician; and how much of serious truth resides in that opinion, we perhaps shall see if next we turn our notice to our great poets' second object of non-comprehension in the realm of Drama, to wit the singularity of *Shakespeare* and his artistic method.—

To the French, as representatives of modern civilisation, Shakespeare, considered seriously, to this day is a monstrosity; and even to the Germans he has remained a subject of constantly renewed investigation, with so little positive result that the most conflicting views and statements are forever cropping up again. Thus has this most bewildering of dramatists—already set down by some as an utterly irresponsible and untamed genius, without one trace of artistic culture—quite recently been credited again with the most systematic tendence of the didactic poet. Goethe, after introducing him in "Wilhelm Meister" as an "admirable writer," kept returning to the problem with increasing caution, and finally decided that here the higher tendence was to be sought, not in the poet, but in the embodied characters he brought before us in immediate action. Yet the closer these figures were inspected, the greater riddle became the artist's method: though the main plan of a piece was easy to perceive, and it was impossible to mistake the consequent development of its plot, for the most part pre-existing in the source selected, yet the marvellous "accidentiæ" in its working out, as also in the bearing of its dramatis personæ, were inexplicable on any hypothesis of deliberate artistic scheming. Here we found such drastic individuality, that it often seemed like unaccountable caprice, whose sense we never really fathomed till we closed the book and saw the living drama move before our eyes; then stood before us life's own image, mirrored with resistless truth to nature, and filled us with the lofty terror of a ghostly vision. But how decipher in this magic spell the tokens of an "artwork"? Was the author of these plays a *poet*?

What little we know of his life makes answer with outspoken naïvety: he was a *play-actor* and *manager*, who wrote for himself and his troop these pieces that in after days amazed and poignantly perplexed our greatest poets; pieces that for the most part would not so much as have come down to us, had the unpretending promptbooks of the Globe Theatre not been rescued from oblivion in the nick of time by the printing-press. *Lope de Vega*, scarcely less a wonder, wrote his pieces from one day to the next in immediate contact with his actors and the stage; beside Corneille and Racine, the poets of *façon*, there stands the actor *Molière*, in whom alone production was alive; and midst his tragedy sublime stood *Æschylus*, the leader of its chorus.—Not to the Poet, but to the Dramatist must we look, for light upon the Drama's nature; and he stands no nearer to the poet proper than to the *mime* himself, from whose heart of hearts he must issue if as poet he means to "hold the mirror up to Nature."

Thus undoubtedly the essence of Dramatic art, as against the Poet's method, at first seems totally irrational; it is not to be seized, without a complete reversal of the beholder's nature. In what this reversal must consist, however, should not be hard to indicate if we recall the natural process in the beginnings of all Art, as plainly shewn to us in *improvisation*. The poet, mapping out a plan of action for the improvising mime, would stand in much the same relation to him as the author of an operatic text to the musician; his work can claim as yet no atom of artistic value; but this it will gain in the very fullest measure if the poet makes the improvising spirit of the mime his own, and develops his plan entirely in character with that improvisation, so that the mime now enters with all his individuality into the poet's higher reason. This involves, to be sure, a complete transformation of the poetic artwork itself, of which we might form an idea if we imagined the impromptu of some great musician noted down. We have it on the authority of competent witnesses, that nothing could compare with the effect produced by Beethoven when he improvised at length upon the pianoforte to his friends; nor, even in view of the master's greatest works, need we deem excessive the lament that precisely these inventions were not fixed in writing, if we reflect that far inferior musicians, whose penwork was always stiff and stilted, have quite amazed us in their 'free fantasias' by a wholly unsuspected and often very fertile talent for invention.—At anyrate we believe we shall really expedite the solution of an extremely difficult problem, if we define the Shakespearian Drama as *a fixed mimetic improvisation of the highest poetic worth.* For this explains at once each wondrous accidental in the bearing and discourse of characters alive to but one purpose, to be at this moment all that they are meant to seem to us to be, and to whom accordingly no word can come that lies outside this conjured nature; so that it would be positively laughable to us, upon closer consideration, if one of these figures were suddenly to pose as poet. This last is silent, and remains for us a riddle, such as Shakespeare. But his work is the only veritable Drama; and what that implies, as work of Art, is shewn by our rating its author the profoundest poet of all time.—

From the countless topics for reflection afforded by this Drama of Shakespeare's let us choose those attributes which seem of most assistance to our present inquiry. Firstly then, apart from all its other merits, it strictly belongs to the class of effective *stage-pieces*, such as have been devised in the most dissimilar ages by skilful authors either sprung from the Theatre itself or in immediate contact therewith, and such as have enriched, for instance, the popular stages of the French from year to year. The difference between these true dramatic products, similarly arisen, simply lies in their *poetic value.* At first sight this poetic value seems determined by the dignity and grandeur of the subject-matter. Whereas not only have the French succeeded in setting every incident of modern life with speaking truth upon the stage, but even the Germans—with their infinitely smaller talent for the Theatre—have done the like for the narrower burgher province of that life, this genuinely reproductive force has failed in measure as the scene was to picture forth events of higher life, and finally the fate of heroes of world-history and their myths, sublimely distant from the eye of everyday. For here the mime's improvisation fell too short, and needed to be wielded by the poet proper, i.e. the inventor and fashioner of Myths; and his genius had to prove its pre-election by raising the style of mimetic improvisation to the level of his own poetic aim. How Shakespeare may have succeeded in raising his players themselves to that level, must remain to us another riddle; the only certainty is, that our modern actors wreck their faculties at once upon the task he set. Possibly, what we above have called the grotesque affectation peculiar to English actors of nowadays is the remains of an earlier aptitude, and, springing from an inborn national idiosyncrasy, it may once have led, in the fairest age of English folk-life and through the contagious example of the poet himself, to so unheard a climax of the player's art that Shakespeare's conceptions could be realised thereby. If we are indisposed to assume so great a miracle however, we perhaps may explain this riddle by instancing the fate of great Sebastian Bach, whose difficult and prolific choral compositions tempt us at first to assume that the master had the most unrivalled vocal forces at command for their performance; whereas, on the contrary, we have unimpeachable documents to prove his complaints of the mostly altogether pitiable condition of his schoolboy choir.* Certain it is, that Shakespeare withdrew very early from his business with the stage; for which we may easily account by the immense fatigue the rehearsing of his pieces must have cost him, as also by the despair of a genius that towered high above the "possibility" of its surroundings. Yet the whole nature of this genius is explicable by nothing but that "possibility" itself, which assuredly existed in the nature of the mime, and was therefore very rightly presupposed by the genius; and, taking all the cultural efforts of the human spirit in one comprehensive survey, we may regard it as in a certain sense the task bequeathed to Shakespeare's aftercomers by the greatest Dramatist, to actually attain that highest possibility in the development of histrionic art.

To fulfil this task, appears to have been the inner aspiration of our great German poets. Starting, as here

* A story, now become a commonplace among musicians, tells us how the master contrived to get his excessively difficult works performed at all: it concerns one of Bach's former choristers, who made the strange confession, "first he thrashed us, and then—it sounded horrible."—R. WAGNER.

was indispensable, with the recognition of Shakespeare's inimitability, every form in which they cast their poetic conceptions was dictated by an aim we can readily understand on this assumption. The search for the ideal Form of the highest work of art, the Drama, must necessarily lead them away from Shakespeare to a fresh and ever deeper consideration of Antique Tragedy; in what sense they thought to draw profit thence, we have explained before, and we had to see them turning from this more than dubious path to the strangely powerful impression made on them by the noblest products of a genre that yet appeared so highly enigmatic, the genre of Opera.

Here were two chief points of notice: firstly, that a great master's music lent the doings of even poor dramatic exponents an ideal charm, denied to the most admirable of actors in the spoken play; secondly, that a true dramatic talent could so ennoble even entirely worthless music, as to move us with a performance inachievable by the selfsame talent in the recited drama. That this phenomenon must be accounted to nothing but the might of *Music*, was irrefutable. Yet this could apply to Music solely in the general, and it still remained incomprehensible how the dramatic poet was to approach the singularly paltry fabric of her forms without falling into a subjection of the very vilest sort.—Now, we have appealed to Shakespeare to give us, if possible, a glimpse into the nature, and more especially the method, of the genuine dramatist. Mysterious as we found the most part of this matter too, yet we saw that the poet was here entirely at one with the art of the mime; so that we now may call this mimetic art the life-dew wherein the poetic aim was to be steeped, to enable it, as in a magic transformation, to appear as the mirror of life. And if every action, each humblest incident of life displays itself, when reproduced by mimicry, in the transfiguring light and with the objective effect of a mirror-image (as is shewn not only by Shakespeare, but by every other sterling playwright), in further course we shall have to avow that this mirror-image, again, displays itself in the transfiguration of purest Ideality so soon as it is dipped in the magic spring of Music and held up to us as nothing but pure Form, so to say, set free from all the realism of Matter.

'Tis not the *Form* of Music, therefore, but *the forms which music has evolved in history*, that we should have to consider before arguing to that highest possibility in the development of the latent powers of the mimo-dramatic artwork, that possibility which has hovered before the earnest seeker as a voiceless riddle, and yet a riddle crying out aloud for answer.

Music's Form, without a doubt, is synonymous with *Melody*; the latter's special evolution makes out the history of our music, just as its need determined the development of Lyric Drama, once attempted by the Italians, into the "Opera." If one meant to imitate the form of the Greek Tragedy, the first glance shewed it falling into two main sections, the choral chant and a dramatic recitation that mounted periodically to *melopöe*: so the "drama" proper was handed over to Recitative, whose oppressive monotony was at last to be broken by the academically-approved invention of the "Aria." In this last alone did Music here attain her independent Form, as Melody; and it therefore most rightly gained such a preponderance over the other factors of the musical drama, that the latter itself eventually sank to a mere pretext, a barren prop on which to hang the Aria. It thus is with the history of Melody chained to the Aria-form, that we should have to occupy ourselves, were it not sufficient for our present purpose to consider that one particular shape in which it offered itself to our great poets when they felt so deeply moved by its effect in general, but all the more bewildered at the thought of any poetic concern therewith. Beyond dispute it was always the particular genius, and he alone, who knew to put such life into this cramped and sterile cast of melody as to make it capable of that profound effect: consequently its expansion, its ideal unfolding, could be awaited from no one but the Musician; and the line of this development was already to be traced, if one compared the masterpiece of Mozart with that of Gluck. And here the greater store of musical invention turned out to be the unique measure of Music's dramatic capacity, since Mozart's "Don Juan" already displayed a wealth of dramatic characterisation whereof the far lesser musician Gluck could never have dreamt. But it still was reserved for the German genius to raise musical Form, by the utmost vitalising of its tiniest fraction, to the infinite diversity the music of our great *Beethoven* now offers to a wondering world.

Now, Beethoven's musical fashionings bear marks that leave them equally inexplicable as those of Shakespeare have remained to the inquiring poet. Whilst the power of effect in both must needs be felt as different at once and equal, upon a deeper scrutiny of its essence the very difference appears to us to vanish, for suddenly the one unsolved peculiarity affords the only explanation of the other. Let us select the peculiarity of the Humour, as that most swiftly seizable, and we discover that what often seems to us an unaccountable caprice in the sallies given off by Shakespeare's characters, in the corresponding turns of Beethoven's motive-moulding becomes a natural occurrence of the utmost ideality, to wit a melody that takes the mind by storm. We cannot but here assume a blood-relationship, which to correctly define we must seek it, not between the musician and the poet, but between the former and the poet-mime.

Whereas no poet of any artistic epoch can be compared with Beethoven, we find his fellowship with Shakespeare in the very fact that the latter, as poet, would forever remain to us a problem, could we not detect in him before all else the poet-*mime*. The secret lies in the directness of the presentation, here by mien and gesture, there by living tone. That which both directly mould and fashion is the actual Artwork, for which the Poet merely drafts the plan,—and that itself successfully, only when he has borrowed it from their own nature.

We have found that the Shakespearian Drama was definable the most intelligibly as a "fixed mimetic improvisation"; and as we had to suppose that this Artwork's high poetic value, resting in the first place on the elevation of its subject, must be ensured by the heightening of the *style* of that improvisation, we can scarcely go astray if we look for the possibility of such an utmost heightening in a mode of music which shall bear thereto the same relation as Beethoven's Music to just this Drama of Shakespeare's.

The very difficulty of thus applying Beethovenian Music to the Shakespearian Drama might lead, when conquered, to the utmost perfecting of musical Form, through its final liberation from each remaining fetter. What still distressed our great German poets in regard of Opera, and what still left its manifest traces on Beethoven's instrumental music,—that scaffolding which in nowise rested on the essence of Music, but rather on that selfsame tendence which planned the operatic aria and the ballet-tune,—this conventional four-square structure, so wondrously wreathed already with the luxuriant life of Beethovenian melody, would vanish quite away before an ideal ordering of highest freedom; so that Music now would take the ineffably vital shape of a Shakespearian drama, and its sublime irregularity, compared with the antique drama, would well-nigh give it the appearance of a nature-scene as against a work of architecture, a scene whose skilful measurement would be evinced by nothing but the unfailing sureness of the artwork's effect. And in this would lie withal the untold newness of this artwork's form: a form ideal alike and natural, and thus conceivable in no modern racial language save the German, the most developed of them all; a form, on the other hand, which could be misconstrued only for so long as the artwork was measured by a standard it had thoroughly outgrown, whereas the new and fitting standard might haply be sought in the impression received by the fortunate hearers of one of those unwritten impromptus of the most peerless of musicians. Then would the greatest dramatist have taught us to fix that impromptu too; for in the highest conceivable Artwork the sublimest inspirations of them both should live with an undying life, as the essence of the world displayed with clearness past all measure in the mirror of the world itself.

Now if we abide by this definition, "a mimo-musical improvisation, of consummate poetical value, fixed by the highest artistic care," we may find experience throw a startling light on the practical side of our Artwork's execution.—Taken in a very weighty sense, our great poets' prime concern was to furnish Drama with a heightened Pathos, and finally to discover the technical means of securely fixing its delivery. Markedly as Shakespeare had derived his style from the instinct of mimetic art, for the performance of his dramas he nevertheless stayed bound to the accidental greater or less degree of talent in his players, who all, in a sense, would have had to be Shakespeares, just as he was certainly at all times the whole character he personated; nor have we any reason to suppose that in the representations of his pieces his genius would have recognised aught beyond his own bare shadow cast across the boards. What so chained our own great poets' hopes to Music, was its being not only purest Form, but the most complete physical presentation of that Form; the abstract cypher of Arithmetic, the figure of Geometry, here steps before us in a shape that holds the Feeling past denial, to wit as Melody; and whereas the poetic diction of the written speech falls prey to every personal caprice of its reciter, the physical reproduction of this Melody can be fixed beyond all risk of error. What to Shakespeare was practically impossible, namely to be the mime of all his rôles, the tone-composer achieves with fullest certainty, for from out his each executant musician he speaks to us directly. Here the transmigration of the poet's soul into the body of the player takes place by laws of surest technique, and the composer giving the beat* to a technically correct performance of his work becomes so entirely one with the executant that the nearest comparison would be that of a plastic artist and his work achieved in stone or colour, were it possible to speak of a metempsychosis into this lifeless matter.

If to this astounding might of the Musician we add that attribute of his art which we recognised at starting,—namely that even indifferent music, so long as it does not positively descend to the grotesque vulgarity of certain operatic genres in vogue to-day, enables a good dramatic artist to achieve results beyond his reach without it, as also that noble music virtually extorts from even inferior actors achievements of a type unreachable elsewhere at all,—we can scarcely doubt the reason of the utter dismay aroused in the Poet of our era who desires nobly to succeed in Drama with the only means at his disposal, that selfsame speech in which to-day the very leading-articles address us. Precisely on this side, however, our hypothesis of the perfection destined for the Musically-conceived Drama should rather prove encouraging than the reverse, for its first effect would be to purge a great and many-sided genre of art, the Drama in general, from those errors which the modern Opera alike has heightened and exposed. To clear up this point, and at the same time to gain a survey of their future field of prosperous work, our dramatists perhaps might deem advisable to trace back the pedigree of the modern Theatre; not seeking its roots in Antique Drama, however, whose form is so distinctly a native product of the Hellenic spirit, its religion, ay, its State itself, that to assume the possibility of a modern imitation must necessarily lead to the gravest errors. No: the path of evolution of the Modern Theatre has such a wealth of products of the greatest worth to shew, that it fitly may be trodden farther without shame. The

* It is all-important that this beat should be the right one, however, for a false tempo will undo the spell at once; as to which I have therefore expressed myself at length elsewhere.—R. WAGNER.

thorough "stage-piece," in the modernest of senses, assuredly would have to form the basis, and the only sound one, of all future dramatic efforts: for success in this, however, the very first essential is to rightly grasp the spirit of theatric art, which rests upon mimetic art itself, and to use it, not for the bolstering-up of tendences, but for the mirroring of scenes from actual life. The French, who not so long ago did admirably in this line, were certainly content to not expect a brand-new Molière every year; nor for ourselves would the birthdays of new Shakespeares be recorded in each calendar.

Coming at last to the contentment of ideal aspirations, from the working of that all-powerful dramatic Artwork itself we might see, with greater certainty than has hitherto been possible, the length to which such aspirations were justified in going. Their boundary would be found at the exact point in that Artwork where Song is thrusting toward the spoken Word. By this we in no sense imply an absolutely lowly sphere, but a sphere entirely different, distinct in kind; and we may gain an instant notion of this difference, if we call to mind certain instinctive transgressions on the part of our best dramatic singers, when in the full flow of song they have felt driven to literally *speak* a crucial word. To this, for example, the Schröder-Devrient found herself impelled by the cumulative horror of a situation in the opera "Fidelio"; in the sentence "one further step and thou art—*dead*," where she aims the pistol at the tyrant, with an awful accent of desperation she suddenly *spoke* the closing word. The indescribable effect upon the hearer was that of a headlong plunge from one sphere to the other, and its sublimity consisted in our being given, as by a lightning-flash, a glimpse into the nature of both spheres at once, the one the ideal, the other the real. Plainly, for one moment the ideal was unable to bear a certain load, and discharged it on the other: seeing how fond people are of ascribing to Music, particularly of the passionate and stirring type, a simply pathologic character, it may surprise them to discover through this very instance how delicate and purely ideal is her actual sphere, since the material terror of reality can find no place therein, albeit the soul of all things real in it alone finds pure expression.—Manifestly then, there is a side of the world, and a side that concerns us most seriously, whose terrible lessons can be brought home to our minds on none but a field of observation where Music has to hold her tongue: this field perhaps may best be measured if we allow Shakespeare, the stupendous mime, to lead us on it as far as that point we saw him reach with the desperate fatigue we assumed as reason for his early withdrawal from the stage. And that field might be best defined, if not exactly as the soil, at least as the phenomena of History. To portray its material features for the benefit of human knowledge, must always remain the Poet's task.

So weighty and clearing an influence as this that we here could only undertake to sketch in broadest outline—an influence not merely upon its nearest relatives in Drama, but upon every branch of Art whose deepest roots connect with Drama—most certainly could never be made possible to our "Musically-conceived-and-carried-out Dramatic Artwork" until that Artwork could present itself to the public in an outward garb entirely corresponding with its inner nature, and thus facilitate the needful lack of bias in the judgment of its qualities. 'Tis so closely allied to "Opera," that for our present purpose we might justly term it the fulfilment of the Opera's destiny: not one of the said possibilities would ever have dawned on us, had it not already come to light in Opera, in general, and in the finest works of great Opera-composers in particular. Quite surely, too, it was solely the spirit of Music, whose ever ampler evolution so influenced the Opera as to enable those possibilities to arise therein. Once more then, if we wish to account for the degradation to which the Opera has been brought, we certainly must seek its reason in the attributes of Music herself. Just as in Painting, and even in Architecture, the "piquant" has taken the place of the "beautiful," so was it doomed that

Music should turn from a sublime into a merely pleasing art. Though her sphere was that of purest ideality, and her effect on our mind so deeply calming and emancipating from all the anguish of reality, through her displaying herself as nothing but pure Form,—so that whatever threatened to disturb the latter, either fell away of itself, or had to be held aloof from her,—this very unmixed Form, when set in a relation not completely suitable, might easily pass current for a mere agreeable toy; thus, once set in so indefinite a sphere as that on which the Opera rested, it could be employed in this sense alone, and finally be made to serve as a mere surface fillip to the ear or feeling.

On this point, however, we have the less need to dwell just now, as we started from the outcry raised against the Opera and its influence, whose ill effect we can express no better than by pointing to the notorious fact that the Theatre has long been given over to an intense neglect by all the truly cultured in the nation, though once they set great hopes thereon. Wherefore, as we cannot but desire to bring our suggested Artwork to the only notice of profit to it, namely of those who have turned with grave displeasure from the Theatre of to-day, it follows that we must shun all contact with that Theatre itself. But although the neutral ground for this must locally be quite cut off from our theatres' field of action, it could prove fruitful only if it drew its nurture from the actual elements of mimetic and musical art that have already developed in their own fashion at the theatres. In these alone consists, and will consist, the truly fertile material for genuine dramatic art; each attempt in other directions would lead, instead of Art, to a posing Artificiality. 'Tis our actors, singers and bandmen, on whose innate instinct must rest all hope of the attainment of even artistic ends as yet beyond their understanding; for it is they to whom those ends will become clear the swiftest, so soon as their instinct is rightly guided to a knowledge of them. That this instinct has been led by the tendence of our theatres to the exclusive development of the worst propensities in the profession,—it is this that needs must make us wish to snatch these irreplaceable artistic forces at least periodically from the influence of that tendence, and give them such a means of exercising their own good qualities as would rapidly and surely fit them for the realising of our Artwork. For only from the natural will of this mimetic fellowship, cutting so sorry a figure in its present misdirection, can issue now—as from of old have issued the best of things dramatic—the perfect Drama meant by us. Less by them, than by those who without the slightest calling have hitherto conducted them, has the downfall of the theatric art of our era been brought to pass. To name in one word what on German soil has shewn, and goes on proving itself least worthy of the fame of our great victories of to-day, we have only to point to this *Theatre*, whose tendence avows itself aloud and brazen the betrayer of German honour. Whoso should link himself to this tendence in any shape or form, must needs fall victim to a misconstruction that would assign him to a sphere of our publicity of the most questionable nature, whence to rise to the pure sphere of Art would be about as difficult and fatiguing as to arrive from Opera at what we have termed the Ideal Drama. Certain it is, however, that if Art has fallen solely through the artists,—according to Schiller's saying, here not exactly accurate,—it can be *raised again by the artists alone*, and not by those who have dishonoured it with their favour. *But to help forward from without, as well, that restoration of Art by the artists, would be the fitting national expiation for the national sin of our present German Theatre.*

ACTORS AND SINGERS.

Über Schauspieler und Sänger.

"On Actors and Singers" was written soon after the laying of the foundation-stone of the Bayreuth Festspielhaus, May 22, 1872, and was published in the autumn of that year by E. W. Fritzsch, Leipzig.

TRANSLATOR'S NOTE.

REPEATEDLY, in course of my inquiries into the problem of Dramatic Art and its bearings on a truly national Culture, have I been brought to the crucial question of the nature of the *Mime*,—a term I have used to signify both the *Actor* and the *Singer*, and under which, in virtue of the special light in which these two appear to me, I have seen reason to include the *Bandsman*. What uncommon importance I attach to the art of the Mime, I have proved by publishing my personal surmise that only through the peculiarity of just this art can *Shakespeare* and his artistic method in framing his dramas be explained. Moreover, when discussing the longed-for establishment of a truly German theatric art, and its fulfilment of the highest artistic tendences reserved for Drama, I have never lost sight of the fact that the possibility of this realisation is subject to conditions which I thus defined in an earlier writing, and now repeat.* "'Tis our actors, singers and bandsmen, on whose innate instinct must rest all hope of the attainment of even artistic ends as yet beyond their understanding; for it is they to whom those ends will become clear the swiftest, so soon as their instinct is rightly guided to a knowledge of them. That this instinct has been led by the tendence of our theatres to the exclusive development of the worst propensities in the profession,—it is this that needs must make us wish to snatch these irreplaceable artistic forces at least periodically from the influence of that tendence, and give them such a means of exercising their own good qualities as would rapidly and surely fit them for the realising of our Artwork. For only from the natural will of this mimetic fellowship, cutting so sorry a figure in its present misdirection, can issue now—as from

* *Über die Bestimmung der Oper* ("The Destiny of Opera"), Leipzig, E. W. Fritzsch. See page 154.

of old have issued the best of things dramatic—the perfect Drama meant by us. Less by them, than by those who without the slightest calling have hitherto conducted them, has the downfall of the theatric art of our era been brought to pass; and certainly *by them alone* can that art be raised again."

After this preamble I surely need have no fear of being misunderstood by the associates of mimetic art; and my further efforts to lay bare their veritable needs by a searching inquiry into the nature of that art will not, I trust, give me the appearance of labouring under any feeling of disparagement thereof. However, still more decidedly to meet the possibility of such an appearance, I will at once sum up in the most definite terms my own sincere opinion of the nature and value of mimetic art.

In the first place, then, I point to the experience common to everyone acquainted with the effect of stage-performances upon the public and himself, that it proceeds directly from the doings of the actors or singers; and indeed, this effect is so pronounced, that a good performance will disguise the worthlessness of a dramatic work, whereas an excellent stage-poem can produce no effect when badly rendered by incompetent performers. Hence we cannot but conclude that, taken strictly, the *artistic* share in theatrical representations must simply be ascribed to the performers, whereas the author of the piece has no more to do with the "art" itself than insofar as he has planned his poem with a thorough calculation of the effect it is to produce when acted. In that, despite all maxims hammered into it, the public really holds by nothing but the doings of the players, and regards them as the only substance of all the artistic show, does it still evince a truly unspoilt art-sense; in a manner, it thereby tells us the true aim of Art in general.

If we look a little closer at the characteristics of a first-rate actor's work, we are amazed to find in it the basic elements of each and every art, in utmost multiplicity, ay, and with a strength unreachable by any other art. What the plastic artist models from Nature, the mime will copy from her to the most deceptive likeness; and hereby he exerts a power over the spectator's phantasy coequal with that he exercises as by magic on himself, his outmost person and his inmost feeling. This powerful, nay, this despotic effect can necessarily be never equalled by any other art; for the wondrous thing about it, is that the intent to deceive and be deceived is denied by neither side, all possibility of the admixture of a material pathologic interest—which would destroy the game at once—is rigorously excluded, and yet the actions and passions of purely fictitious persons thrill us in exact degree as the performer himself is steeped in them, nay, possessed to the point of yielding up his whole real personality. After the last Act of a representation of *King Lear* by *Ludwig Devrient* the Berlin public for a while stayed rooted to its seat, and not amid the usual noisy outburst of applause, but scarcely whispering, hushed and motionless, as though bound by a magic spell which no one felt the strength to combat, whilst to each it seemed incomprehensible how to placidly start homeward and re-enter the groove of a life from whose habits he had just been rapt so infinitely far away. Beyond dispute, the highest grade of the effect of the *sublime* was here attained; and it was the *mime* who raised us to it, whether one call him *Ludwig Devrient* or *Shakespeare* himself.

Starting with the knowledge of such effects, it might seem almost impossible that in further course of our review of the operations of our actors and singers we should reach a point where their art inspired us with such misgivings that we must straightway decline to let it rank as Art at all. And yet the observation of their daily traffic must bring us wellnigh to that pass. What is offered us in the usual representations at the theatre has quite the character of a strange, in sooth a very dubious trade, which seems plied with the exclusive object of displaying the actor's person to the best advantage. All concealment of the actor's personality, an illusion alike æsthetically pleasing and conducive to the most sublime effect, we here see dropped entirely out of count; in fact a truly shameless abuse of the peculiar resources of his art is practised by the actor to dispel any such illusion and throw his person into high relief. How it became possible to pervert the tendence of theatric art in such a manner, and set the resulting type of public entertainment in place of that which owed its development to the pleasure in dramatic illusion,—to explain this, we needs must cast a glance at the nature of Modern Art in general.—

Art ceases, strictly speaking, to be Art from the moment it presents itself as Art to our reflecting consciousness. That the Artist does the right thing without knowing it, the Hellenic mind discovered when itself had lost its own creative power. Indeed it is both instructive and affecting, to see how the rebirth of the arts among modern nations issued from the rebellion of popular instinct against the traditional dogma of antique criticism. Thus we find the actor coming earlier than the poet who wrote pieces for him. Was this latter to follow the classic rules, or the form and substance of the improvisations of those actors? In Spain great *Lope de Vega* forwent the fame of a classical art-poet, and made for us the Modern Drama, that Drama which brought forth in *Shakespeare* the greatest poet of all time. Yet how hard it must have seemed to the critical understanding to comprehend this unique and genuine artwork, we see at once from its careful disintegration by the antiquarian counterthrusts of so-called art-poets. These latter held the field in France; here the drama was given an academic cut, and rules invaded the player's art. Plainly, these rules were less and less directed toward that lofty Illusion which we can but regard as the end and aim of theatric art in especial; one had determined to stay at all hours fully conscious that one here was dealing with an "art," an "art-achievement." To maintain this mood at all costs, was still a duty falling less to the poet than to the player, and for him was paramount: how this *acteur* played, his reading of this or that character, with what art he applied to it his natural gifts, or made up for those he lacked in, became the object of the savant public's most diligent inquiry.

We repeatedly see a reaction against this tendence arising among free-thinking nations. When the Stuarts returned to England, they brought with them French "*Tragédie*" and "*Comédie*": but the "regular theatre," established by them for this purpose, found no suitable actors among the English, nor any lasting hold; and the players of the olden times, dispersed beneath the Puritan supremacy, gathered toilsomely their sere remains together, to prepare for a *Garrick* that soil whereon at last the *player*, and the player only, republished to the world the wonders of genuine dramatic art; for *he* it was, who in *Shakespeare* reawoke and saved for it the greatest poet.—

A like lustre once seemed dawning for the Germans, when from the very soil of true theatric art there sprang at last a *Sophie Schröder*, a *Ludwig Devrient*.—Having already attempted in a lengthy treatise upon "German Art and German Policy" to trace the outer causes of the Theatre's so swift decay in Germany too, after scarcely coming into bud, I here may rather devote myself to that ruin's inner grounds. In the two great players last-named one might easily be tempted to see nothing save a pair of natural geniuses, such as come to light but seldom on the field of any art: in the character of their artistic practice, however, there remains a something not the individual's gift alone, but of the very essence of their art itself. This "something" must be fathomable, and a judgment to be drawn from its discovery. The state of transport into which the Berlin audience was rapt by that performance of *King Lear*, was assuredly the same in kind as that experienced by the great mime himself upon that evening; for neither of them did the actor *Devrient*, or the Berlin audience, any longer exist; they each had passed entirely outside themselves. Now, upon applying this reflection to the opposite case, we may learn the secret of all the emptiness that so disgusts us in the traffic of the stage: it stands confessed before us when, in midst or at the close of a performance, we witness the habitual noisy, hollow tokens of applause on the part of the public, and the corresponding signs of simulated thanks on that of the actor. Here the audience stays as conscious of its private self, as the actor stays preoccupied with the sense of his own personality, for all the world as if outside the theatre. The mutual figment of a dramatic illusion becomes a sheer convention, according to which the one side plays at practising, the other at judging an "art."

To the best of my knowledge, this convention was first matured into a system in France. Its origin dates from the rise of so-called "later Attic Comedy," which, adopted by the Roman Theatre, was thereafter developed on the lines of an "Art-comedy" among all nations of Latin descent or admixture. Here sits the connoisseur before the stage, whereon the *acteur* takes due pains to "play his rôle well": conventional signs of favour or distaste inform him whether he has succeeded in that object; on these depends the mime's good fortune, and we may judge what store must be set on "playing comedy" if we reflect that the divine *Augustus* himself desired on his deathbed to be held a good comedian.

Notoriously, the French have brought this art the farthest. Nay, it has become the Frenchmen's art par excellence; for their dramatic writers, too, are only explicable by the maxims of their Art of Comedy, and on it rests the perfect balance (*Sicherheit*) of their works, the whole plan alike with the tiniest detail of its execution being modelled on the selfsame rules whereby the acteur has to woo the public's favour for his own artistic efforts on the stage. Moreover this supplies us with the reason why these, the most assured stage-artists in the world—a title we must grant the French without dispute—are promptly and completely disconcerted when asked to play a piece not based on that convention. Each attempt to get Shakespeare, Schiller, or even Calderon performed by French comedians, has always been foredoomed to failure; and nothing but the misunderstanding of this other type of drama could have moved them to invent a grotesque genre in which Nature, by exaggeration, has been turned forthwith into Un-nature. The canon still remained in force, that the Theatre's province is the art of "playing comedy," i.e. the actor must never forget that he is playing to an audience which seeks its only excitation in this his art of playing at disguise in every sense.

How ill this art must turn out with the Germans, is easy enough to comprehend. One might sum up the position by saying that comedy is played both here and there, but the French play it well, the Germans badly. For the gratification of seeing a man play comedy *well*, the French will forgive him everything: of Louis XIV., for all their clear perception of the utter hollowness of the rôle he played, they are truly proud to this day, from sheer and imperturbable delight in his having played that rôle superbly.

If we are to see in this an artistic spirit, then that particular art-sense is undeniably no property of the Germans. Toward a German Louis XIV. as monarch our political public would behave about the same as our good burghers in the theatre toward the playing of an actor, taking him in sober earnest for the hero whom he represented; for, in face of all assurance to the contrary, they would believe this was expected of them, whereas the schooled spectator is really asked to do no more than forget the imaged hero in the art of the actor who plays his part so capitally. And this in fact is the demand now addressed, in accordance with the French convention, to the German spectator who, without an inculcated art-sense, seeks at the theatre a real emotion such as can only be evoked by an illusion completely effacing the artistic person of the actor and leaving nothing save the individual portrayed. Notwithstanding the extreme rarity of those cases in which this sublime illusion can be compassed by truly talented performers, the theatre is opened nightly for the German public, and that the "theatre of all sorts"; and to this end the indispensable accessories of French theatrical convention are pressed into our service.

Even were it possible for the German to "play comedy" as excellently as the Frenchman, it still would be a question whether he is capable, as spectator, of appreciating this art to the same extent as the French public does. That, however, is an inquiry quite beyond our purview, for simple reason that we never get comedy played to us in that perfection. What with regard to the cultivation of artistic aptitudes the modern world terms *talent*, is possessed by the German in the very scantiest measure, ay, wellnigh not at all; whereas, a natural endowment of the Latin nations, in the form of a predisposition to give effect to inculcated culture-tendences, it is showered broadcast on the French. Whether a like power is latent in the German, could only transpire when he found himself surrounded by a culture all his own, and quite in keeping with his inborn nature; for by *talent*, at bottom, we can mean nothing else than the natural capacity and inclination to acquire eminent dexterity in the practical application of existing artistic forms. Thus was the plastic art of the Greeks pursued through centuries by nothing but this Talent, and even to-day the artificial culture of the French, albeit tottering to its irrevocable downfall, is still kept upright by this Talent. But that culture is just what we Germans lack, and our only substitute for it is the scarecrow of a culture not arisen from our nature, a culture never really understood by us; as we here behold in the cultivation of our Theatre, for which we therefore very naturally possess no talent.

To convince ourselves of this, we have only to attend the first stage-performance that offers. Be it the sublimest product of dramatic art, on which we light, or the trivialest concoction of a "free" translator or adaptor from the French, we always recognise one thing at once: the craze for "playing comedy," in which both Scribe and Shakespeare go equally to ground before our eyes in a ridiculous coil of travesty. Granted that the *good* French acteur keeps a constant eye upon the effect produced on the spectator by his declamation, his gestures, his whole demeanour, and can never be betrayed into shewing himself in a light distasteful to the public for sake of the character he represents,—the German histrion believes it his first duty to turn this lucky chance of commending himself to the public's confidence to his own best personal advantage. Has he to display emotion, or utter some particularly sapient saying, he promptly faces toward the audience, and casts on it the glance that seems to him too eloquent to waste upon his colleagues. For this is a main characteristic of our stage-hero: he always plays to the audience, and thus forgets his rôle so far that, after a masterstroke of this kind of correspondence, he often altogether loses the tone in which he should continue his speech to his fellow-actor. We are told that *Garrick* in his monologues, with open eyes, saw no one, spoke solely to himself, forgot the universe. I, on the other hand, have seen and heard one of our most famous actors expound the self-murder monologue of "Hamlet" with such a fervour of familiarity that he grew hoarse, and left the stage in a bath of perspiration. His eternal care to make a striking personal impression on the audience, be it as a pleasant man or a "thinking artist," compels him to maintain throughout a corresponding cast of features, and he is simply put out of countenance by everything to the contrary in the nature of his rôle. Once I saw a celebrated 'leading lady' of our day in the painful predicament of having to play the Regent "Margareta" in "Egmont"; the character of this intriguing, but weak and timorous woman, did not become her: from first to last she aired a quite heroic fury, and so far forgot herself as to scold Machiavelli for a traitor—a rating which the latter most politely took without the least offence.

Thus a personal vanity, devoid of all capacity for artistically dissembling its end, gives our mimes the constant appearance of glaring stupidity. The ballet-dancer, or even the concert-singer, may be excused if at the close of a brilliant tour de force she turns with her best graces to the public, as though to ask if she has hit their taste; in a certain sense, she is keeping to her rôle: but the actor proper, who has been given an individual character to depict, has to convert his whole rôle into that one question to the public; and this, considered calmly, must set him in the light of senseless ridicule from beginning to end of his work.

As the Frenchman loves society and intercourse above all else, as though to gain from the perpetual clash of wits his only chance of growing conscious of himself, so his great mimetic assurance, nay, the correct portrayal of his rôle, comes first to him in the so-called Ensemble. A French theatrical performance has all the air of a highly polished conversation between persons mutually interested in some engrossing topic: hence the marvellous exactitude in the rehearsing of this Ensemble; nothing is allowed to break the artistic convention, here raised to the pitch of Illusion; the puniest member of the whole must be just as fitted to his task as the foremost acteur in the situation, and the latter would straightway fall out of his rôle if his interlocutor proved unequal to his. But the German actor is saved from any such mishap: he can never fall out of his rôle, since he never is in it. His is one long monologue addressed to the audience, and his whole rôle becomes for him an "*a parte.*"

The tendence of this *a parte* offers us the best insight into the peculiar nature of German acting. In his passion for turning everything he has to say into such an "aside" the actor plainly shews us how he seeks to save his person from the awkward plight of being expected to play comedy well, and what pains he takes to give himself a certain look of superiority to the whole untoward situation.

It is highly instructive to note how this peculiar penchant for "asides" has inspired our playwrights with their own specific style, in particular for Tragedy. Take Hebbel's

"Nibelungen" for instance. This multipartite piece at once affords us the impression of a parody on the Nibelungenlied, after the fashion of Blumauer's travesty of the "Æneid." Here the modern man of letters seems manifestly mocking what he considers the grotesqueness of the medieval poem by ridiculous exaggerations: his heroes go behind the wings, there carry out some monstrous feat, and return to the stage to tell us all all about it in much the same depreciatory tone as Baron von Münchhausen upon his exploits. As all his dramatis personæ adopt a similar tone, and thus are really mocking one another, it is obvious that these speeches and narrations are addressed to no one save the audience, as if each hero wished to let it know that the whole thing was a mere farce,—thereby meaning not only the Nibelungen, but the German Theatre itself. And in truth one might take it as an intentional skit on the whole attempt of our "moderns" to deal alike with the heroic Saga and the Theatre, an attempt which neither the well-bred poet, nor the mime he has in eye, could satirise pronouncedly enough in the exercise of their respective arts. The singular position into which we thus have fallen toward ourselves, toward our pretended purpose, we may admirably illustrate by the scene in Shakespeare's "Midsummer-night's Dream" where good actors, in their own esteem, get the heroic romance of "Pyramus and Thisbe" played to them by bad comedians: they are vastly diverted, and make a thousand witty observations, most suitable for the cultured gentlemen they have to represent. But imagine for a moment that these sprightly gentlemen are nothing but players themselves, taking part in the performance of "Pyramus and Thisbe" pretty much as the author of the "Nibelungen" and his actors behave to that old heroic poem, and we at once are confronted with a picture of the most repulsive kind. Yet it is none other than the picture of the modern German Theatre. For here, regarded closer, one thing is unmistakable: no one will admit that he is joking, but pretends to take the thing in solemn earnest. Never for an instant does the poet cease to strut as world-sage and get himself displayed as such by his comedians, into whose mouths he drops the deepest-going comments on the action in its very thick. But the resulting compound is further planned to create the utmost theatrical Effect, and for this one loses sight of nothing the latest French school, with *Victor Hugo* in particular, has introduced upon the stage. There was some sense in the revolutionary Frenchman, in full revolt against the maxims of the Académie and classic Tragédie, deliberately dragging into vivid daylight everything they had tabooed; and though it led to a baleful eccentricity in both the construction and the wording of pieces, it was at once an act of vengeance most instructive for the history of our culture and a not uninteresting spectacle, since the Frenchman's indisputable talent for the theatre came out in even this. But what figure do Victor Hugo's "Burgraves" cut, for instance, when transposed into the German Nibelungenlied? So fatuous a one, that we may readily excuse the poet's and the actor's inclination to self-ridicule. And the worst of it is, that all this not merely is given, but also taken for earnest, and dubbed right good on every hand. Our actors see such plays accepted by their Intendants as equally sterling coin with the strangely ironical farragos of our historical painters on the grand scale, now bought by our art-patrons: music, of course, is made for them, and so the Mime must set to work to push the thing a little farther with the rankest of his mannerisms.

Now, upon this ruin of theatric art, a few of whose characteristic traits I have tried to set before the reader, a fully-organised relation has been founded, which we may term *the stage-system of to-day*. In this an "acting *class*" [or "actors' standing"—Schauspieler-*Stand*] has come to be acknowledged: a word that warns us we here are dealing with no mere organisation of the most fleeting of all artistic pursuits, but with an arrangement to protect the civic interests of all who seek their livelihood in the practice of mimetic art. To them a certain indulgence is still extended, much as to our sons for so long as they are students at the University, keeping sober citizen society in a state of constant watchfulness and some disquiet: which, again, may account for the former's somewhat freer attitude towards the latter. Just like our students, however, our actors are subject to a certain "censure," enabling their genteel Intendants to engage in serious dealings with them.

If *Goethe* was already of opinion that "a comedian might instruct a clergyman" at times, it need not surprise us that nowadays almost the whole of our more elegant burgher-world has moulded itself on the teachings of stage decorum and propriety. We gladly would equal the French in this, with whom no difference is any longer to be detected between the actor in the ministerial cabinet, or the porter's lodge, and the actor on the boards. Were our actors as representative of true German nature as theirs are of the French, there might be something for our town-society to expect from their instruction: but, since we are obliged to disallow them any stricter talent for the stage, the sole result of their spurious theatric culture being brought into contact with our burghers' nature is the fostering of similar ill propensities in social life to those which have led themselves to a wholly false and utterly un-German style of art. The actor's Class, with its subdivision into "hero," "villain," "heavy father," "utility" and the like, remains an utter mystery to us, and no real father would so lightly bring himself to give his daughter to a "tragic lover." Despite the growing spread of theatricalism all over Germany, the actor's class is still regarded by our burgher-world with shakings of the head and Philistine astonishment, and the taste for mingling in its company is limited to certain frivolous circles of non-burgher society.

Concerning this, and the change that must needs come over the actor's class if the Theatre is ever to be saved by it, in the course of my personal experience I have met with two completely opposite opinions. They were those of two men, each of whom was called in his time to lead a theatre.

Karl von Holtei confessed without ado that he could make nothing of a so-called "solid" company: since the theatre had been run into the planished grooves of citizen propriety it had lost its sterling tendence, to which he should soonest hope to restore it with a troop of strolling actors. By this opinion the anything but witless man abode, and turned his back on the theatre entrusted to his care after many a fair beginning of success had ended in his being forced to there abandon the prosecution of his tendence.

In the most glaring contrast to this man's opinion stood that of *Eduard Devrient*, who thought needful to demand the elevation of the actor's calling to a civic rank. By getting the *dignity* of the Theatre decreed by edict of the State he hoped to see its operative factors settle down of themselves, with the aid of a little good discipline. It was certainly to the credit of this learned but not very talented actor, above all to wish to see the neglected theatrical system stamped with a tendence under whose ennobling influence the deficiency in natural gifts might be passably made good by school and training. But, for the pursuance of his views a deeply earnest-minded prince bestowed on him a theatre arranged with the utmost regard to propriety, and alas! the results of his exertions proved so completely null that this selfsame theatre—from whose conduct Devrient withdrew at last—has now been relinquished to the maxims of our ordinary directorate, presumably in consequence of an indifference sprung from disappointment.

Now, it can but be instructive to explore the inner reason of two tendences apparently so different, as those of Devrient and Holtei. It then will transpire that the ghost which hovered before them both was that of *mimetic genius*. Holtei sought it on the rugged footpaths of its distant home, and shewed in that a spark of genius;

Devrient, more cautious and mistrustful, thought it safer to find a substitute for that "genius," from whose ghost he had had enough to suffer. He recognised that on Holtei's path one could barely reap the vulgar licence, to say nothing of the old creativeness, of the comedian ; whereas it had become patent to him that the most indigenous moulders of the German actor's calling, as he could demonstrate by *Eckhoff*, *Schröder* and *Iffland*, had been solid, nay, quite moral men in the strictest burgher sense. To take its standard from these fathers, and form and regulate thereby, must seem to him the surest way of healing for the German Theatre. Unfortunately the Genius sought by Holtei appeared to Devrient in none but the guise of the modern histrionic virtuoso ; to hold it at arm's length, as a troubling presence, he may well have deemed imperative: but his zeal appears to have misled him into warding off whatever threatened to disturb him, and I fancy he simply squandered on this object the whole pains of his theatric management, losing himself at last in the eternal defence of his tenets against all possible concussions. Whence, however, could have come to a man grown-up in the thick of our present Theatre the *judgment* whereby to discriminate between phenomena all strange to him ? Such a man would himself have had to own the eye of Genius, of that same genius in which he had no faith because he knew it merely as a ghost. Here everything, quite naturally, could only end in stubbornness, and upon an institute of the most absolute sterility and tedium in its doings the dignity of civic rank could only be conferred in vain.—

Various other attempts to help the Theatre on, no matter how, have led in desperate cases to a combination of these two diverging tendences: in this way the old Hofburg-Theater of Vienna lost the last nimbus of its quondam excellence, which had reposed on a certain conventional burgher-like solidity in its acting system. Since some definite line of study must be taken up, particularly when literati meddled with the stage, one made for the

Frenchman's smartness (*Gewandheit*), a thing which anyone who had ever seen a play in Paris must recognise we plainly lacked in:* one also veered from Devrient's principle to that of Holtei, and tried to lift the theatre into the sphere of the *amusing*. Here one worked oneself up into wondering that people who knew nothing of playing comedy should venture to write for the stage: how quickly this art could be mastered, on the other hand, one fancied one proved in propriâ personâ by the rapid conversion of a decaying scholar into a hale and hearty first-comedian,—a thing which refused to succeed with others, you know, Messrs *Gutzkow* and *Bodenstedt* for instance.

Now, whether it was the scholar or the actor himself, to whom one committed the conduct of the Theatre, it was always on the supposition that something was here to be taught, and probably also learnt; so that it only remained to settle who should be the teacher, the actor or the man of letters? And even the most enlightened must have endorsed this opinion if he felt obliged to deny to the Germans in general, especially in comparison with other nations, a talent for the theatre.

How astonished would *Frederick the Great* have been, if his Court-intendant had one fine day proposed to him to found a German theatre! French *Comédie* and Italian Opera were the only forms under which one then could conceive of the Theatre at all, and it is much to be feared that, if the great king were suddenly to-day to step into his Berlin Court-theatre, he would turn his back on the joys of the since-established German Theatre with the same disgust as though one had presumed to play him a sorry joke. Pursuing this idea, it would be interesting upon the other hand to imagine the impression which that performance of "King Lear" by Ludwig Devrient, let us say, would have produced on the same great Frederick:—

* A writer now credited with ample wit, Herr *Paul Lindau*, enthusiastically extols the Director here referred to, informing us that once he stopped an actor at rehearsal with the cry: "Pause!—That was a joke: let the audience have time to digest it!"—R. WAGNER.

conjecturably an amaze as at the foundering of a world! It would surely have been impossible, however, that genius should have stayed unrecognised by genius.

'Tis from it alone, from Genius, that we have in any case to await the ransom of our Theatre. We find it not, when we seek it; for we seek it in Talent, where it certainly cannot just now be present to us Germans: it is only to be recognised when unexpectedly it shews itself; and to sharpen our eyes for that, is the only preparation we can make for its appearance. And since the whole history of our culture points us to the maintenance of our native gifts—so hemmed from their natural evolution—by earnest, open-minded cultivation, it is on this very path we have with most regardless truth to first grow conscious of the nature of our Judgment; much as upon the path of criticising Thought itself *Kant* lit for us the torch of right knowledge of things in general.—

Now if we view our Theatre in the proper light, we soon shall see why we have no talent for the art there practised: namely, because the whole art as practised by ourselves is not in keeping with our nature, but consists of foreign elements which we are unable to assimilate save by attempting to fit ourselves to *them*, in the same way as we try to fit our bodies and deportment to the fashion of French clothes. What has become a second nature to the French, with us becomes un-nature. As in our garments, so upon our stages, we play at one perpetual masquerade, in which we have passed at last beyond all recognition even of ourselves. If this masquerade has been broken through at times by the genuine spirit of the nation, as "genius" itself, and if we therefore must bear ourselves the strangely-sounding testimony that, though far behind other nations in point of Talent, we are the only people among whom the rare phenomenon of Genius can shew itself in all its grandeur, we nevertheless do not imply thereby that Talent is denied to us in every province: on the contrary, the observation of just that kind of mental gifts and acquisitions, which we denote by the term, on our own realms of art and science has commonly led to the verdict that the German has more talent, the Southern nations of Europe, for instance, more genius. This verdict holds good to to-day, as applied to our achievements in those sciences where we have remained true to ourselves and not been led astray by foreign strivings for effect: and even in respect of Art it finds most cheering proof if we regard the plastic art of the Reformation era, when, beside a few exceptional geniuses, *i.e.* inventors of the highest rank, we see in active life throughout all German countries a spirit of the best and noblest exercise of the invented, most deftly turning it in ever novel use and transformation to the service of domestic art (*Kunstgewerbe*). Whilst if we add to this the abundant manifestments of the German spirit in that province which has come to be entirely our own, the realm of Music, and more especially of Instrumental music, we may advance to the conclusion—so full of lofty hope for all the German future—that not only has genius been vouchsafed to us in emanations as numerous as to the Italians, but, these emanations having been of richer and more powerful type, we likewise may ascribe to that aptitude of the German in virtue whereof the appearances of Genius, divorced in time and space, are united by the amplest outcomes of a national productive art-sense, the quality of *Talent* in its very highest meaning.

Consequently we need not hesitate to assume that the German will prove no whit less fitted for dramatic art as well, once its own domain is freely opened, ay, but left open to his genius, instead of being concealed, as now, behind the fumes of an un-German muck-heap. What a difficult problem I now have mooted, with this allusion to "our own domain" in the Theatre, escapes the eye of no one less than myself: let me therefore approach the attempt at solving it with great precaution.

In this sense my foremost aid must be a reference to the various hints and more precise suggestions to whose publication I have been already moved by earlier conjunctures. First I would refer to my appeal for an *Original-theatre*, embodied in my letter to Franz Liszt upon the "Goethe-stiftung" *; secondly to my working out of the idea contained in that appeal with special regard to narrower accidental, local circumstances, as set forth many years ago in a pamphlet styled "A Theatre in Zurich." † The assents I received, particularly to the latter treatise, were not of an encouraging nature; they mostly came from persons who believed they saw in my proposal a decent pretext for indulging their hobby of so-called private theatricals with an appearance before the assembled public in actual comedy. More intelligent friends found it simply inconceivable how anything at all to be tolerated could be reaped for the theatre from just those elements of town society I had in view, if only for reason of the ugly dialect there current. That there would be any dearth of poets, no one feared however; for everybody thought himself quite competent to write a good stage-piece.

Now I fancy that if my suggestion for the gradual establishment of an original theatre at Zurich were taken up to-day by some imposing power, a wealthy limited company for instance, and addressed to the whole of Germany, the assent would fall out pretty much as then: of actors, since all Germany could be drawn on for the dialect, there would be no greater lack than of poets; the latter in particular would hail with more than patriotic glee the exclusion of every foreign product, and hold the German Theatre's originality for guaranteed thereby; whilst perhaps the only person to object, would be a certain Viennese Director whose experiences of the last two decads have made him

* "See *Gesammelte Schriften und Dichtungen*, Vol. V." R WAGNER.—Vol. III. of the present series.—Tr.

† Ibidem.

think it impossible for a German theatre to be kept up without French pieces,—till even he at last would find himself turning his hand once more to native production. The thing would wear a more difficult aspect, however, if our imaginary shareholders came to take the requirement of Originality in fuller earnest, and deemed needful to have this term "originality" defined by genuine experts in order that the doings of the Theatre might be henceforth judged thereby. And this point in truth, namely how that Originality should certify itself, would be the one we should have to weigh before all else with cold-blooded exactitude.

I believe I have already paved the way for settling this point from many sides, and in particular by my contributions to a criticism of the unoriginality of the modern German Theatre; not to repeat myself, I therefore refer my readers to the remarks hereon in "German Art and German Policy," "A Music-school for Munich," and the close of "Opera and Drama." The harm done to the German Theatre by this unoriginality is so great and startling that one might recommend, as the simplest means of testing the originality of any German piece which claimed it, that our players should be given the piece to read aloud, and note be taken as to whether the tone into which they promptly fell was natural to them or affected. Give them the most admired "original" piece of our highest-flying modern poet, and, so soon as one found them falling into unnatural pathos or casting eyes to right or left towards the audience, request them to speak and behave exactly as accustomed to in somewhat similar situations of actual life: when they did so, they all presumably would burst out laughing at the would-be poetical artwork. If anyone should think this test unsuited to the character of theatric art, I have only to ask him to apply it to French actors and the most eccentric of French plays, and he at once will perceive that the poet's most extravagant stage-pathos makes not the slightest alteration in the actor's tone and bearing, as become a second nature in situations at all resembling these in actual life: for thus does the

Frenchman speak and behave, and, because he always watches this and keeps it carefully in mind, thus also, and not otherwise, does the playwright write. But to the German all approach to this French pathos is unnatural out and out; if he deems needful to employ it, he has to seek its imitation in a laughable disguising of his voice and a screwing-up of all his usual accents.

That we find this un-nature so rife among our actors, proceeds alas! from our having accustomed ourselves to see the same absurd comedy enacted far outside the theatre: it is played, with us, by everyone called to deliver any kind of speech in public. Some time ago I was assured with regard to a fairly famous professor of philology that, given the opportunity, he would also play an important rôle in politics, since he had studied the art of rhetoric so systematically as to have become a past master in every conceivable form of expression, even where the object was to raise a smile or an actual laugh. It once was granted me to convince myself, at a funeral ceremony, of the art of this otherwise most estimable man: he had just been chatting pleasantly with me in the most pronounced of dialects, when suddenly his official speech began, and voice, language, expression, changed in so outrageous a manner that I thought I had a spook before me. Eh! get our best poet to read his verses to us, he promptly mounts into falsetto, and trots out all those pompous fooleries to which we at last are almost as accustomed as if they were matters of course. We hear that *Goethe* became quite painful, through unnaturalism, when reading out his poetry; and of *Schiller* we know that his exaggerated pathos made his pieces quite irrecognisable. Should not all this make us very doubtful as to the relation in which the Higher Tendence may stand towards our natural means of expression? Plainly, we must recognise that here we have an affectation wellnigh grown into a second nature, and to be traced at bottom to a false assumption; perhaps to the poor opinion of our natural faculties that has been drilled into us by a foreign Culture so unconditionally accepted as a higher one that, even at risk of making ourselves ridiculous, we have felt compelled to seek our welfare in its utmost possible assimilation.

Abstaining, for sake of our immediate object, from any criticism of this fatal feature in the German plan of culture, we here have merely to record the fact that the best-educated, alike with the most gifted, German is constantly exposed to Affectation in both his rhetorical and his plastic methods of expression. We have already mentioned that *Goethe* does not appear to have escaped this danger on all occasions, yet, with his usual penetration, he gives us a very drastic glimpse into the evil: on the one hand his "Wilhelm Meister" seeks to free his person from its burgher habits by aid of the theatre; on the other the wretched pedant who desires to make progress in the art of delivery, appealing to the proverb that a comedian may instruct a parson, receives from his "Faust" the pregnant answer: "To be sure! if the parson's a comedian." It will not be without profit for us, to take the thought expressed in this reply as a text for more extended application.

If for "parson" we read all those who in the practice of some higher calling deem needful to adopt a stilted mode of speech and carriage, so as to assert that calling's special dignity, and for "comedian" those who make it their calling to imitate by simulated voice and gesture the natural man in his various grades of character and occupation, it will be evident that here the comedian alone can be the teacher, and presumably the parson will have much to learn before he equals his master. But, strictly speaking, the nickname of "comedian" denotes the man who tries by an assumed demeanour to make himself seem either interesting or specially important, wishing to be taken in fact for what he gives himself out as; it thus would apply to the Mime when he did not seek to objectify by his art an individuality from real life, *as such*, but seriously endeavoured to deceive us as to his actual person by means of borrowed airs and graces. This latter class, however, includes all those who in real life are addicted to the so-called *theatrical* manner; termed "comedians" when they strut upon our boards, 'tis they who wellnigh fill our civic world in all dimensions and directions: so that the honest mime has almost nothing left to copy from it, save the motive of comediantic affectation.

Where the whole of life is filled with this comedianism, the search for purer motives for mimetic art to picture would of itself conduct to proper criticism of the real Originality beseeming us. When I expressed the opinion that a modern tragedy declaimed in a natural tone by our actors would at once betray the absurdity of both its style and its entire conception, my object was to mark the universal affectation in which we unconsciously have lost ourselves, and which comes out in daily life, with its practical interests, the very instant we deem fit to clothe ourselves in a certain borrowed theoretic dignity. The undisfigured, natural man is only to be met to-day in commonest life, nay, hardly anywhere but in the lowest spheres of life; and it therefore need not startle us to find the art of comedy original in none but pieces copied from this life and based on motives taken from these spheres.

So it is, however. Only in the humblest genre is the Play still good in Germany, and the performances of this genre, as concerns the essence of the actor's art, in no wise fall behind the excellence of the French Theatre; ay, here we often meet with more than ordinary talent, with the very Genius of Comedy, albeit pining in a lowly sphere. But just as the so-called Folk-theatre is dying out in every German town, or, where it still subsists in name, is becoming turned into an odious caricature through inoculation with all the tainted motives of our affectation: so even this last refuge of the native German histrionic spirit is shrinking to an ever narrower round, in which we soon shall barely light on aught beyond the *Kasperltheater* * of our yearly fairs.

Indeed it was from a chance encounter with one of these

* Almost identical with our Punch and Judy show.—Tr.

street-shows, that I lately gained a last ray of hope for the German Folk's productive spirit; and that just after all my hopes had been sunk to zero by the performance of a "higher" comedy at an illustrious court-theatre. In the showman of this puppet-theatre and the quite incomparable feats wherewith he held me breathless, while the street-audience seemed to have clean forgotten all its daily avocations in its eager interest, the Spirit of the Theatre once more appeared alive to me, since Heaven knows when. Here was the improviser poet, manager, and actor all in one, and through his magic his poor dolls took life before me with all the truth of sempiternal native characters. He could grip us by the selfsame situation as often as he pleased, perpetually surprising with its each recurrence. And his action centred in a notable being, a being strung to the Dæmonic, that German "Kasperl" who rises from the calmly gluttonous "Hans Wurst" to the indomitable layer of all Priest-and-Devil ghosts, gets the better of the preposterously affected Count by his unanswerable mother-wit, triumphs over Hell and Death, and keeps his bones all whole and safe from Roman Rights in every form of Justice. I was unsuccessful in my attempt to personally hunt out the wonder-working genius of this most genuine of all the stage-shows I ever have witnessed: presumably I was spared thereby a sad revisal of my verdict. Yet, come what might, I felt that Holtei's ideal was a sorry jade against that genius.—

Certainly we should study our history in more places than our books, since it may often be met in full and speaking life upon the very streets. In that Kasperl-theatre I had the birthplace of the German Play before me, and correctly to estimate this origin to me seemed more instructive than all the "essays" of our ignorant and self-opiniated writers on the Theatre. Through such a study one would also gain a proper knowledge of the incredible decay of German public art, and realise at last the reason why the only truly German original-piece of superlative poetic value—namely Goethe's *Faust*—could *not* be written for our stage albeit its every feature springs so clearly from the native German Theatre, and belongs so inwardly thereto, that whatever makes it seem impracticable for our puling modern stage can be explained by nothing but that parentage. Before a fact so patent to the man of average insight and attention, this fact of the unheard position of the most original German stage-piece towards our modern theatre of the Comedians, stands our Art-judgment in its dotage, and can draw nothing from it but the lame conclusion that *Goethe* after all—was no real playwright! And to such a judgment is one asked to make oneself intelligible, ay, to go hand-in-hand with it in a search for the sources of the German Theatre's originality!—

Allow me, therefore, to altogether turn my back on that Art-judgment of our "moderns," and approach a definition of what can alone be meant by Originality in German acting.

In Goethe's "Faust" I point our German players to a piece of the very highest poetic worth, yet a piece whose every rôle and every speech they must by their own nature be equipped to act and speak, if they have an atom of talent to shew for the Theatre. Here no pathos of voice is required for even God Almighty, who "speaks with the Devil himself as man to man;" for he is German like the rest, and speaks the tongue we all know well, the accents each has heard outgoing from the kindly heart and lucid mind. Should it ever come to a general muster of our actors and a sifting-out of the unfit, I would give to each the rôle he might select from "Faust," and make his retention at the Theatre depend on how he took it. This would be the test of the actors' originality, the converse of that proposed above for the originality of the pieces. If we carried out this trial to the point of dismissing every actor who fell into affectation, drawling, or playing for effect, to the great company of comedians outside the theatre, I fear we should end by hardly finding one play-actor for our Faust-performance; unless, perhaps, we dived into our stage's humblest spheres, there to meet at least the traces of those gifts we sought. For my part, some years ago I attended a performance of "Faust" at the Viennese Burgtheater, after the first act of which I departed with the advice to the Director, that at the very least he should make his actors speak their lines exactly twice as fast as they were doing, and get this measure carried out with watch in hand; for thus alone did I think it feasible, in the first place to somewhat cloak the boundless absurdity into which the wretches floundered with their tragedising, in the second to force them to a really natural, perchance an even common mode of speaking, wherein the plainest elementary meaning of their speeches might haply dawn upon them. Of course this suggestion was thought unseemly, and I was told it would make the actors drop into the tone of the so-called Conversation-piece, their forte indeed, but conducive to a bearing scarcely suitable for a Goethian tragedy. These Conversation-pieces, in their turn, gave an idea of the conversational tone of our German actors: "a German conversation-tone!" The very word is sufficient, and involuntarily one thinks of Brockhaus' Konversationslexikon!—To vent on "Faust" this gallimathias of un-nature, of mincing impudence and nigger-like *coquetterie*, must at any rate seem blasphemous even to a modern Theaterdirektor. Only, this is as good as confessing that the Germans' greatest original dramatic piece can absolutely not belong to our own Theatre, as it is; for which reason, also, the Parisians may be complimented on having supplied an "opera" to fill an actual gap in the German Theatre!— —

As it cannot occur to me to tender plans of reform for the German Theatre, which I consider rotten to its deepest root, or haply to suggest a means of giving its repulsiveness a better look, the sole object of my present inquiry must be to furnish the truly gifted mime—upon whom, from various indications, I still may hope to light—with the best clue to his way out of the maze of his surroundings. In Ed. Devrient's "History of German Acting" there lies a very handy guide to this clue, for anyone who weighs the data so perspicuously assembled there. Here we see the raw Folk-theatre, erewhile entirely neglected by the higher-cultured of the nation, falling into the experimenting hands of beaux esprits in the first half of the eighteenth century; from these it escapes to the benevolent care of an honest but narrow-minded Burgher world, whose fundamental note becomes its law of Naturalism; upon this law relies the swift-flowering poetic literature of that century's second half, and rushes the Theatre with it to a bold extravagance of style. To bridle this tendency and lead it to the Ideal, becomes the labour of our greatest poets: the meaning of the astonishment wherewith they paused before the "Opera" I have sought to explain in my treatise "On the Destiny of Opera," at like time setting forth the reasons for the striking of that newer line which brought into our Play false pathos and the academic tone. How we have been led from here into the chaos of the German Court-theatre, with its consequences and dependencies in the Tivoli and hermaphroditic Folk-ballet Theatre, belongs to a special history, upon which I also have thrown some light already, but from whose results we must turn aside, to draw from all we now have learnt and suffered a sound conclusion as to the lamentably maimed and broken character of original German acting.

It will not be easy to rightly denote this character, without hurting someone's feelings. If there's truth in Goethe's dictum, "in German one lies when one is courteous," it is unmistakable that our Theatre and Literature are none too truthful when they try to make things pleasant; and the worst of it is, our lying is such a laughable misfit that no one believes us, for we never can cheat a creature with it. Courtesy, again, we practise in our own peculiar fashion: where we're cramped and bony we give "the German heart" its play, the stiffness of our female world in crinoline and chignon we paraphrase as "noble German womanhood," and "German sturdiness" peeps out from every squinting eye. But with all our euphemisms we cannot even gain a semblance of the tone to which men lend belief, and they do no more than travesty our nature. There's nothing for it: the only thing to help the German is full sincerity, however little this may please at first. So we must keep returning to this tone, the tone we now meet nowhere saving in the humblest spheres, particularly of our Theatre. And who shall gainsay its highly plastic productivity? We need not go so far as our supremely glorious "Faust,"—the witness also of our deepest shame; still closer to those lower spheres, and thus more influential on the practice of the stage, we find significant developments from out this sphere. From the Viennese popular farce (*Volksposse*), with its types still clearly shewing their relationship to Kasperl and Hans Wurst, we see the magic-plays of *Raymund* mounting to the region of a truly dainty poesy; and to cite a stage-work of the highest excellence upon the worthiest side of thorough German nature, we have only to name *Kleist's* wonderful "Prinz von Homburg."

Can our actors still play this piece?

If they are no longer able to hold the interest of a German audience from beginning to end of this particular play, they have only to sign a deposition to their incapacity for practising the art of Comedy in the German sense at all, and may retire from the make-believe of performing Schiller and Shakespeare. For as soon as we touch the realm of higher Pathos, we are treading a field where none but the *genius* can give us a true thing, and however honestly we may have trained our native acting talents to this point, they here are lost at once in that peculiar German "courtesy" which nobody believes. But this Genius is a rare affair at any time, and it would be perfectly absurd of us to ask to see its feats, the "out of the common," on every evening our scattered national German stage throws wide its doors. All that we might recommend as conducive to our Theatre's improvement, would be such an organising of its tendences as to keep the soil in constant readiness for the appearance of this mimic genius; and that can only be accomplished by a faithful tillage of the German's healthy native talents for the theatre.

We have seen how an auspicious turning in the revival of the English Theatre made it possible for a *Garrick* to appear there. What smoothed the ground for our *Ludwig Devrient*, at the German Theatre? Plainly, the sound direction which that Theatre had struck, and in its weightiest respects still followed, when it brought forth performers like Fleck, Schröder, Iffland, ay, and contemporaneously with the great tragedian an Esslär, an Anschütz and others. Were a Garrick possible on the present English stage? Or shall we conjure up the light in which the Theatre of to-day would appear to a Ludwig Devrient, were he to meet it in guise of the Berlin Hoftheater? Perhaps his highly sensitive imagination would have warned him by a premonitory shudder, and thereby spared the great-hearted mime the life-destroying shock.—If, however, we mean to aim at the steady cultivation of an Original German style of acting, it is evident that we must first of all reduce the ridiculous pitch of our theatrical tone to the degree of mimic pathos natural to the German, try to become at home again in that, and thus at least provide a healthy subsoil for the god-sent genius to root in.

And the date of its appearance would lie entirely in our own hands. We should merely have to constitute the German Theatre in a truly German-political sense, according to which there are many German States but only one Reich, a body called upon to execute the Great and the Uncommon, beyond the individual capacity of its component parts. If consequently all our various theatres confined their labours to that loyal cultivation of a sound theatric art, and never overstepped the circle which I drew around Kleist's "Prinz von Homburg," it would then behove a union of the choicest forces of these theatres to also pitch its efforts higher than that sphere, provided this took place but seldom and only in response to the appearance of exceptional gifts.

With these hints at a real organisation of our theatres for practical purposes, I touch the selfsame thought that prompted the proposed stage-festivals at Bayreuth. Whoever has noticed in that matter how from first to last I abstained from even the proposal to attempt an organisation of all our theatres for co-operative action, will need no telling that I still less feel called to elaborate the foregoing hints into a definite scheme. The conduct of our theatres is left at present to the judgment of people who, however superior they may think themselves, owe their understanding of the thing to nothing but the badness of our general theatric system : all hope of seeing that understanding widened to a knowledge of the Theatre's true needs, I have long since given up. Wherefore, as I can count on nothing save the healthy instinct of our mimes and bandsmen for any good to be done in the theatre, I also turn to them alone with an expansion of my hints for the better employment of their natural parts.

My root-idea I have already propounded to the æsthetic reviewer of the various types of Drama in my paper "On the Destiny of Opera." I now desire to bring it nearer to the conscience of our actors and singers. For the former [the actors] I have suggested a boundary-line for the training and development of their faculties in harmony with the basic German character, to ensure their avoidance of un-German affectation and the consequent ruin of their art. If after the most conscientious deliberation, however, circumstances proved favourable to the overstepping of this line, accordingly should one have here and there observed conspicuous mimetic talents whose skilful combination might reasonably take the form of a noble national festival, it then would remain for careful experiments to shew whether the didacto-poetic pathos so largely represented by *Schiller* were really beneficial to that idealising of the Drama here certainly aimed at, *i.e.*, while lifting the performer to a higher sphere, whether it still allowed his feet to touch the terra firma of his art. In any case this is a problem yet to solve, and in propounding it I by no means wish to imply a foregone unconditional doubt.—From the mere standpoint of effective stage-pieces Schiller's dramas are of such uncommon worth, simply through the movement of the plot they chain us so irresistibly, that it can but repay the trouble, to seriously attempt to overcome the difficulties which appear so much to hinder their performance in even a natural sense. The bent which prompted our great poet to mature that "didacto-poetic pathos," through whose extraordinary sweep of wing he strove to elevate the substance of his dramas and set them in a rarer atmosphere, at any rate lies deeply rooted in the German's nature. Nevertheless the means of achieving the task here set the mime, of keeping intact the inalienable character of a Dramatic action when it is intercepted at every instant by an appeal to the judgment-seat of Ethics—this means has first to be discovered and confirmed. By the consequences of the entry of "poetic diction" into dramatic style, we have seen to what ruin of all good propensities in the German Play a shallow reading of this task could lead. To my knowledge, it has been supportably accomplished only by the sound though sober sense of a handful of good actors from the olden school, as shewn, for instance, by the able Esslär within the memory of the riper generation of our day: here the ethical-didactic content of the sentence was stripped of Pathos, and sensibly delivered with a tinge of due emotional colour. Only once does Schiller's ideal appear to have been thoroughly attained, when for that content the gifted Sophie Schröder found withal the transfiguring *musical tone* of voice, melting the very didactic core into the sphere of unadulterated Feeling, and thus restoring it itself to the passionate accent of the dramatist.

Think *ye* ye may venture to enrich your style with the winning of this accent, this incommunicable soul-possession of a great genius?

At all events I should deem it prudent to venture such an attempt in none but the extraordinarily favouring circumstances already stipulated, for here it is a question of applying their best results to an actual discovery of the laws of an intrinsically German ideal Style; whereas Shakespeare's dramas point us to a histrionic style for which there seem in truth to be no laws at all, as it forms itself the fundamental law of *naturalism* in all mimetic playing worth the name.

Shakespeare, in fact, is to be explained in virtue of no national school, but only through our seizing the pure essence of mimo-dramatic art in general. With him all schematism of Style—i.e. each formal or expressional tendence imposed from without, or adopted through reflection—resolves into that one root-law from which the natural lifelike imitation of the mime derives its wondrous power of illusion. Through Shakespeare's ability, beneath the mask of his performers, to let each human individuality observed by him express itself according to its most natural demeanour, he was enabled also to seize and express according to its proper features all that lay beyond his life-experience. All his figures bear the stamp of faithfulness to nature in such a marked degree, that the first pre-requisite for mastering the tasks he set appears to be mere freedom from affectation: but what a claim we here have stated, is manifest to anyone who reflects that our whole modern Theatre, and particularly its "higher pathetic" tendence, is based on affectation. Let us suppose this affectation put aside by following the principles laid down above, there here would remain, as there with Schiller's didacto-poetic pathos, that overpowering height of purely *passionate* pathos of characters whose eccentricity appears to us—however versed in the experiences of actual life—no whit less supranatural than those cothurnus-mounted heroes of Antique Tragedy. To apply to this Shakespearian pathos that pathos of Schiller's, no matter how successfully matured on the above conditions, would lead in all good faith to the same confusion as was brought about by the false pathos common everywhere to-day.

Here our first business would be to discover the exact principle on which the mimetic naturalism of Shakespeare's dramas is to be distinguished from what we call by that name in the case of almost every other dramatic poet.

I venture to deduce this principle from the *one* fact that Shakespeare's actors played upon a stage surrounded by spectators on all sides, whereas the modern stage has followed the lead of the French and Italians, displaying the actors only from one side, and that the front side, just like the painted 'wings.' Here we have the academic theatre of the art-Renaissance, modelled upon a misunderstanding of the antique stage, in which the scene is severed from the public by the orchestra. The special-privileged "friend of art," who erst preferred to sit on each side of this modern stage as well, our sense of seemliness has finally sent back into the parquet, to leave us an untroubled view of a theatrical picture which the skill of the decorator, machinist and costumier has almost raised to the rank of a generic work of art.

Now, it is both surprising and instructive to see how a trend toward rhetorical Pathos, intensified by our great German poets to the didacto-poetic pitch, has always preponderated on this Neo-european stage, miscopied from the antique; whereas on Shakespeare's primitive folk-stage, which lacked all blinding scenic glitter, the interest was centred in the altogether realistic doings of the meanly clad play-actors. Whilst the later, academically ordered English Theatre made it the actor's imperative duty under no circumstances to turn his back on the audience, and left him to sidle off as best he could in case of any exit toward the rear, Shakespeare's performers moved before the spectator in all directions with the full reality of common life. We may judge what a power the naturalistic mode of acting had here to exert, since it was backed by no auxiliary illusion, but in every gesture had to set in closest neighbourhood to us the poet's marvellously true and yet so curiously uncommon figures, and make us believe in them to boot: here was need of the very highest dramatic pathos, if only to maintain our belief in the truthfulness of this playing, which would otherwise have proved quite laughable in situations of great tragic moment. Admit that in such circumstances nothing but the most unwonted mimic art could be conceived as producing the right effect, the art of those geniuses of whose protean nature and unusual power of dominating the hearer's imagination those famous anecdotes have come down to us in witness. Most certainly their rareness was the reason of the so speedily appearing reaction of educated art-taste against this Popular Theatre and the line prevailing in its dramatic poetry; for poor and affected actors were manifestly insufferable in such naked proximity, whereas if set in a more distant frame, and bolstered up with stylish academic rhetoric, they could be made quite pleasing to that art-taste.

It is in this latter style that the Modern Theatre and its art of Acting have been bequeathed to us: what a figure it cuts, we now perceive; and how the Shakespearian Drama here comes out, we likewise witness. Here we have coulisses, views and costumes, turning the whole drama into a senseless masquerade. Nearly as this Drama is related to the German spirit, equally remote does it stand from modern German theatric art; and we shall not go very far wrong if we incline to the supposition that Shakespeare's Drama—as it in fact was wellnigh the only truly original product of the newer European spirit, the only thing that escaped all influence of the antiquising Renaissance—stands also alone as such, and utterly inimitable. This fate it might be said to share in an eminent degree with Antique Tragedy itself, to which in other respects it stands in the most complete antithesis; and we may add that, should the hoped-for maturation of the world-rescuing German spirit be ever blessed with a Theatre as entirely its own, it must be an Artwork arising with equal inimitability, and no less self-dependence, between that pair of opposites.

To the as yet unknown, but in this case absolutely indispensable genius that shall some day spring from our Theatre, it may be left to regenerate the German acting-stage on the lines above suggested, to regenerate it in such a sense that, returning without affectation to its natural departure-point, it may happily pass through each partly lapsed, in part suppressed by evil outward influences, each broken or aborted stage of evolution of its healthy nature, as if retrieving its steps with waking consciousness, to thus arrive at last at full development of all the good and individual qualities as yet observable in it. We then should expect that genius so dextrously to plan the scene of its activity—including Schiller's Ideal tendence—that, if not the Shakespearian Drama itself, at least the leading feature of its art of representation should there be able to approach us in familiar nearness, on the one hand, whilst the other would make possible that ideal distance in which to set the boldest figures of the most original of German pieces, Goethe's "Faust." What a fundamental transformation of the present theatre we necessarily imply, above all in respect of its architectural arrangement, is clear from what has gone before; that such a thing would be inconceivable at our modern semi-theatre, with its scenes presented to us merely on the flat, *en face*, must be obvious to anyone who seriously thinks the matter over: before that stage the spectator stays entirely withdrawn into himself, awaiting passively from there above, and finally from there behind, fantastical contrivances to bear him to a world from whose real midst he wishes to remain aloof. Further, it will be evident that here the successfully aroused imagination of the spectator alone can facilitate, in fact make possible, the representation of scenic incidents which, so to speak, are to cluster round us on all sides; consequently, that it can be no question of elaborations, but merely of suggestive hints, such as Shakespeare's stage employed to signify the place of action. But the Shakespearian stage

N

already shews us what a wealth of scenic motives may accrue from an ingenious use of simple architectural conditions and the assumptions formed thereon; and its remote imitation at our theatre has enabled an intelligent expert to so far overcome the difficulties presented in the mounting of the "Midsummer-night's Dream" that he may actually be termed the first to have made it possible. Now, if we conceive those simple architectural conditions of the Shakespearian theatre extended and enriched with the modern improvements in all mechanical art, it finally might need no more than a bold appeal to the spectator's fancy, to set him in a world of magic where the scene is changed before his eyes "from heaven through earth with all due speed to hell." *

To realise this, would be the true task for our Theatre, if ever it meant to prove itself worthy of its own great poets. Should no genius be able to take this path once more, it then must be admitted that our Theatre has strayed on one side to the abyss of deepest degeneration, and that its noblest destiny can only be rescued by leading it right away from its former path, by striking an altogether new direction, albeit primally its own.—

Let us now turn our eyes to German "Opera."—

As to the high destiny which I believe reserved for Opera I have spoken at length in the special paper already mentioned more than once, in which I took my principal stand on the fact that a leaning toward the Operatic has always been inherent in modern Drama. Referring to that essay for everything in this particular connection, I now will link my most earnestly-meant demands on Opera directly to the last-considered characteristic of the modern stage and the relation into which the spectator is brought thereto. Here it is evident that, even in its architectural

* From the Prologue to Goethe's *Faust*.—Tr.

construction, the modern theatre has turned away from any sound development of the so-called Recited Play, and toward the Opera.

Our theatres are opera-houses, and their structure is only explicable by the Opera's requirements. Their origin lies in Italy, the specific land of "Opera." Here the ancient amphitheatre, with the box-like storeys of the Colisseum, has been transformed into the glittering assembly-room of the richer entertainment-loving circles of the town's society, a hall in which the audience feasts its eyes upon itself before all else, and where "the ladies lend their dress and persons for an unpaid rôle." * But, just as the whole pretence of Art was here derived from the academically-misread Antique, there neither lacked the orchestra with the stage upreared behind it. From the orchestra rang out the introduction or the ritornel, as a herald's cry for silence; upon the stage appeared the singer in the hero's costume, gave forth his aria accompanied by the instruments, and departed with a signal to the audience to resume its rapturous entertainment of itself.

However great the disfigurement, in this convention one still can trace the outlines of the antique theatre, of which we have distinctly retained the orchestra as link between the public and the stage. In this position the orchestra indisputably is called to act as idealiser of the play upon the stage; and herein lies the radical distinction between this theatre and that of Shakespeare, in which the play was offered us in bare reality, and thus could hold the spectator's interest in a higher, ideal sphere through nothing but the mime's consummate power of illusion. The antique "orchestra" is the magic tripod, the fruitful mother-womb of the Ideal Drama, whose heroes—as has rightly been remarked †—only shew themselves in plane upon the stage, whereas the magic welling from the

* Again from Goethe's Prologue to *Faust*.—Tr.

† Apparently an allusion to Friedrich Nietzsche's "*Geburt der Tragödie*," with chapter 8 whereof the present section has many points in common. See my preface, also page 198.—Tr.

Orchestra alone is able to fill out in amplest scale each possible dimension in which their individuality can be conceived as extending. Now, if we consider to what significance the modern orchestra has developed from those scant beginnings of Italian Opera, we may well infer its high vocation for the Drama; and we shall find that inference surprisingly supported by the triumph of the modern theatre, with its originally mistaken copy of an antique model, over the playhouse of Shakespeare. Certain it is, that in this modern theatre the native Neo-european Play has fallen to such flatness that it could but yield before the rivalry of Opera: nothing is left but the mere flat surface on which the stage-figures are drawn; and, robbed of the omnipresent magic of the orchestra, the theatrical Pathos which our great poets sought to better with ennobling sentences—under such circumstances in vain—must necessarily degenerate to empty platitude.

This point we must clear up, to understand the reasons of the characteristic faults and imperfections of the modern Theatre.

In the antique Orchestra, almost completely surrounded by the amphitheatre, the tragic Chorus stood as in the public's heart: its songs and dances, instrumentally accompanied, rapt the nation of spectators to a state of clairvoyance in which the hero, now appearing in his mask upon the stage, had all the import of a ghostly vision. Now, if we think of Shakespeare's stage as pitched within the Orchestra itself, we at once perceive what an uncommon power of illusion must have been expected of the mime, if he was to bring the drama to convincing life under the spectator's very eyes. To this stage transplanted to the orchestra our modern proscenium bears the relation of that *theatrum in theatro* of which Shakespeare makes repeated use, presenting the performers of his actual drama with a second piece performed upon that doubly fictive stage by players playing at being players. I fancy this feature proves an almost conscious knowledge, on the poet's part, of the original ideality of those scenic conventions which he here employs according to their traditional misunderstanding and abuse.* His Chorus had become the drama itself, and moved in the Orchestra with so realistic a naturalism that it well might end by feeling itself the audience, and expressing in that capacity its approval or disapproval of, or even but its interest in, a second stage-play acted to it. Highly characteristic, too, is the light in which the poet sets this second play: the "Murder of Gonzago" in Hamlet shews us the whole rhetorical-pathos of Academic Tragedy, to whose actors the poet gets sent from the orchestral main-stage itself the cry to "leave their damnable faces." We here might be looking on French tragédie transplanted to the German stage; whilst the clowns' tragedy in the Midsummer-night's Dream gives us a foretaste of the newest pathos of our "original grim Hagen" poets.†

But academic taste prevailed; the hinder stage with its surface-views was proclaimed the stage itself, the drama banished from the orchestra, and actual musicians put there in its stead, to accompany the singers of the opera up aloft. What a might that orchestra possesses, even when used as mere musical accompaniment; what a power of participation in the whole dramatic performance, in perfect keeping with the ground-lines of the theatre's arrangement—this was to become ever clearer with the waxing of the newer instrumental music in importance. 'Twas not alone the overwhelming might of Song, compared with bare recited Speech, that gained for Opera the earnest notice of distinguished minds in every age, and finally of our own great poets; no, it was the entire element of Music which pervaded the whole drama, in never so exiguous forms, and

* "Ich glaube, dieser Zug des Dichters lässt uns auf ein fast ganz deutliches Bewusstsein desselben von der urherkömmlichen Beschaffenheit der idealen scenischen Konventionen, in welchen er sich nach zunächst überliefertem Misverständnisse und Misbrauche bewegte, schliessen." An exceptionally difficult sentence to interpret.—TR.

† "Das neueste Pathos unserer grimmigen Original=Recken=Poeten." See page 169.—TR.

thus transferred it to that ideal sphere for which the costliest poetic diction had proved inadequate.

The expectations nursed in this regard can never be fulfilled, however, until the relations of the hitherto recognised factors of Opera shall have been considerably modified; and this is the point on which our traditional views must be very substantially amended. The Opera has given us singers, *i.e.* vocal virtuosi on the stage, and in the orchestra a gradually increasing tale of instrumentists to accompany the singing of those virtuosi: with the growth of the orchestra's skill and importance there consequently arose the critical axiom, that of these two factors the orchestra should properly supply the "pedestal," the singer the "statue," and that it was wrong to wish to set the pedestal upon the stage, the statue in the orchestra,* as happened when the latter took too prominent a part. This comparison itself betrays the whole misconstitution of the operatic genre: for there to be any talk of statues and pedestals, one at most can think of the icy rhetoric of French Tragédie, or the no less cold Italian-operatic vocalism of castrati of the eighteenth century; but when one comes to living Drama all analogy with sculpture ceases, for its mother-element is only to be sought in Music, out of which alone was born the Tragic Artwork.† With the Greeks this element obtained its plastic body from the Chorus in the Orchestra; through the shifting of the lines of culture in newer Europe, that Chorus has become the merely audible Instrumental-orchestra, the most original, ay, the only truly new creation entirely peculiar to our spirit, in all the realm of Art. Thus we should rightly phrase it:—Here the infinitely potent orchestra,‡

* The well-known maxim of the fast-decaying older school of critics, applied in particular to Wagner's music, if not actually invented *ad hoc*. See also page 209.—Tr.

† See page 195, the full original title of Nietzsche's essay being "The birth of Tragedy from the spirit of Music."—Tr.

‡ That this orchestra's idealising agency can only be ensured by making it invisible, I have several times remarked elsewhere.—R. Wagner.

there the dramatic mime; here the mother-womb of Ideal Drama, there its issue borne on every hand by sound.—

And now for our "*Opera-singer.*"

By him we mean to-day the absolute Singer, of whom one no longer asks an appearance in recited Play, and whom one forgives with a smile for speaking the dialogue, that still crops up in Opera, so vilely as would never be allowed to any actor.

At the rise, and during a long period of the evolution of German Opera, it was otherwise. That opera had an almost identical origin with the French vaudeville, and was performed by the selfsame actors who played in every species of the spoken drama. Even after the unpretending little vocal pieces that gave the *Singspiel* its name had been expanded into the later Opera, the singers remained attached to the Play, and that for its most important parts. K. M. von Weber undertook the establishment of a German Opera in Dresden with the co-operation of the same company as acted in the Play: at Leipzig some years ago I saw the actor Genast, now recently deceased, appear in the principal rôles of both opera and play; and the brothers Emil and Eduard Devrient began their stage-career as singers and actors alike. For this highly laudable class of performers the operas of Mozart—originally written for Italian companies—were translated into German, with dialogues in place of the recitatives; and these dialogues were even lengthened by additions, to give them the wonted natural animation. In such a guise the "Seraglio" (*Entführung*), "Don Juan," and "Figaro" entered the same class with products of the true French school, such as the "Water-carrier," "Joseph" and others, which only needed to be translated, to supply our Opera with a repertoire that could very well be sustained by an aptly chosen company of actors.

But a so-called "coloratura" lady had soon to be expressly added: for here it was a matter of special art-dexterity, the attainment and keeping-up of which appeared to exclude all cultivation of strictly mimetic gifts, and therefore could scarcely be expected of an actress skilled in her own department. With her was next associated the "coloratura" tenor, called to this day the "lyric" tenor in distinction from the "dramatic," who for long had to continue his services as actor proper. This pair of rarities, who lived apart from the remaining personnel of the theatre in a seclusion hedged as much by their stupidity as by their virtuosity, became the actual poles of modern Opera, and in particular the ruin of its German type.—When the Princes were obliged to curb their luxury, and dismiss from court the Italian troops of singers maintained at their expense before, the repertoire specific to Italian Opera had also to be shouldered by the German acting-companies. And here things went pretty much as I myself experienced with the once so famous music of the Catholic church in Dresden when the Italian castrati had either been discharged or were dying out, and poor little Bohemian choristers had to wrestle with bravura pieces reckoned for those terrible colossi, as people deemed them indispensable. So the whole opera now sang coloratura, and the "singer" became a sacred being, to whom one presently could not so much as dare to speak: where dialogue survived, it must be curtailed, reduced to a nothing-saying minimum, and entirely suppressed wherever possible in the case of the leading personages. What words and speeches remained for pure singing, moreover, at last became that double-Dutch we hear to-day in Opera, for which one really might have spared oneself the trouble of translation, since nobody can guess what language it belongs to.

Thus we see Opera falling into precisely the same ruin as the Play, a ruin already characterised at length by me elsewhere. If Goethe and Schiller could only hear a "Prophète" or "Trovatore" performance of to-day, they certainly would laugh at their hopes aroused by performances of "Don Juan" and "Iphigenia" as an error to be rectified with all despatch. And if the Opera is ever to fulfil the noble destiny then dreamt for it, it will have to be through an entire new-birth; my views on which I now will lay to the heart of those through whom alone it is attainable, first taking our singers back to the starting-point of their so degenerated art, to where we find them acting still as players.

Here we shall see what distinguishes our own stage-singer so completely from the Italian opera-singer that the attempt to combine their natural tasks was bound to end in just the senseless opera-screaming (*Opernsingerei*) of to-day.

Italian Opera is the singular miscarriage of an academic fad, according to which, if one took a versified dialogue modelled more or less on Seneca, and simply got it psalm-sung as one does with the Church-litanies, it was believed one would find oneself on the high road to restoring Antique Tragedy, provided one also arranged for due interruption by choral chants and ballet-dances. Here the singer, with his affected pathos and unnatural stilted prosing, was the departure-point of the practical execution: as his psalmodising became unbearably tedious, one soon allowed him to reward himself and his audience for the thankless task of Recitative by the production of vocal fireworks, eventually quite separable from the text; precisely as the stiffly antiquising dancer was at last accorded the pirouette and entrechat. As a logical consequence there hence evolved a vocalistic specialism, best cultivated in the long run by expressly adjusted human instruments, in other words Castrati.

Now, what has our honourable German singing-actor in common with this strange creation of Italian vocal art? However charming and truly delightful that art itself may have become in the hands of eminent masters, it is altogether foreign to the German's nature. If he *can* acquire it, it is only by abandoning his native aptitudes and

Italianising himself, of which we have had a good many instances: but he thereby is cut off from all part or lot in the German Theatre. If Italian singing is practicable in a German throat, it can only be through acquisition of the Italian tongue; no other language could engender or sustain so sensuous a pleasure in sheer vocalism, to use the musical term, *solfeggio*. And with the Italians this revelling in the sensuousness of vocal tone—only to be fully glutted in Pathetic song—is so great that this richly gifted nation has relatively but little cultivated its talent for the more popular genre of wellnigh merely chattered *Buffa*, always preferring the whining drawl and ornate affectation, the so-called *Lamento* of the supposed Tragic style to the very cleverest products of that humbler sphere.

From France alone, did our German Singspiel get a food at all assimilable; for in many respects, such as the character of his language and the derivation of his vaudeville from that character, the Frenchman was debarred as much as the German from adopting the Italian mode of Song. And it was in France, in return, that a German succeeded in bringing certain principles of naturalism to an almost ceremonial notice, at least through the stand he made against the Italian type of "aria." Yet, *Gluck* having necessarily based his reputed reforms upon French "tragédie," his efforts had no permanent result in the formation of a healthy German-operatic style. Whilst so-called "Grand Opera"—i.e. an opera sung throughout, with recitatives to piece the arias and ensembles together—remained to us a foreigner, our native element pursued its path of simply enlarging the *Singspiel*. And it is here that we must take it up, from here lead on our singers, if we mean to stand secure on our own feet.

First of all, then, we have to settle what alone can be meant by "*song*" in German chanted drama. The German language, which of course we intend to use, gives the needful answer into our very hands. The Italian "*canto*" is inexecutable in this language, and, be it as rich and sweet as our gourmands think it, we must abstain from it in toto. If we insist on speaking our mother-tongue to that "canto," it becomes a jumble of inarticulate vowels and consonants, which simply hinder and distort the singing without being understood as speech.

That even supportable German singers are growing rarer every day, and at last must be paid their weight in gold and precious stones by our lordly Theatre-Intendants, does not arise from any progressive incapacity of the Germans, but simply from their perverse training to nonsensical accomplishments. If to-day I seek out singers for a passably correct performance of my own dramatic works, it is not by chance the "scarcity of voices" that alarms me, but my fear of their having been utterly ruined by a method which excludes all sound pronunciation. As our singers do not articulate properly, neither for the most part do they know the meaning of their speeches, and thus the character of any rôle entrusted to them strikes their minds in none but general hazy outlines, after the manner of certain operatic commonplaces. In their consequent frenzied hunt for something to please, they light at last on stronger tones (*Tonaccente*) strewn here and there, on which they rush with panting breath as best they can, and end by thinking they have sung quite "dramatically" if they bellow out the phrase's closing note with an emphatic bid for applause.

Now it has been almost amazing to me, to find how quickly such a singer, with a little talent and good will, could be freed of his senseless habits if I led him in all brevity to the essentials of his task. My compulsorily simple plan was to make him really and distinctly speak in singing, whilst I brought the lines of musical curvature (*die Linien der Gesangsbewegung*) to his consciousness by getting him to take in one breath, with perfectly even intonation, the calmer, lengthier periods on which he formerly had expended a number of gusty respirations; when this had been well done I left it to his natural feeling to give the melodic lines their rightful motion, through accent, rise and fall, according to the verbal sense. Here I seemed to observe in the singer the salutary effect of the return of an overwrought emotion to its natural current, as if the reducing of its unnatural and headlong rush to a proper rate of motion had spontaneously restored him to a sense of wellbeing; and a quite definite physiological result of this tranquillisation appeared forthwith, namely the vanishing of that peculiar cramp which drives our singers to the so-called head-note (*Gaumenton*, lit. "palatal tone")—that terror of our singing-masters, which they attack in vain with every kind of mechanical weapon, although the enemy is but a simple bent to affectation, which takes the singer past resistance when once he thinks he has no longer to speak, but to "sing," which means in his belief that he must do it "finely," i.e. make an exhibition of himself.

I believe that every decent German singer is susceptible of a similar speedy cure, or in fact rebirth; and I hold it labour absolutely lost, to waste the arts of our singing-masters on such as are not at once amenable to the mode of guidance sketched above. If you want the "canto" of the Italians, send your rarely suitable voices straight to Italy! What the German needs, to fit him for a dramatic style of singing in keeping with his natural parts, consists in something altogether different from the teaching-apparatus there in vogue. For all that the German singing-actor (as I may call him) requires, besides recovery of his scandalously neglected naturalism in speaking as in singing, lies solely on the *mental* plane.

By this "mental plane" I certainly do not mean the domain of our Schools of Music and the Stage, where the Herr Professor mouths his lectures on Æsthetics, Art-history and the like; things he has carefully read up in divers books to give himself the air of knowing something of them.* No: we have here to do with a popular gift, from whose cultivation we cannot keep our doctrinaire maxims too far away, to learn from its quite natural development by its own true instincts what may be the rightful style of Drama for ourselves.

It can only be a question of *what tasks* we set our mimic artists for the practice of their art. Has the actor or singer himself acquired a comprehensive culture, so much the better for him as man. Such an education, however, can have absolutely no influence upon the practice of his special art: soundness in this will only come to him through his gift for mimetic portrayal, guided and determined by the *right example*. By nature an imitative bent, it becomes a thing of higher art through learning to pass from imitation to interpretation.† As bent-to-imitation it contents itself with the immediate appearances of daily life; here is its root, deprived of which the mimic spirit, as Stage-affectation, floats holdless through the miasms of our whole affected Culture. But to hold before this primal bent a picture of the Ideal of all realities, raised high above the common sense-life of the experiential world, and thus to point it to the interpretation of the never-seen and ne'er-experienced—is to give it the *example*; which example, if clearly and plainly expressed, will at once be understanded of the mime, for whom imprimis it was reckoned to a nicety, and now will be copied by him in the same manner as formerly the phenomenon or incident of actual life.

That example is the main requirement, then; and, in the special case here dealt with, we mean by it *the work of the dramatic musician*. Now, it is manifestly absurd to ask our modern opera-singer to sing and act naturally, when an unnatural example is laid before him. But the

* If our Princes, Chambers of Deputies, and other Art-protectors to whom has lately been delegated the duty of manning and maintaining "solid" schools and conservatories, but knew on what their money is wasted, I feel sure they would gladly agree to its being spent instead on our poor starving Folk-school teachers.—R. WAGNER.

† *Nachahmung* and *Nachbildung*; see Vol. IV., page 76.—TR.

unnaturalism of our Opera resides in the utter vagueness of its Style, which oscillates between two completely opposite sides; and these two sides I may briefly term *Italian Opera* (with its *canto* and *recitativo*) and *German Singspiel* upon a basis of dramatic dialogue.

I have already proved that the German must stand entirely aloof from Italian Opera, and devote himself to maturing the German Singspiel. This also has been done by our best composers: we have Mozart's "Magic Flute" ("*Zauberflöte*"), Beethoven's "Fidelio," and Weber's "Freischütz." The only failing in these works, is that the dialogue could not as yet be wholly set to music. Here was a difficulty to overcome, whose solution we were only to approach by many a side-way, to vanquish it at last through nothing but the full unveiling of the Orchestra's gigantic power. Those masters found no field for their musical inventiveness save that of Aria and Ensemble, bequeathed to them beside the high road of the dialogue, and cleared for more and more luxuriant cultivation. This tempted them, e'en them, to come to terms with Italian *canto*, since the very isolation of those single pieces inclined them to the character of the Cabaletta etc. The German composer seemed to dread the charge of heaviness, on the part of amateurs, of "unthankful" rôles on that of the singers, and met them by concessions, such as the vocal colorature strewn here and there—whose execution, on the other hand, did not so much as set his talent in a favouring light.* The rift in this whole style of composition seemed reparable only by discovery of the means of getting the dialogue sung as well, to do away with the isolation of the vocal numbers, and thus avoid the temptation to treat them undramatically. But each attempt to apply the Recitativo proper to our dialogue miscarried, and to it

* "Der deutsche Komponist schien den Vorwurf der Plumpheit von Seiten der Kunstliebhaber, sowie den der "Undankbarkeit" ihrer Partien von Seiten der Sänger zu fürchten, und begegnete diesen durch Konzessionen, wie sie selbst hier und da eingeflochtene Coloraturen für die Gesangsstimme ausdrücken, deren Ausführung andererseits nicht einmal seine Geschicklichkeit in einem günstigen Lichte erscheinen lassen konnte."—

Weber owed his "Euryanthe's" disappointing effect on the public. For the subsequent greater habituation to dialogue composed throughout, and rendered in recitative, we have to thank the marked ascendance which French Grand Opera appeared to be taking: that Opera presented us with a few uncommonly impressive works in which the recitative, delivered with unwonted fire and flanked by a richer orchestral accompaniment, took all our usages by storm; thenceforth it became a point of honour with our own composers also, to set every line of their text-books, "durchkomponiren" as one called it. So we fell without a struggle into the utterly un-German recitative, with the distinctive feature that its style was borrowed this time from French rhetoric, and the German tongue was handled on a system plainly taken from our bad translations from the French.—

I now must be allowed to demonstrate by my own works the phases of evolution from the last-named labyrinth to a good sound German style—at least, according to my way of thinking—since a similar demonstration by the works of my opera-composing German contemporaries has not yet become clear to me.

What was always bound to confuse the German musician's view of Opera, was its division into two halves, a dramatic and a lyrical, whereof the latter alone was meant for him; leading him to elaborate and adorn his share in the sense of his own specific art, i.e. according to a formula quite out of touch with the dramatic action. Thus *Weber*, compelled to leave to spoken dialogue the highly dramatic scene of Max's enlistment by Kaspar through the fatal loan of the magic-bullet, found his only chance of expressing the excitement of the situation in the setting of a few lines of verse to an aria for the hellish tempter, the utter nonsense of which solo he naturally sought to remedy by most undramatically prolonging it for sake of a purely-musical effect; wherefore, also, he felt it impermissible to omit the coloratura, so appropriate in the eyes of many composers, upon the word "revenge" ["*Rache*,"—end of act i.]. Well, the long preceding scene in dialogue was afterwards "composed throughout" by Berlioz in the style of French Recitative, for the Paris production. Whereupon the entire unsuitability of the spirited German dialogue for such a treatment was manifest, and to myself it became quite evident that this scene should never have been worked out with the usual Recitative, however animated, but with music of quite another stamp, in which the dialogue itself would have been made so musical that the appending of a special aria, like that of Kaspar, would have seemed a work of supererogation even from the musical standpoint. The raising of the dramatic dialogue to the real main subject of musical treatment—it being already the factor of greatest weight and interest in the drama itself—must consequently so affect the aggregate purely-musical structure that the vocal pieces sandwiched hitherto between would have entirely to disappear, as such, to breathe their musical essence without cease throughout the texture of the whole, nay, to be broadened to that whole itself.

To make plainer what I mean, let us pursue this example from Freischütz, and figure what a fertile use Weber would have made of the musical constituents of the preceding drinking-song and Kaspar's closing aria, how he would have expanded and enriched them by new combinations, had he but worked them into a musical setting of the whole scene that lies between, and that without having to alter or omit one word of the dialogue for sake, we will say, of turning it into an operatic "arioso." Let us suppose that some necessity or other had moved Weber to do this thing, and in particular to let the orchestra not merely accompany the dialogue in the fashion of Recitative, but carry it in Symphonic style, pervading it from beginning to end as the blood the veins of a man who shews himself now thus now otherwise, now passionate now tranquil, sad or merry, resolved or hesitating; and if from many analogies supplied us by Weber's characterisation of musical motives—for instance, in the closing scene of the last act of Euryanthe—we may infer the telling and thrilling manner in which the orchestra would have pinned our sympathy to the situation developing in right-accented dialogue before our eyes, without ceasing for a moment to delight our artistic feeling as a well-made tissue of pure tone,—then with this single scene we should have had to thank the glorious composer for an already fulfilled ideal of dramatic art.

To seek out the possibilities which here lay still concealed from *Weber*, was the instinctive impulse that shaped the future course of my development, and I believe I shall best denote the point I reached in their discovery by instancing the one result, that I was able in time to bring my dramatic poems to such a complexity of dialogue that those to whom I first imparted them could only express their wonder how I was ever going to set a purely interlocutory play to music*; whereas, when the scores of these very poems were completed, it had to be admitted that they shewed a ceaseless flow of music as yet unknown. Every kind of contradiction found voice in the judging of this artistic phenomenon: the equality of my orchestra's elaboration itself gave rise to wrath; folk said I now had plunged the statue in the orchestra from top to toe and left nothing but its pedestal to career about the stage, whereby I had done my "singer" to death.† But it so happened that our singers, and the best of them, took a great liking for the tasks I set them, and "sang in my operas" with such a zest at last that their chief achievements, and those received the warmest by the public, have issued just from them. Never have I been more heartily contented with an opera-company than upon the occasion of the first performance of the "Meistersinger." At the

* Referring to *Die Meistersinger* in particular, as appears from the remainder of the paragraph.—Tr.

† See the reminiscence of Ludwig Schnorr as "Tristan," in Vol. IV.—Tr.

close of the dress-rehearsal I felt driven to express to every one of the assistants, from the first of the Masters to the last of the Apprentices, my incomparable joy at finding that they had so speedily put off each operatic habit and adopted with the most self-sacrificing love a mode of representment whose propriety may already have appealed to their deepest feeling, but now, that they had made its full acquaintance, had also been so willingly attested by them. Upon taking my leave I therefore could assure them of my renewed conviction that, if the Play has indeed been ruined through the Opera, it is only through Opera that it ever can be raised again.

And to this bold assertion it was just the "*Meistersinger*" that might beguile me. What I above have termed the "example" to be given to our performers, I believe I set the plainest with this work: though a witty friend has compared my orchestral score to a continuous fugue transformed into an opera, my singers and choristers know that with the acquittal of their so difficult musical tasks they arrived at the mastery of a continuous *dialogue*, which came to them at last as easily and naturally as the commonest talk of everyday. They who before, when "opera-singing" was the word, had thought needful to fall at once into the spasms of false pathos, now found themselves led to take that dialogue sharp and crisp with the utmost truth to nature and only from this starting-point to gradually attain the pathos of emotion; which then, to their own amazement, had an effect they never could bring about with their most convulsive strainings.

If I thus may claim for my musical signs the merit of having given the singer the surest guide to a natural mode of dramatic delivery, now totally lost by even the 'reciting' actor, I have inversely to explain the hitherto unwonted fulness of my later scores by the sheer necessity of discovering for the singer that correct indication of a thoroughly natural rendering.—

It is to no solution of this problem, if solved I now may call it, that I owe the success of my "Tannhäuser" at

German theatres: I must modestly admit that that success has reposed as yet on a mere pleasure in certain lyric details, whereas the performances which I have witnessed of this opera have left me with the somewhat humiliating impression that the "Tannhäuser" conceived by myself had never been performed at all, but merely this and that from my score; of which the chief part, namely the drama itself, had been discarded as superfluous. For this mishap I will not hold our operatic factors' mindless treatment of my work exclusively responsible, but confess, as outcome of these very experiences, that I had not yet marked out the said "example" sufficiently definitely and distinctly in that score. Here nothing but the purely individual genius of the performer could supply the lack; who thus would have had himself to set that "example" which I henceforth felt obliged to give him.

Now, whoever may choose to think that I meant to fetter the life of a spirited performance by mechanical minutiæ, is simply confounding the natural with the affected, and I have only to point him to the effect of the marks in my scores upon the Rendering alike of the bandsmen and singers, whose natural instinct tells them that those marks are but the picture I hold up to them to follow. Oh! it is natural enough for the uncommon shallowness of just these regions of our Criticism to take offence at the complexity of the technical apparatus employed to trace that picture, since they opine that a more superficial sketch should leave the exponent singer a seemlier freedom to indulge his personal inspirations, of which freedom I would rob him by my tiresome orders. This surely is the same opinion, dressed in different clothes at times, as that which takes offence at Antique Tragedy for its metric and choreographic wealth, and even wants to have the antique subjects set before it in the sober garment of Iambic diction beloved of our modern poets. But he to whom that seeming overwealth of choreographic apparatus has become intelligible; he who has the wit to explain what we now have merely as a literary monument by the spirit of its lost, once sounding music; who can form a lively notion of the tragic hero summoned by the incantations of that music, and, with his badge of mask and cothurn, now rising up before us from that pregnant distance,—he will also comprehend that the work of the dramatic poet rested almost more upon his deeds as choreograph and choregus, than even on his purely poetical power of fiction. What the poet invents and circumstantially prescribes in that capacity, is the exactest illustration of the image he saw when conceiving, which image he thus holds before the fellowship of mimes for conversion into actual represented Drama. On the contrary, it is a token of the Drama's decline, from the rise of so-called Later Attic Comedy down to our own day, for the poet to leave a vaguely drawn and flatter subject to the individual fancies of the mime, the "histrio" proper of the Romans. That herewith mime and poet both degenerated and fell down, is equally sure as that the mime has only risen to his feet again when the true poet allied himself anew with him, and plainly marked for him the model whereof we have an instance in Shakespeare's dramas, an artwork no less incomprehensible as literature than are those antique tragedies themselves.

Before us Germans lies an equally uncomprehended artwork, a riddle still unsolved, in Goethe's *Faust.* It is manifest, as I have already insisted, that we possess in this work the most consequent outcome of the original German Play: if we compare it with the greatest creations of any nation, those of Shakespeare not excepted, it reveals an idiosyncrasy exclusively its own, ranking it for the present as theatrically-speaking impracticable, for simple reason that the German Stage itself has shamefully made away the originality of its own development. Only when this shall have been recovered, when we possess a Theatre, a stage and actors who can set this Germanest of all dramas completely properly before us, will our æsthetic Criticism also be able to rightly judge this work: whereas to-day the coryphœi of that Criticism presume to crack bad jokes and parodies upon its second part. We then shall perceive that no stage-piece in the world has such a scenic force and directness (*Anschaulichkeit*) to shew, as precisely this maligned (no matter what the pose adopted!) and un-understood second half of the tragedy. And this work, which roots in the plastic spirit of the German Theatre as ne'er another, had to be written by the poet in the air: the only signs by which he could fix its type, or the "example" as I have called it, were rhyming metres taken chiefly from the rugged art of our old folk-poet, Hans Sachs. Yet if we want a witness to the supreme ideality whose germ lay lurking in the homeliest element of the German Folk, awaiting its development by a faithful chosen spirit, we have only to regard this wonder-building raised by Goethe on that so-called knittel-verse [doggerel]: he seems to never quit this basis of the most completely Popular, and yet he soars above it to the highest art of antique Metrics, filling link upon link with fresh inventions of a freedom unknown to the Greeks themselves, from smiles to grief, the wildest bluntness to the tenderest sublimity. And these verses, in a tongue the truest to our German nature, our actors cannot even speak!

Could they sing them, perchance?—

Haply with Italian "*canto*"?—

Verily there was something to discover here: namely, a singing-tongue wherein an ideal naturalism should take the place of the unnatural affectation of our actors ruined by un-German rhetoric; and to me it seems as if our great German musicians had mapped the way for us, giving into our hands a melismus pulsing with exhaustless rhythm, whereby to fix beyond all doubt an infinitely varied life of discourse. Perhaps the model founded on their art might then resemble one of those said "scores," which at anyrate will remain as much a riddle to our æsthetic Criticism [as *Faust* itself] until they shall have one-day fulfilled their purpose, namely to serve as technically determinate model for a finished dramatic performance.—

But that model is just what mimetic art has need of, and in its circumstantial plainness resides its power of working on the bent-to-imitation, to raise it to an ideal art of Interpretation. And thus we reach the point where the nature of the Mime, the main object of these inquiries into the state of our "Actors and Singers," must itself be taken into closest consideration if we are to determine alike the artistic and the social standing of these the weightiest factors in the Drama and its Theatre.—

It is as absurd to ask an actor or singer to indue with dramatic truth and nature the fabrication of an affected literature-poet or musician, as it is foolish to expect from him productive power at all. His whole essence is reproductiveness, whose root we find as the bent to copy with all possible deception the individuality of other persons and their demeanour in the incidents of daily life. When we add hereto the dramatic poet's unique power of guiding this bent to the portrayal of an image above and beyond the experience of daily life, consequently of an ideal life, we have said everything there is to say about the *dignity* of mimetic art—a dignity already misconstrued into a raising of the actor's status to official "respectability."

What the Mime may be outside his art, an educated or an ignorant, an upright, orderly, or a loose and flighty man, has nothing in common with what he is within his art; if it happens to Professors to get drunk and come to fisticuffs, far rather may it happen among actors; and that Margrave of Bayreuth, who allowed himself to be deterred by a drunken buffoon on their tavern-steps from inquiring into the condition of a German strolling company, may be pardoned as a spoilt gentleman with a weakness for French Play and Italian Opera, though we cannot credit his sense of histrionic art with any particular earnestness. On the other hand, after all I have said above, I hope to escape the charge of siding with that earlier-mentioned Director in his desperate preference for a company composed of dissolute comedians: it transpired that the poet here, to arrive at any influence, must necessarily become a comedian himself. We may take it for granted, however, that he who feels within himself the calling of a dramatic poet, will not pass by in arrogance the humblest sphere of the actor's art: here, where the mime gives speaking portraits of his landlord, the tapster, the police-sergeant, and whomsoever else he has mixed with, to revenge himself at night for all the worries of the weary day, whilst seeming all the time to entertain you out of pure good humour,—here has the poet to learn pretty much what Shakespeare learnt before he turned his raw comedians into kings and heroes. A puppet-show, remember that! inspired Goethe with his "Faust."

If we abide by the view that the honour to which mimetic art is elevable can only be conferred on it through a change in the model to be imitated, transferring it from the common experience of physical life to the sphere of an ideal intuition, we certainly may presume that with this transference the Mime himself will also enter a new social condition.*

The latter is quite primly defined by Ed. Devrient, in his book already mentioned, when he demands of the Mime the truly Republican virtue of *self-denial.*

At bottom this implies a notable extension of those qualities which make out the mimetic bent itself, since that bent is chiefly to be understood as an almost dæmonic passion for *self-divestment* (Hang zur *Selbstentäusserung*). The question then would be: In whose favour, and for what profit, does the act of this self-divestment, so singular per se, take place? And here we stand before an utter

* "Bleiben wir bei der Ansicht, dass die Würde, zu welcher jenes Mimenwesen zu erheben ist, ihm einzig durch die Vertauschung des von ihm nachzuahmenden Vorbildes, vermöge der Versetzung desselben aus der gemeinen, sinnlichen Lebenserfahrung in die Sphäre der idealen Weltanschauung, verliehen werden kann, so ist allerdings anzunehmen, dass mit dieser Versetzung der Mime selbst auch in einen neuen sozialen Zustand eintritt." The singular—I might almost say purely Wagnerian—use our author makes of the term *Wesen* (essence, or being), both in compound words and by itself, forces one to a merely approximate translation of a sentence bristling with other difficulties. See also page 205.—Tr.

marvel, at the brink of an abyss illumined by no consciousness of ours. Wherefore it is here that we must suppose to be set the focus whence proceeds—by the merest turn —either the most wonderful vision of Art, or the most ridiculous of Vanity.

Granted that a real putting-off of our Self is possible, we must assume that our self-consciousness, and thus our consciousness in general, has first been set out of action. In truth the throughly gifted, perfect mime appears in that act of self-divestment to offer up his consciousness of self to such a degree that, in a sense, he never recovers it even in daily life, or never completely. Of this we may convince ourselves by a glimpse into the records of the life of *Ludwig Devrient*, from which it appears that outside that state of wondrous self-divestment the great mime spent his days in progressive unconsciousness, nay, that he violently fought off the return of self-consciousness by intoxication with alcoholic liquors. Plainly then, this extraordinary being's only happy consciousness of life was limited to that marvellous condition in which he had totally exchanged his personal self for that of the individual he impersonated; of the potence of which state one may form a notion if one reflects that here a purely immaterial imagining usurped his person, down to his body's last muscle, in such a way as commonly happens through nothing but the Will's reaction to a material stimulus.

"What's Hecuba to him?"—asks Hamlet, having seen the player moved to tears by the dream-image of the poem, whereas he feels himself but "John-a-dreams" in presence of the sternest call to action.

Manifestly, we are standing before an excess of that mother-force from which springs all poetic and artistic faculty; whilst the latter's most beneficent products, the most fruitful for the weal of man, are due to wellnigh nothing but a certain diminution, or at least a moderation, in the violence of its expression. Let us therefore conclude that we owe the highest art-creations of the human mind to that rarest of intellectual gifts which endows this capability of total self-divestment with the clearest *perspicacity* (Besonnenheit) to boot, in power whereof the state of self-divestment itself is mirrored in that very consciousness which in the case of the mime is wholly dethroned.

Through that capability of self-divestment in favour of a purely visionary image the Poet thus is ure-akin to the Mime, whereas he becomes his master through this other one, of clearest perspicacity. To the mime the poet brings his self-possession * and his lucid brain, and thus their intercourse acquires that incomparable gaiety known only to great masters in their comradeship with dramatic performers, whereas the usual commerce of modern singers and actors with their ostensible chiefs has nothing to shew for itself but the sober-sided seriousness of stupid pedantry. But this gaiety is the element withal that holds the gifted mime secure above the gulf toward which he feels his supernatural trend to self-divestment impelling him in the practice of his art. Whoso can stand with him at brink of that abyss, will shudder at the peril of this playing with one's personality, that a given moment may turn to raving madness; and here it is just that consciousness of *play* which saves the mime, in like manner as the consciousness of his self-divestment leads the poet to the highest creative discernment.

That saving consciousness of play it is, that lends the gifted mime the childlike nature which marks him out so lovably from all his lesser-gifted colleagues, from his whole surrounding burgher-world. My most delightful and instructive experiences in this regard I was privileged to make through an artistic intimacy with the glorious *Wilhelmine Schröder-Devrient*, by whose example I might illustrate my every view on noble mimicry. Through this

* The term "*Besonnenheit*" may be used either in this sense or in that of "perspicacity"; it signifies the possession of a clear eye and tranquil reason, in fact an æsthetic "presence of mind." One is reminded, here again, of Nietzsche's definition of Greek Tragedy as springing from the union of what he calls the Apollinian, with the Dionysian element. See Preface and page 139.—TR.

wonderful woman I became acquainted, in a truly startling manner, with the saving return of a consciousness lost in fullest self-divestment to the sudden remembrance that it was nothing but play. In the middle of a most agitating scene, throughout which she held her hearers spellbound in that ecstasy that borders upon terror, she had to quit the stage for a brief interval: these scanty seconds she spent on an outburst of the wildest spirits, merrily snatching from her old teacher the handkerchief with which he was drying his passionate tears, to wipe away her own, and throwing it back to him with the playful reproof: "What have you to cry about, old friend? Leave that to me!"—whereupon she rushed back to the stage with the heart-rending cry: "What sight have I seen!"

Hearing of such a scene behind the wings, the uninitiate might feel disposed to regard the transaction on the stage, by which the artist plunged us all into the deepest emotion, as an arrant piece of conscious jugglery: he would be surprised to learn how impossible it was for any episode of ordinary consciousness to shake her from her self-divestment. Even her habitual lot, to find herself allied with players who never ceased to stand and move before her in their own ridiculous person, made not a jot of change; though off the stage she might vent the most indignant complaints, one never could detect a trace of their reaction so soon as she had rapturously stepped upon the boards to face her fate. As "Desdemona" on her knees before her father, at the heart-broken question: "Canst thou cast off thy child?" * she once seized the hem of "Brabantio's" gown, whereat the worthy basso was so alarmed that he hastily drew his mantle round him and retired; the effect was so ridiculous that it convulsed the whole audience, but not a sign of it was legible upon the features of the artist: not an eyelash blinked across the unspeakably expressive glance that had put to hare-like flight the wretched "Brabantio," who should have cursed his child unshaken.

Who has not seen the graces of our prime donne in a

* In Rossini's *Otello*?—Tr.

so-called grand finale, when, flanked by the chorus, the singers stand before us in a row, not one of them knowing what the other is singing or aiming at? I have watched the Schröder-Devrient in the last finale of the "Freischütz," and declare that never have I gained a higher idea of the art of dramatic portrayal than from her bearing toward this somewhat banal scene, the customary dénouement of an operatic plot, in which Agathe has but twice to make herself heard, almost episodically, while, banned to a knoll of grass, she takes but a suffering share in the action. But in this suffering share, of the maiden waking from the jaws of death to the most agonising of discoveries; in the slow transition of her loving soul to revival of the brightest hopes; in the final glance she fixed on her lover leaving for his year of probation—there was expressed a poetry that none of us had suspected in the drama, and which we nevertheless were to find, of all places, at its touchingest in this seemingly wearisome and undramatic, this so often disgracefully scrambled "finale."

Concerning this artist I have again and again been asked if her *voice* was really so remarkable, since we glorified her as a singer—the voice being all folk seem to think about in such a case. It constantly annoyed me to answer this question, for I revolted against the thought of the great tragedian being thrown into one bevy with the female castrati of our Opera. Were it asked once more to-day, I should answer somewhat as follows:—No! She had no "voice" at all; but she knew how to use her breath so beautifully, and to let a true womanly soul stream forth in such wondrous sounds, that we never thought of either voice or singing! Moreover, she had the gift of teaching a composer how to compose, to be worth the pains of such a woman's "singing": this she did through that "example" aforesaid, which she, the mime, gave this time to the dramatist, and which, among all to whom she gave it, has been followed by *myself* alone.—

And not this Example only, but all my knowledge of mimetic art (*des mimischen Wesens*) I owe to this grand woman ; and through that teaching can I point to *truthfulness* as that art's foundation. The art of sublime Illusion, as practised by the chosen mime, comes not by any form of lying ; and this is the wall that parts the genuine mimic artist from the bad comedian whom present taste delights to load with gold and laurels. These pigmies always on the watch for gain, and therefore always puling, are quite incapable of that serenity whose godlike solace rewards the others for the tremendous sacrifice of their self-divestment. We know of a great actor who in response to a storm of applause from the audience, after a performance which his own feeling told him he had failed in, cried out "The Lord forgive them ! They know not what they do !" The *Schröder-Devrient* would have died of shame, had she owed a demonstration of approval to the employment of spurious means ; just as it would have been impossible for her to court the men with the ridiculous fashions of our greater and our lesser female world, such as a towering chignon or the like. And yet the spontaneous outburst of applause was the only element upon whose waves the strain of that creative self-divestment could feel itself securely borne. This wondrous playing with the Self, wherein the player clean forgets himself, is no pastime for one's personal pleasure ; 'tis a mutual game, in which all the winnings fall to you spectators. But you must gather them for yourselves : the sublime illusion, on which the mime stakes his whole personality, must search you through and through ; and from you must his own relinquished soul make answer to him, or he slinks away a lifeless shadow.

And here, in this nature-law of the barter of his wondrous art for the enthusiasm directly manifested in the public's applause, should we have to seek the demon that so oft has cast the genius into chains and sent instead the gnomes and spectres to our modern theatre. 'Tis it that well may ask us with satanic irony : "What is truth ?" What here is truth, where all is reckoned for illusion ? Who knows if vulgar love of admiration converts this feigning to its personal ends, or the most gifted individuality employs it for its putting-off-of-self?

This difficult problem brings us back to the commencement of our last inquiry: namely the question whether the Theatre might haply benefit by a Republican constitution with its members bound to self-denial?

What may stand for "self-denial" here, we have learnt from the character of true mimetic art itself—which manifests its force through self-divestment. But who shall lay down for this which enters of itself, whenever the art of the mime is genuine, that law of self-denial?

We see at a glance that the thing is a contradiction in terms, the purest nonsense; unless one means that mimetic art in every form is an art of sheer vanity and love-of-admiration, and to make the best of these elements, to give them quite another look—that of attaining the highest goal of dramatic art—one deems needful to frame Republican laws for the comedians, and get them sanctioned by edict of State.

Indeed, upon closer inspection, the ambitious dream of a recent type of Directors appears to dissolve into this phantom. It must have irked them to see that lovely virtue of Self-denial simply enjoined on the personnel of a theatre, as done by the high-and-mighty Intendants when need arose: it seemed more humane, to *teach* it; and as virtue-master one got oneself appointed, quite seriously to set to work on the singular problem of teaching what under no circumstances can be learnt. Into talentless actors, however, it was not so very hard to drill a due obedience to the orders of the Herr Director; it might even be done by his assuming high-and-mighty airs himself, making little movements with the hand, speaking curtly, and at the proper moment giving no answer at all. Only, no sterling talent must venture here; it would have upset the whole laborious arrangement.* The mime must be carefully bottled, neatly ticketed, and placed on the repositorium; from which the dramaturgic virtue-apothecary then reached him down, brewed him into the mixture prescribed by the recipe of the no less virtuous Herr Theatre-poet, and poured the healing dramatic arcanum down the public's throat at night as plaudit-vomitory.

To some, however, this kind of stage-practitioner did not seem quite the right one, and many deemed the literate by far the fitter man, if so be he had decided to try his fortune at the theatre.† Now this gentleman, no sooner made Director, became the rival of his players: he wanted to please, as much as they; and to him it seemed that, taken strictly, the public's applause would be more just if allotted to him instead of to the actors, for was he not the author of the recipe after which those arcana had first been set in operation? So the actors were employed in a way to turn the whole light of admiration, especially that streaming from the daily press, forever on the brilliant "total" of the representation; thereby glorifying, if not the Director's translations or actual "original pieces," at least the acting-versions furnished by his master-hand. Even Shakespeare was seized of a sudden, and bestowed on the German public for the first time in an orderly form. And all this with players not worth mentioning, especially in the eyes of their eclipser, the dramaturg himself; for 'twas his pride to earn with his sorry troop, and some play that formerly had ranked as thankless, a similar praise to that wherewith folk flattered Meyerbeer, namely that he had composed a preposterous subject so wonderfully.‡

That nothing much will come of this either, in its turn seems to stay not quite unheeded; and finally uncurbed Comedianism breaks down at every point the artificial fence one thought one had devised to check its vanity. With a contemptuous smile the full-blown virtuoso tumbles

* Ed. Devrient, *vide antea*, p. 173.—Tr.

† Obviously Carl Gutzkow, who followed E. Devrient in the management of the Dresden Court-theatre.—Tr.

‡ The Prophète, *vide* contemporary German criticisms.—Tr.

down the house of cards. Where everyone is bidding for applause, how should it be withheld from him to whom alone it falls by right? And this—if the applause is intended seriously—is obviously the mime, the mime who at this moment stakes his all, himself, his past and future, upon the immediate evidence of that immense effect produced on you by his self-divestment.

So much has been said and sung about the transience of the mime's renown; but few will have measured the whole tragedy of this fame for which "posterity no garland weaves." I therefore will quote from my personal memoirs an incident which definitely supplies that valuation. —In the year 1835 I happened to be in Nuremberg at the same time with Frau *Schröder-Devrient*, who had arrived there for a brief 'starring' engagement. The local opera-troupe allowed of no great choice of pieces to be given; beyond "Fidelio" there was nothing for it but the "Swiss Family" *—about which the artist complained, as this was one of her earliest juvenile rôles, for which she was scarcely fitted any longer, and moreover she had played it till she was sick of it. I also looked forward to the "*Schweizerfamilie*" with ill humour, wellnigh with apprehension, for I could but fancy that the vapid opera and the old-fashionedly sentimental rôle of "Emeline" would weaken the deep impression hitherto invariably made by this artist upon the public, as upon myself. How great was my surprise, and my emotion, when I found that this evening was to be the first to teach me the overwhelming grandeur of this unfathomable woman! That a thing like the impersonation of this Switzer maid can not be turned into a monument and handed down to all futurity, I still must count as one of the sublimest sacrificial conditions under which alone the marvels of dramatic art reveal themselves; wherefore, whenever such phenomena appear, that art can not be held too high and holy.

To lay down laws of Self-denial for such a woman! Mayhap in favour of the score of the "Swiss Family,"

* By Joseph Weigl, 1766-1846.—Tr.

or of the Nuremberg town-theatre? The pair live on in peace together, without the smallest recollection of that wondrous evening.—

There is one, and only one, to outvie the inspired mime in his self-offering: the author who *entirely forgets himself* in his joy at the mime's achievement. He alone understands the mime, and to him alone the mime gives glad submission. In the wholly natural relation of these two to one another resides the only surety of the healing of Dramatic Art.

If ye can find a law to plainly express this relation, in that ye will have before you the sole authentic theatre-law. Here ceases each dispute of rank, and all subordination vanishes, since it is voluntary. The poet's control of the mime is boundless so soon as in his work he upholds to him the right example, and its rightness is only to be proved by the mime's being able to altogether put aside himself in its adoption. With this adoption comes about that wonderful exchange in which the poet clean forgets himself to reappear in the mime, no longer as poet, but as the highest artwork won through that man's self-divestment. Thus do the two become one, and the poet's recognition of himself in this mime accords him that unspeakable joy which he tastes in the mime's effect on the heart of the audience—a joy he would kill at once, did he snatch at a personal share in that effect itself, as lingering remnant of the personal poet! The poet "called" at the close, as the custom is, and bowing his acknowledgments to the public, would then be evidence forever of the complete miscarriage of the mimo-dramatic venture; it would also say that the whole had been nothing but a make-believe. But none knows better, than the mime, whether the illusion compassed is a lofty truth or a foolish lie; and naught expresses his knowledge of the truth more plainly than his affectionate enthusiasm for the poet, who hovers now above him but an incorporeal spirit, whilst the mime is conscious of his full possession of the riches left him by the poet.—

Having thus defined the only road for the mime's attainment of true dignity, everything else connected with his social standing, as also with the general constitution of the Theatre, results of itself; though it will not be easy, perhaps will be impossible, to rule that standing or that constitution by pattern of a law.

To what well-meaning person has it not occurred at some time, to wish the Theatre placed under tutelage and supervision of the State? But it always transpired that our State and our Theatre were too heterogeneous of descent. Whereas in the State we are striving our utmost to strengthen its ancient props, since its maintenance depends on just the force of olden usage: in the development of our Theatre we have been led away from all ancestral German habitude, and have in it a rootless plant, whereof nothing save its draggling want of self-reliance still is German, and whose unnatural life can only be preserved according to the laws of that disease. Here everything therefore is unintelligible to the helmsmen of our State, and we may rest assured that if once we tried to lay our thoughts before those regions, we should be told to talk the matter over with the Herr Hoftheater-Intendant.* A little while ago, when an "art-ministry" was appointed in Berlin, it contented itself with new labels at the museums and arrangements for an Exhibition of Paintings: since then we have heard no more of it. As we cannot but just

* About this time the author approached the German Chancellor, Bismarck, on the subject of the Bayreuth Festspielhaus, but in vain. See the account of the "performances of 1876" in vol. x. of the *Ges. Schr.*, to appear in the next volume of the present series.—TR.

have seen, this had its very rightful reason: the Theatre is not included in Art, and least of all in German art.

Nothing remains for us but the curious freedom, where nobody understands any more, to do what we understand —and presumably to be plagued with no interference.

As all depends on the right example, we ourselves have now to give it to those who can form no notion of a thing they have never experienced, and, so doing, to silence all the objections—as to your capacity for self-denial etc.— upon which is based the whole routine of our sluggards' wretched conduct of the Theatre. Their verdict on the moral value of your calling, ye actors and singers, will then have also to be revised: as your vanity upon the boards, so your graspingness when off them, has been the standard for their measurement of all their commerce with you. Shew them that your vices are the outcome of their bad administration of your most intimate affairs; but shew them further that through a spiritual elevation, such as certainly cannot be summoned by the orders of the Herr Intendant or the arrangements of his Regisseur, ye forthwith step into a rank that ranges you as noblemen and kings above them.—

I have said that it does not concern his art, whether the mime is uncultured or learned, moral or dissolute. But I had no intention of endorsing the blatant verdict of malignity, which parts the artist from the man to give itself the right to trounce a great artist after the measure of an evil man. On the contrary, it has been proved that a high-souled art, i.e. an art discharged with self-denial, cannot possibly be borne upon a petty heart, the source of all badness of character; for truthfulness is the irremissible condition of all artistic being, and no less of all worthiness of character. If the Artist's passions are, admittedly, peculiarly excitable, he pays for it through being the only one to suffer from them; whereas the cold-blooded can always find the wool to warm him. And what he may lack in learning, ay, in education, he makes good by what no ever so learned education can supply,—the eye for something he alone can see, for a thing the cultured only spies when able to pierce through all his education and see with *your* eyes: the image (*Bild*) itself, to which all culture (*Bildung*) owes its being, and which I have described above as that "*example.*"

So I will conclude by once more instancing that remarkable woman, whose nobleness of life is unforgettable by all who knew her.* She was passionate, and therefore was she often cheated: but she was incapable of taking vengeance for the meannesses put on her; she might be swept into injustice of opinion, but never of action. Unsatisfied by a life of teeming changes, her boundless heart was all compassion; charitable to the point of royal lavishness, to her the griefs of others were the only griefs unbearable. Upon the boards the character she represented, and that alone, in private life she was entirely herself: the possibility of pretending to be a thing she was not, lay so remote from her imagination that its very absence stamped her with that gentility which Nature had so markedly intended for her. In dignity and ease of bearing she thus might sit as model for any queen. Her lightly won, but dearly cherished education often shamed the beaux esprits of various nations who came to pay her homage, whom she would playfully introduce to one another in their respective tongues, thereby plunging them at times into an embarrassment from which she alone could extricate them. Through her wit she could cloak her education in the presence of uncultured Sirs, for instance our Court-theatre Intendants; but she gave that wit free rein among her equals, as whom she gladly looked upon her colleagues of the theatre without a touch of pride. One sorrow ran throughout her life: she never found the man completely worth her making happy; and yet she yearned for nothing

* Frau Schröder-Devrient died on January 26, 1860.—Tr.

so much as the tranquil pleasures of domestic life, which her perfect gift as manager and hostess would have made as homelike as refined. Never could aught but those weirdly blissful throes of soul-translation, in that matchless double-life upon the stage, make her forget what she often deemed a life's path missed. Yet even as artist, her conscience could never feel truly at peace: she taxed herself with lacking her mother's genius, the genius of great *Sophie Schröder*.

What may have filled her with such a doubt?

Can it have been that she recognised her great moral superiority to her mother, whose questionable character inspired her with a filial awe, as if to that must be ascribed the origin of this woman's supernatural genius?

Or was she ashamed of her indebtedness to the *spirit of Music* for that which raised her to a level with her mother? As though she asked herself: "What were I, but for Music?"— —

To the comrades before whom I lay this string of thoughts upon their art I believe I finally can no better express my friendly feelings of esteem, than by herewith dedicating it *to the memory of great Wilhelmine Schröder-Devrient.*

THE RENDERING OF BEETHOVEN'S NINTH SYMPHONY.

Zum Vortrage der neunten Symphonie Beethoven's.

These notes upon the "Ninth Symphony," which were so bitterly attacked by Gounod, originally appeared in the Musikalisches Wochenblatt *of April 1873.*

TRANSLATOR'S NOTE.

T a performance I lately conducted of this wondrous tone-work certain reflections touching what I deem the irremissible *distinctness* of its Rendering forced themselves so strongly on me, that I since have meditated a remedy for the ills I felt. The result I now lay before earnest musicians, if not as an invitation to follow my method, at least as a stimulus to independent study.

In general, I draw attention to the peculiar position in which Beethoven was placed as regards the instrumentation of his orchestral works. He instrumented on exactly the same assumptions of the orchestra's capacity as his predecessors Haydn and Mozart, notwithstanding that he vastly outstripped them in the character of his musical conceptions. What we may fitly define as *plastique*, in the grouping and distribution of the various instrumental families, with Mozart and Haydn had crystallised into a firm agreement between the character of their conceptions and the technique of the orchestra as formed and practised until then. There can be nothing more adequate, than a Symphony of Mozart's and the Mozartian Orchestra: one may presume that to neither Haydn nor Mozart there ever occurred a musical thought which could not have promptly found expression in their Orchestra. Here was thorough congruence: the *tutti* with trumpets and drums (only truly effective in the tonic), the quartet passage for the strings, the harmony or *solo* of the wind, with the inevitable *duo* for French horns,—these formed the solid groundwork, not only of the orchestra, but of the draft for all orchestral compositions. Strange to relate, Beethoven also knew no other orchestra than this, and he never went beyond its employment on what then appeared quite natural lines.

It is astonishing, what distinctness the master manages to give to conceptions of a wealth and variety unapproached by Haydn or Mozart, with identically the same orchestra. In this regard his "*Sinfonia eroica*" remains a marvel not only of conception, but also, and no less, of orchestration. Only, he already here exacted of his band a mode-of-rendering which it has been unable to acquire to this day: for the execution would have to be as much a stroke of genius, on the orchestra's part, as the master's own conception of the score. From this point then, from the first performance of the "*Eroica*," begin the difficulties of judging these symphonies, ay, the hindrances to pleasure in them—a pleasure never really arrived at by the musicians of an older epoch. These works fell short of full *distinctness* in achievement for simple reason that it no longer lay ensured in the use to which the orchestral organism was put, as in the case of Haydn and Mozart, but could be brought out by nothing save a positively virtuosic exploit of the individual instrumentists and their chief.

To explain: now that the opulence of his conceptions required a far more complex material and a much more minute distribution thereof, Beethoven saw himself compelled to exact the most rapid change in force and expression from one and the same bandsman, after the fashion acquired by the great virtuoso as a special art. For example the characteristically Beethovenian *crescendo*, ending, not in a *forte*, but in a sudden *piano*: this single nuance, so frequently recurring, is still so foreign to most of our orchestral players, that cautious conductors have made their bandsmen reverse the latter part of the *crescendo* into a sly *diminuendo*, to secure at least a timely entry of the *piano*. The secret of this difficulty surely lies in demanding from one and the same body of instruments a nuance that can only be executed quite distinctly when distributed between two separate bodies, alternating with one another. Such an expedient is in common practice with later composers, at whose disposal stands the increased orchestra of to-day. To them it would have been possible to ensure great distinctness for certain effects devised by Beethoven without any extravagant claims on the orchestra's virtuosity, merely through the present facilities of distribution.

Beethoven, on the contrary, was obliged to count on the same virtuosity in his band as he himself had before acquired at the pianoforte, where the greatest expertness of technique was simply meant to free the player from all mechanical fetters, and thus enable him to bring the most changeful nuances of expression to that drastic distinctness without which they often would only make the melody appear an unintelligible chaos. The master's last piano-compositions, conceived on these lines, have first been made accessible to us by *Liszt*, and till then were scarcely understood at all. Exactly the same remark applies to his last Quartets. Here, in certain points of technique, the single player has often to do the work of many, so that a perfect performance of a Quartet from this period may frequently delude the hearer into believing he listens to more musicians than are really playing. Only at quite a recent date, in Germany, do our quartettists appear to have turned their virtuosity to the correct rendering of these wondrous works, whereas I remember hearing these same Quartets performed by eminent virtuosi of the Dresden Kapelle, Lipinski at their head, so indistinctly that my quondam colleague Reissiger might hold himself justified in calling them pure nonsense.

The said distinctness rests, in my opinion, on nothing other than a drastic marking of the *melody*. I have shewn elsewhere * how it became possible to French musicians to discover the mode-of-rendering here required, before the Germans: the secret was that, adherents of the Italian school, they looked on melody, on song, as the essence of all music. Now, if true musicians have succeeded on this only rightful path, of seeking out and giving prominence to the melody, in finding the proper rendering for works of Beethoven's which erewhile seemed past understanding; and if we may hope that they will further be able to establish it as a normal standard, in the way already done

* In the essay on "Conducting"; see Vol. IV.—TR.

so admirably by *Bülow* with Beethoven's pianoforte-sonatas: then in the great master's necessitation to make his utmost of the technical means at hand—the pianoforte, the quartet, and finally the orchestra—we might perceive the creative impetus to a spiritual development of mechanical technique itself; and to this, in turn, we should owe a spiritualising of execution never yet displayed by virtuosi. However, as I here am dealing with the Beethovenian Orchestra and the main principle of ensuring its *melody*, I have now to consider an evil which at first seems wellnigh irremediable, since it contravenes that principle in a way no ever so spirited virtuosity can possibly amend.

Unmistakably, with the advent of Beethoven's deafness the aural image of the orchestra in so far faded from his mind that he lost that distinct consciousness of its dynamic values which now was so indispensable, when his conceptions themselves required a constant innovation in orchestral treatment. If Mozart and Haydn, with their perfect stability of orchestral form, never employed the soft wood-instruments in a sense demanding of them an equal dynamic effect to that of the full 'quintet' of strings, Beethoven on the contrary was often moved to neglect this natural proportion. He lets the wind and strings alternate with each other, or even combine, as two equally powerful engines of tone. With the manifold extension of the newer orchestra, it certainly is possible to do this most effectively to-day; in the Beethovenian orchestra it could only be accomplished on assumptions that have proved illusory. True, that Beethoven succeeds at times in giving the wood-wind the necessary incisiveness, through allying with it the brass: but he was so lamentably hampered by the structure of the 'natural' horns and trumpets, the only ones then known, that their employment to reinforce the wood has been the very cause of those perplexities which we feel as irremovable obstacles to the plain emergence of the melody. The musician of to-day I have no need to warn of the last-named drawbacks in Beethovenian orchestration, for, with our now universal use of the chromatic brass, he will easily avoid them; I have merely to state that Beethoven was compelled to suddenly arrest the brass in outlying keys, or to let it sound a shrill note here and there, as the nature of the instrument permitted, utterly distracting one's attention from the melody and harmony alike.

As it surely is superfluous to produce a schedule in support of this assertion, I will proceed to instance the remedies which I myself have tried in single cases where the obscuring of the master's plain intention had at last become unbearable. One obvious cure I have found in a general order to the second horn, or second trumpet as the case may be, to play the high note missing from the lower octave in passages such as

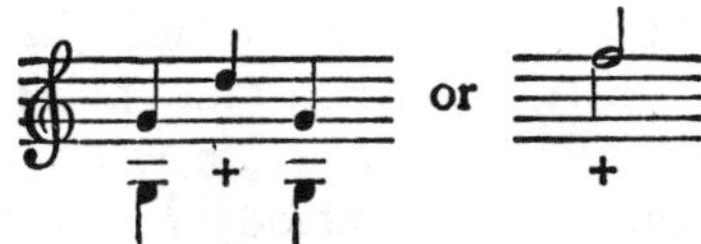

taking it thus:

which is quite easy of execution upon the chromatic instruments alone employed in our orchestras of to-day. This simple expedient has in itself removed great obstacles. Less easy is it to help, however, where the trumpets have dominated everything up to a certain point, and suddenly break off for mere reason that the passage—though intended to be as loud as ever—here strays into a key for which the natural instruments have no corresponding interval. As example I cite the forte passage in the Andante of the C-minor Symphony:

Here the trumpets and kettle-drums, which for two bars long have filled the whole with splendour, pause suddenly for close upon two bars, then re-enter for a bar, and cease again for over another. Owing to the character of these instruments the hearer's attention is inevitably diverted to this colour-incident, inexplicable on purely musical grounds, and therewith is distracted from the main affair, the melodic progress of the basses. The only remedy I have been able to devise till now, is to rob those intermittent instruments of a portion of their glare by ordering them to play less loudly, which at any rate is advantageous to a greater distinctness in the melody of the basses.—As to the highly disturbing effect of the trumpets in the first *forte* of the second movement of the Symphony in A, however, I at last arrived at a more energetic resolve. Here Beethoven had very rightly felt the necessity for the two trumpets, but unfortunately their simplicity of structure debarred them from co-operating in the fashion needed: I made them play the whole theme in unison with the clarinets. The effect was so excellent that not one of the audience felt it other than a gain, yet not as any change or innovation.

An equally thorough cure of a different though kindred defect in the instrumentation of the second movement of the Ninth Symphony, its great Scherzo, I could never yet decide upon, since I had always hoped to compass it by purely dynamic means. I refer to the passage, first in C, the second time in D, which we must take as that movement's second theme:

Here the weak wood-wind, two flutes, two oboes, two clarinets and two bassoons have to assert a bold and trenchant theme against the whole weight of the string-quintet accompanying them in continual fortissimo with the four-octave figure :

The support they receive from the brass is of the kind described above, i.e. a 'natural' note strewn here and there, which rather mars than aids the theme's distinctness. I challenge any musician to say with a clear conscience that he has ever plainly heard this melody in any orchestral performance, nay, that he would so much as know it if he had not spelt it from the score or played it from the pianoforte-arrangement. Our usual conductors do not even seem to have hit upon the first expedient, that of considerably decreasing the *ff* of the strings ; for, whatever bandsmen I have got together for this Symphony, they invariably began this passage with the utmost fury. That expedient I myself had always adopted, however, and believed it would prove successful enough if only I could get the wood-wind doubled. But experience has never verified my theory, or most inadequately, since it demanded of the wood-wind instruments a greater penetrativeness of tone than consists with their character, at least in the present combination. If I had to conduct this Symphony again, I can think of no better remedy for the undeniable indistinctness, if not inaudibility in which this extraordinarily energetic dance-motive is lost, than to allot a quite definite share in the theme to at least the four horns. This might perhaps be done as follows:

We should then have to try whether the theme was now sufficiently strengthened to allow the string-quintet to take the figure of accompaniment in the *ff* prescribed by the master—a matter of no less importance; for Beethoven's present idea is clearly the same exuberance of spirits that leads to the unparalleled excess at the return of the principal theme of the movement in D minor, a thought which nowhere yet has found expression but in the most original inventions of this unique wonder-worker. For this very reason I had already deemed it a sorry makeshift to emphasise the wind by deadening the strings, as that must tame the passage's wild character past recognition. So that my last advice would be, to go on fortifying the theme of the 'wind,' even by bringing in the trumpets, until it plainly pierces through and dominates the strings' most strenuous *fortissimo*. The trumpets in fact are introduced at the passage's return in D, but alas! again, in a way that merely blurs the wood-wind's theme; so that I here have found myself compelled, as before, to enjoin on strings and trumpets alike a characterless moderation. In deciding all such points, the question is whether one prefers to go for some time without hearing anything of the tone-poet's intentions distinctly, or to adopt the best expedient for doing justice to them. In this respect the audience of our concert-rooms and opera-houses is certainly accustomed to a quite unconscious act of self-denial.

For another drawback in the instrumentation of this Ninth Symphony, arising from the selfsame grounds, I decided upon a radical cure at the last performance I conducted. It concerns the terrifying fanfare of the wind at the beginning of the last movement. Here a chaotic outburst of wild despair pours forth with an uproar which everyone will understand who reads this passage by the notes of the wood-wind, to be played as fast as possible, when it will strike him as characteristic of that tumult of tones that it scarcely lends itself to any sort of rhythmic measure. If this passage is plainly stamped with the 3/4 beat; and if as usual, in the conductor's dread of a change of time, this is taken in that cautious tempo held advisable for the succeeding recitative of the basses, it necessarily must make an almost laughable effect. But I have found that even the boldest tempo not only left the unison theme of the 'wind' still indistinct, but did not free the passage from the tyranny of a beat which here should certainly appear to be discarded. Again the evil lay in the intermittence of the trumpets, whilst it was impossible to dispense with them and yet observe the master's intentions. These clamorous instruments, compared with which the wood-wind is little more than a hint, break off their contribution to the melody in such a way that one hears nothing but the following rhythm:

To give prominence to that kind of rhythm was in any case entirely outside the master's aim, as is plainly shewn by the last recurrence of the passage, where the strings co-operate. Thus the limitations of the natural trumpets had here again prevented Beethoven from thoroughly fulfilling his intention. In a fit of despair quite suited to the character of this terrible passage, I took upon myself this time to make the trumpets join with the wood-wind throughout, playing as follows:

At its later return the trumpets again took the passage as the first time.

Light was won : the fearsome fanfare stormed across us in all its rhythmic chaos, and we knew at last why the "Word" must come.

Harder than this *restitutio in integrum* of the master's intention, was the finding of a remedy for cases where no mere reinforcement or completion, but an actual tampering with the structure of the orchestration, or even of the part-writing (*Stimmführung*), seems the only way to rescue Beethoven's melodic aim from indistinctness and misunderstanding.

For it is unmistakable that the limits of his orchestra—which Beethoven enlarged in no material respect—and the master's gradual debarment from the hearing of orchestral performances, led him at last to an almost naïve disregard of the relation of the actual embodiment to the musical thought itself. If in obedience to the ancient theory he never wrote higher than for the violins in his symphonies, whenever his melodic intention took him above that point he had recourse to the wellnigh childish device of leaping down to the lower octave with the notes that would have overstepped it, heedless that he thereby broke the melodic train, nay, made it positively misleading. I hope that every orchestra already takes the phrase for the first and second violins and violas in the great Fortissimo of the second movement of the Ninth Symphony, not as it is written :

from mere dread of the high B for the first violins, but as the melody requires :

I also presume the first flute can now take

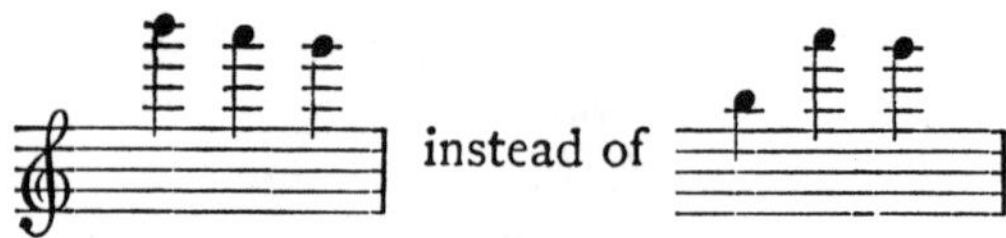

without alarm.—Though here and in many similar cases the remedy is easy enough, the really serious demands for more radical change occur in phrases for the wind where the master's principle of avoiding any violation of the compass accepted for an instrument, and quite particularly the flute, led him either to utterly distort the earlier melodic curve, or to introduce this instrument with notes not contained in, and disturbing to the melody. Now the flute, as extreme upper voice, inevitably arrests the ear so soon as ever it enters, and if the melody does not come out clearly in its notes it necessarily leads the ear astray. Of this ill effect our master appears to have grown completely heedless in course of time: for instance he will give the melody to the oboe or clarinet in soprano, and, as if determined to introduce the upper register of the flute notwithstanding its incapacity to take the theme itself an octave higher, he assigns it notes outside the melody, thereby distracting our attention from the lower instrument. It is quite another matter when an instrumental composer of to-day, with the modern facilities, desires to make a principal motive in the middle and lower registers stand out beneath a canopy of higher voices: he strengthens the sonority of the deeper instruments in due degree, choosing a group whose distinct characteristics [of timbre] allow of no confusion with the upper instruments. Thus was I myself enabled in the Prelude to "Lohengrin," for instance, to plainly sound the fully harmonised theme beneath instruments playing high above it all the while, and to make that theme assert itself against every movement of the upper voices.

But it is no question of this practice—to whose discovery great Beethoven himself first led the way, as to every other genuine invention—when considering the indisputable hindrances whose removal we have now in view. Rather is it a disturbing ornament, strewn-in as if by chance, whose hurtful effect on the melody's clearness we would fain tone down. Thus I have never heard the opening of the Eighth Symphony (in F) without my attention to the theme being troubled in the sixth, seventh and eighth bars by the unthematic entry of the oboe and flute above the melody of the clarinet; whereas the flute's participation in the first four bars, although not strictly thematic, does not disguise the melody, because the latter is here given utmost prominence by the mass of violins in forte. But this evil of the wood-wind is so serious in an important passage of the first movement of the Ninth Symphony, that I will choose that instance as my principal text.

It is the eight-bar *Espressivo* of the wood-wind, beginning in Breitkopf und Härtel's edition with the third bar of the nineteenth page, towards the end of the first section of the movement aforesaid, and returning in a similar fashion at bar three of the fifty-third page. Who can declare that he has ever heard this passage, with distinct perception of its melodic content, at any of our orchestral performances? With that insight so peculiar to him, *Liszt* was the first to set this melody in its proper light through his wonderful pianoforte-arrangement of the Ninth Symphony, among the rest; disregarding the mostly disturbing notes for the flute until it takes over the theme from the oboe, he lowers that continuation a full octave, and thus preserves the master's prime intention from all misunderstanding. According to Liszt these melodic phrases read as follows:

Now, it might seem presumptuous, and not in character with Beethoven's instrumentation—which has its most legitimate idiosyncrasies—if we here were to omit the flute altogether, or employ it as mere unisono reinforcement of the oboe. I should therefore leave the flute-part essentially as it stands, only making it keep perfect faith with the melody where it takes the lead, and instructing the player to subordinate both force and expression to the oboe where the latter claims our full attention. Accordingly, as continuation of its phrase in the upper octave, fifth bar,

the flute would have to play the sixth bar

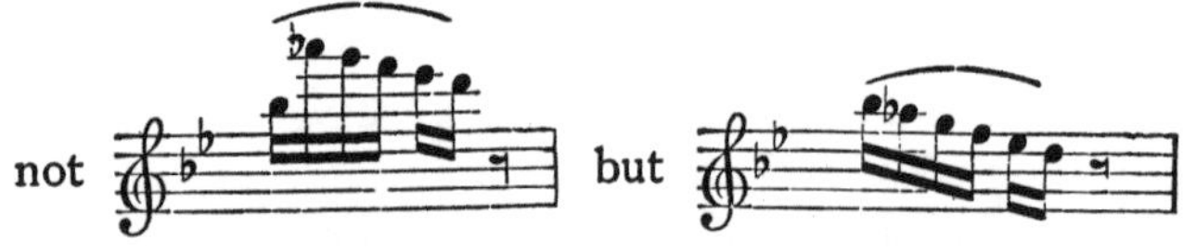

and thus the line of melody would be more correctly followed than was possible to Liszt with the technique of the pianoforte.

If we further were to effect one simple alteration in the second bar, making the oboe give the phrase in full, as it does in the fourth bar: thus

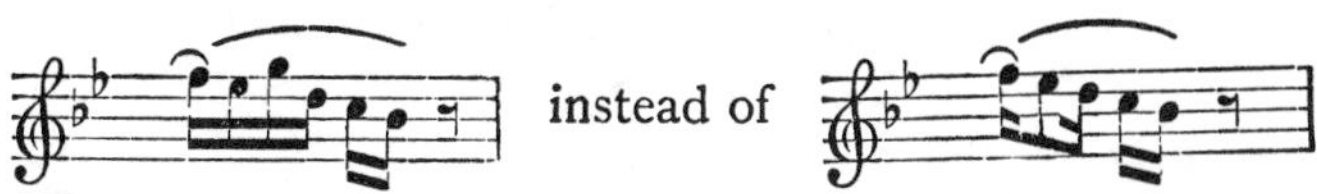

all we should need to give the whole passage its due pronounced expression, entirely lost at present, would be to somewhat slacken speed and observe the following nuances —which really are nothing but corollaries of the master's own notation:

In bars seven and eight, on the other hand, a fine and at last quite strong *crescendo* would suitably lead up to the expression with which to throw ourselves on the piercing accents of the following cadenza.

Where the passage returns in the movement's second section, in a different key and register, it will be much harder to bring about a like intelligibleness of its melodic content. Here, the clef being raised, the flute has necessarily the principal part to play; but as even *its* compass does not extend high enough, changes have been made in the melody that positively obscure it and contradict the sense expressed at like time by the other instruments. Let us compare the flute-part in the score:

with the melody to be deciphered from a combination of the notes for the oboe, the clarinet and the flute itself, answering to the earlier form at the close of the first section, namely:

After this comparison we can only regard the written flute-part as a serious distortion of the musical thought, since it quite distracts us from the melody.

As a thorough restoration here seemed audacious, since it would have meant the changing of a whole interval twice over, namely in the third bar of the flute

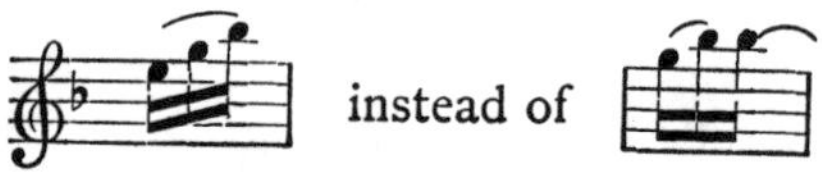

as also in its fifth bar

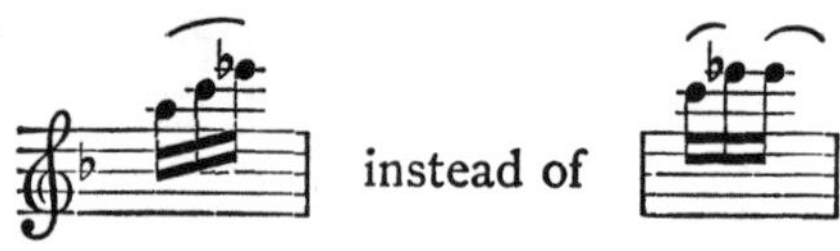

Liszt himself abstained from the bold attempt, and left the passage a melodic monster; as which it appears to everyone who attends our orchestral performances of this Symphony, and here experiences a gap, *i.e.* complete unclearness of the melody, for eight bars long. Having repeatedly suffered under the same distressing impression myself, I now should decide, upon occasion, to get these eight bars played by the flute and oboe in the manner following:

The second flute would have to be omitted from the fourth bar, but in the seventh and eighth, by way of partial compensation, the second oboe would play thus:

Beyond the nuances already recommended for the *Espressivo*, in every second bar we should have to mark the more strenuous ＜, to do justice to the variation in the melos; whilst a special *molto crescendo* would have to emphasise the last of the eight bars, thereby also setting in its true decisive light the desperate spring of the flute from G to the high F sharp:

which I here consider to be in thorough keeping with the master's real intention.—

If we reflect of what unique importance it is to every musical message, that the melody shall hold us without cease, even though the art of the tone-poet often parcels it into its tiniest fractions; and that the correctness of this melodic language can lag in no respect behind the logical coherence of a thought expressed in abstract word-speech, without bewildering us by indistinctness as much as does an unintelligible sentence: then we must admit that nothing is so worth the utmost study as the attempt to clear the meaning of a phrase, a bar, nay more, a single note in the message handed down to us by a genius such as Beethoven's. For every transformation, however startling, of a being so eternally sincere, arises solely from the godlike ardour to lay bare to us poor mortals the deepest mysteries of its world-view. As one should never quit a knotty passage of a great philosopher before one plainly understands it; and as, this rule neglected, the farther one reads the less one heeds the teacher: so one should never glide over a single bar of a tone-poem such as Beethoven's without having distinctly grasped it—unless one proposes to merely beat time in the usual way of our well-appointed academic concert-mongers, by whom I am quite prepared to find myself treated as a vain outrager of the sacredness of the letter.

Despite that fear, however, I cannot desist from the attempt to prove by a few more instances that a well-considered alteration of the letter, here and there, may promote a proper understanding of the master's intention.

So my next example shall be a nuance of dynamic expression that obscures its just intention in the carrying out. The stirring passage of the first movement (p. 13, Härtel's edition):

is immediately worked-out by a triplication of the melodic thought of the first two bars, thus spreading the *crescendo* sentence over six whole bars; of these the master gives the first couple to a detachment of the wind to play quite *piano*, and only lets the real crescendo enter with the third bar and the accession of fresh wind-instruments; finally, the third onset of the same melodic thought is given to the now predominant strings, with force emphatically increasing till it reaches a *fortissimo* at bar seven. Now I have found that the crescendo prescribed for the ascending figure of the strings in contrary motion at the second onset of the wind [bar 3 of this six-bar passage] was detrimental to an emphatic effect of the *più crescendo* of the violins at the third onset,

for it prematurely withdrew attention from the wind and its none too forcible assertion of the main melodic thought, and at like time made it difficult to give the thematic entry of the violins [bar 5] its characteristic stamp, namely the arrival of the true crescendo. Here, where the evil is but slightly marked, it might be altogether conquered by that discreet *poco crescendo* which alas! is wellnigh unknown as yet to our bandsmen, but which must necessarily precede a *più crescendo*; and one of my reasons for discussing this passage at length, is to commend that important dynamic nuance to special practice and adoption.

Even the most careful observance of that precept, however, would not remedy the evil consequences of the master's missed intention where the passage recurs in the last section of this movement, since the dynamic disproportion of the alternate groups of instruments here makes it quite impossible to treat with a gentle hand the nuances prescribed. This remark applies in particular to the first two bars of the kindred passage on page 47 of the score, where the first violins with all the other strings have to start a crescendo which the clarinet, taking it up with the answering phrase, is quite unable to carry forward with due force and climax: here I have had to decide on a total abandonment of the crescendo in the first two bars, reserving it for the wind to execute, and that most energetically, in the two bars following; and this time, as it already reaches an actual *forte* with the fifth bar, the strings may also fearlessly support it. For the same reason of dynamic disproportion, at the further return of the passage with the last bar of page 59 the first two bars must be taken quite piano; the two succeeding, with a strong crescendo by the wind, a weaker by the strings; and the latter will commence their real swell of sound with the last two bars before the "forte."

As I do not propose to dilate any longer on the character of Beethoven's nuances of expression, or on what appears to me their proper mode of execution; and as I believe that the care with which I have detailed my grounds for a rare amendment of the nuances prescribed by him will have justified my opinion of that mode: in this regard I have only further to say that the sense of these signs must be studied as thoroughly as the theme itself, since in them often lies the only guide to an understanding of the master's intention when conceiving the musical motive. Yet I may add that when I advocated a suitable modification of Beethovenian tempi in my earlier essay on "Conducting" I certainly had no idea of recommending the witty mode in which, as I have seriously been assured, a Berlin Upper Kapellmeister conducts those Symphonies: to make them piquant, so it is said, certain passages are first played forte, next piano, as if in echo, at one time slower, at another faster; pranks that a Kapellmeister's flow of humour will dictate to him in the score of the "Figlia del Regimento" or "Martha," for instance, but of which I should have been the last to dream when making my hardly explicable demands in favour of a proper rendering of Beethoven's music.

With the same motive, which has prompted all my efforts to elucidate the master's intentions, I finally have to discuss an extremely difficult passage in the vocal Quartet, in which after long experience I have at last discovered the ill that robs this marvellous composition of a truly delightful effect at all performances. It is the last passage for the soloists at the Symphony's close, the famous B-natural: "wo dein sanfter Flügel weilt."* The reason of its general,

* In Lady Macfarren's version, the one usually sung in England, this line

nay universal failure, does not consist in the height of the ascent for the soprano at its close, or the scarcely arduous intonation of the D-natural for the alto in the bar before the last: these difficulties are to be completely surmounted, on the one hand by a sopranist with a fairly high compass, on the other by a really musical contralto with a knowledge of the harmonic situation. The real and radical hindrance to a pure and beautiful effect is to be found in the tenor part, which begins its figured motion a bar too soon, and thereby on the one hand mars the clearness of the joint delivery, whilst on the other it assigns the voice a task fatiguing under any circumstances, but here opposed to every law of normal respiration, and using up the singer's strength. If we analyse the passage from the entry of the $\frac{6}{4}$ chord with the signature B-natural (page 264 of the score) its exquisite melodic content resolves itself into a figured phrase for the soprano, taken up in turn by alto, tenor and bass, in free imitation. Abstracting the voices that merely accompany this phrase, we find the master's intention distinctly expressed as follows:

However, at the phrase's second entry the tenor supports the alto throughout in sixths and thirds; so that when we reach the third bar, not only do we lose the import of the

runs: "reconciler sweet of hearts"; a closer translation would be: "where thy fost'ring wings abide."—Tr.

reappearance of the soprano's melismic figure in the tenor part, but the ear, having already been attracted to the latter voice, is deprived of the charm of a fresh entry. Besides the clouding of the master's intention, the effect of this glorious passage is further injured by the tenor's inability to take the two consecutive figured bars with the same ease as he certainly could the second of those bars alone. After mature deliberation I have therefore resolved to spare the tenor in future the difficult figure in support of the alto, preceding his main entry, and merely to allot him its essential harmonic notes; his part would then run thus:

I am convinced that every tenor who has struggled in vain to sing

will be very grateful to me, and now will render all the finer the melodic phrase belonging to himself. To give the latter full expression, I would commend to him the following dynamic nuance:

For a last remark I merely mention, without going into any further argument, that, when the admirable singer *Betz* most kindly undertook the baritone solo at the last performance I conducted of the Ninth Symphony, I induced him without any trouble, instead of

to start with the preceding bar and sing:

To our academic singers of the solid English Oratorio school we may leave it, for all future time, to vent their "Joy" in two strict crotchets.

LETTERS

AND

MINOR ESSAYS.

Sendschreiben und kleinere Aufsätze.

Of the following, No. II. appeared in the Musikalisches Wochenblatt, *January 1873; No. III. in the* Norddeutsche Allgemeine Zeitung, *end of 1871; No. IV. in the* Mus. Woch. *of November 1872; Nos. VI. and VII. in the same journal for October 1872 and March 1873 respectively.*

TRANSLATOR'S NOTE.

I.

LETTER TO AN ACTOR.

DEAR SIR,

THE recent publication of my essay on "Actors and Singers" has so considerably reduced my store of available matter, that I have little left for a contribution to your Almanac beyond the expression of my cordial sympathy with your undertaking. On the other hand I have no wish to imply that that essay is so exhaustive as to leave but little room for supplement: it could never be my aim to exhaust all aspects of such a theme as bears the above-named title, but simply to display my one main-theme in every light, and thus to get it rightly judged by the most diverse of classes. This time, accordingly, I addressed myself to the directest partners in the stage-artwork I have in mind, touching their interests for just so far as to me seemed needful to induce them to combine their own with my comprehensive interest in chief.

Now I should not care to let my vanity entice me from the prudent bounds I there observed, to let your invitation tempt me into discussing those sides of the actor's nature which I have not gauged by personal insight. My intuition may have enabled me to transfer myself to the position of the mime—yet only for that state into which he falls when he loses himself in his impersonation: as to his entity outside that state, I could have no lucid knowledge through assimilation. Yet I believe this to be the very point most worth the closest pondering by all who take an earnest interest in the actor's welfare.

What is the Player outside that state of ecstasy which

alone, on the other hand, should explain and warrant his whole life and labours?

The fate of European Culture has ruled that artistic exercises originally practised by every educated man at infrequent festivals should become the daily avocation of a class. The first glance ought to shew us that a great abuse has developed here, namely the squandering and overtaxing of a purely intermittent (*exzentrisch*) force. The most obvious consequence is in any case a degradation of the artistic exercise itself, through the daily wear and tear of the ecstatic state in which it should proceed: and so, as freemen would not lightly lend themselves to such abuse, it was slaves one drilled at last to histrionic service. Slaves, manumitted for their popularity, trooped through the world until the days when, social classes having undergone a fresh commingling, it became possible for a quite serious class of professional actors to arise. Now it needs must interest us highly, to hear the deliberate opinion of its members upon that class itself; for, as I have already said, it is difficult, nay impossible, by even the greatest stretch of imagination to transfer oneself into the soul of an actor not yet arrived at the state of ecstasy, or never entering that state at all.

Nor do I here refer to the shyness of all reserved or retiring men, about making a so-called public appearance: this is a feeling which everyone may overcome when the spirit moves him, on some definite occasion, to stand up in witness of the highest truth he holds. Rather am I thinking of the very boldest characters, who would fall into the most childish perplexity if one asked them to don the mask and clothing of another, and, thus disguised, to front the favour or disfavour of an audience. Yet this thing, which the ecstasy of artistic self-divestment makes possible without a scruple of the personality, is asked in fact from every member of a class to which, as we are bound to suppose, that ecstasy can come but seldom, and commonly not at all. Here we laymen stand before an utter riddle, which will always fill us with a certain awe of the actor's office.

Since we must assume that by far the largest number of our mimes never arrive at entirely translating themselves into the character they have to represent, the generality are therefore left with nothing but their private person, which they offer to the public's favour in a disguise ridiculous on this assumption. What, then, is the inner attitude of the mime towards an artistic function which for him can only take the light of a disguise deemed good enough by others?

And what a disguise!

To us laymen of the present day there perhaps is little more appalling than a visit to our actors' dressing-rooms just before the commencement of a stage-performance, especially if we are seeking out a friend with whom an hour previously we had chatted in the street. And here the least deterrent are the hideous old or crippled masks, whereas the young heroes and lovers with their false curls, their painted cheeks and over-dressy costumes, may easily fill us with positive horror. From the feeling of extreme depression, that always came over me on such occasions, nothing but a sudden stroke of magic could ever free me: and that was when, from out the distance, I heard at last the *orchestra*. Then did my halting pulses re-win life: everything withdrew before me to the sphere of wonder-dreams; the pandemonium seemed to me redeemed: for the eye no longer *saw* in terrible distinctness a wholly unintelligible reality.

Well, I can but think that a similar spell holds the genuinely gifted actor as soon as he sets his foot on the boards, even without the supporting element of Music, and is fascinated by the public's gaze to such a point that he feels snatched from all consciousness of his material situation. In his case, however, it must be assumed that something else is at work, beyond that fascination, namely the object of his portrayal itself; to whose most faithful mirroring he first is challenged by the very expectancy of the audience. Most surely all depends upon this object's worthiness, without which that fascination could draw forth nothing worthy from the mime's ecstatic state: it here must be an ideal verity, which quite annuls the hollow reality of the actor dressed and painted thus or thus, in this or that surrounding of lighted wings and backcloths.

But what are the feelings of the actor who does not enter that verity, the actor to whom this sordid apparatus, with an audience all agog before it, remains the only visible reality? Can sense-of-duty here suffice to cancel consciousness of a situation as frivolous as it is laughable? This at all events is the reckoning of those who make contracts with actors in much the way the owners of the Roman histrionic bands acquired their slaves—by simple purchase. What can the fulfilment of duty here bring to pass, except a total degradation of the man?

Whilst I thus can only imagine the actor's dignity as bound up with the worthiness of the dramatic task he has to solve, since its character alone can lift him from the common consciousness of his position and inspire him to step outside himself, for those who can have no personal experience of that other state in which this rapt uplifting never comes about it is very difficult to explain the actor's nature, provided they have no wish to sum it up as vanity and love of admiration. On the contrary, if we assume that the fairly well-intentioned actor must here be prompted by a mixture of all the motives that can possibly urge a man to the Theatre and keep him there, it would devolve on a thoughtful actor himself to enlighten us anent that mixture, whose effect on the mind we can only picture as a wellnigh perilous charm. I fancy we then should see cause for a thorough purging of those motives, such as certainly could be accomplished by nothing but a cultivation of the purely artistic element. To this end have Dramatic Schools been formed already, but always with the mistaken notion that one could teach the art of acting. Rather do I believe that only actors born can teach each other; and they would find their best assistance in a stern refusal to play bad pieces, i.e. pieces that hinder them from entering that ecstasy which alone can ennoble their art. Nor should we need to limit ourselves to the absolute "classical," but merely to sharpen our eyes for those products of dramatic literature which have issued from a right and lively knowledge of the actor's art, having regard above all to its German character.

As to the mode in which this sense may be sharpened, I venture to offer you a word of advice. Practise the improvising of scenes, and in fact whole pieces.* Indisputably, in improvising lies the root and kernel of all mimetic gifts, of all true acting talent. The dramatic author who has never figured to himself the force that would flow from his work if he could only see the whole thing improvised before him, has never felt within him the true election to dramatic poetry. The gifted Gozzi declared it clean impossible to write out certain of his characters in prose, still less in verse, and contented himself with a mere sketch of their scenes for the performers to fill up. Granted that such a procedure is a return to the first beginnings of dramatic art, yet those were the beginnings of a genuine art, and a return thereto must always lie open to it in its further evolution, if the soil of art is not to merge into a tenuous artificiality.

Moreover, if energetically pursued, the exercises I here suggest to you in brief would soon enable an acting company to discover those members who have entered it without either the equipment of real aptitude or the motive of true impulse. Severely to weed these out, would be a main concern of each such company; for every falsification, and therewith every degradation of an art, is to be awaited from those who mingle in its exercise without true calling.

You yourself, respected Sir, must be begged for further guidance to the recognition of these incompetents from that side which, as remarked above, is beyond my own experience. Should you then arrive upon this inner path at a general exposure of those elements which so immensely

* We find this practice recommended also by Goethe in his *Wilhelm Meister*, Book II., chap. ix., and Book IV., chap. ii.—Tr.

wrong the actor's office, the path at last would also shew itself whereon a glad regeneration of the actor's class might issue from within itself. Where the whole official conduct of the affairs of your profession is so bad as I myself have found it, it is only upon this inner path that may be reached a rescue craved by none more sorely than by him who has sufficiently set forth to you his views elsewhere, and who now signs himself with all esteem

Yours,

RICHARD WAGNER.

Bayreuth, 9. Nov. 1872.

II.

A GLANCE AT THE GERMAN OPERATIC STAGE OF TO-DAY.

FROM a tour which I lately made through the western half of Germany, for the urgent purpose of acquainting myself with the present state of the opera-personnel to be found there, I have derived so much enlightenment as to the artistic standpoint of the theatres themselves that I may hope an account thereof will not be unwelcome to my friends.

After remaining for so many years without any contact with the theatres, and thus in total ignorance of their present doings, I readily admit the dread with which I was filled by the necessity of putting them to the test once more. Against the impression I was about to receive from the maiming and disfigurement of my own operas I had steeled myself in advance, by a long-accustomed resignation: what I had to expect from our conductors on this field of dramatic music I knew well enough, since my eyes had been opened in the concert-room. My forebodings were outdone however, for I found the same inability to hit the right method displayed in every class of operatic music, Mozart's as much as Meyerbeer's; a thing explained by the simple fact, that these gentry have neither any feeling for dramatic life nor the very commonest notion of meeting the singer's needs. When my poor Tannhäuser has to challenge the whole Wartburg Hall of Minstrels with his Venus-song in mad defiance, I once heard him so over-hurried that the crucial phrase: "Go seek the Hill of Venus!" was understood by no one, nay actually unheard. On the other hand I have found the *tempo di menuetto* of Leporello's famous aria so dragged that its robust young singer could make neither breath nor tone hold out—which the conductor never noticed. Hurry and drag, in these consists the conductor's principal treatment of an opera; to which, if it be not exactly a work of Mozart's or "Fidelio," he adds a shameless paring-down to the effect he deems advisable.

To the educated listener, who strays into the house on such a night, it is incomprehensible that no musicians should ever be appointed to the Theatre save those not only without the faintest idea of their proper relation to the singer's task, but moreover utter strangers to the literature of operatic music. In the little theatre at *Wurzburg* I chanced on a performance of "Don Juan" which surprised me on the one hand by the singers' general excellence of voice, their sound enunciation and natural good qualities, on the other by the diligence with which a worthy time-beater at the conductor's desk seemed trying to shew what his singers could do with even a tempo incorrect throughout. I learnt that the Director had imported this person from Temesvar, after enticing him from a military band with which he used to arrange very popular garden-concerts. In this there was some reason: for when the Wurzburg Magistrate looks out for a financially-solid lessee of his theatre, he's not the man to stipulate for the Director's knowing a little about the requirements of such a thing as Opera. But it also may happen that a rigorist called to the directorship of an important Court-theatre on account of his literary effusions, and desirous of making Opera one of his strong suits, will specially select a musician who had been placed at the conductor's desk in his native city on purely patriotic grounds, and there had proved through a series of years that he would never be able to learn the beating of time either good or bad. This case was reported to me at Carlsruhe, as having just occurred there. What is one to say?

From these and similar instances, one might conclude that the blame for the musical misconduct of Opera at German theatres must be laid to the *Directors'* ignorance. I believe that conclusion would not be far out; only, I also think we should be in error to expect a real improvement from any mere shuffling or shifting of the present factors of theatric management. For example, if one found fault with the Regisseur's not being made director, in my experience there is no such person in the whole domain of Opera. Of the Regisseur's activity in our operatic representations let those speak who know the interior of that curious higgledy-piggledy; the outsider can see nothing but a chaos of solecisms and omissions. In token of the Regisseur's activity I remarked a peculiar movement of the ladies and gentlemen of the chorus at the Carlsruhe Court-theatre, so proud of its former dramaturgic and choreographic control: after gathering right and left as knights and dames in the second act of "Tannhäuser," they bodily changed places with a regular "*Chassé croisé*" from the contredanse. Nor in general did this theatre go wanting for inventiveness, upon occasion. In "Lohengrin" I here had seen Elsa's church-going in the second act embellished by the Archbishop of Antwerp meeting the procession half-way and extending his white-cotton gloves above the bride in blessing. This time I saw Elisabeth rise from her knees, after praying to the prompter's box in the last act of "Tannhäuser," and retire to the depths of the forest instead of ascending the mountain-path towards the Wartburg, the height whither Wolfram gazes after her. As this change of route enabled her to dispense with the gestures pointing heavenwards in her mute dialogue with Wolfram, the Kapellmeister had a welcome opportunity for a dashing cut; whilst Wolfram himself, reminded of the deepening twilight by the sudden entry of the sombre trombones, was absolved from his irksome side-turn of the head towards the mountain, and now might sing his Evening-star straight into the faces of the audience. And thus the thing went on.

As there accordingly was little to hope from the *régie*, which in the "Magic Flute" at Cologne quite calmly let the Queen of Night appear in broad daylight, I turned my attention back to the Kapellmeister. On his part again, it was always Mozart that was worst maltreated. To certify the incredible it would repay the pains of taking the singers' evidence, bar by bar, as to the mode in which I heard the first act of this "Magic Flute" performed: the matchless scene between Tamino and the Priests, where the supposed *recitativo* of the dialogue was drawled to exasperation; the never-ending *largo* of the delicious duettino of Pamina with Papageno; and the tripping burthen, "Would that every honest man might find such bells to tinkle!" spun out into a pious psalm, would in themselves suffice to give a notion of the reading of *Mozart* under care of our music-schools and conservatories of the "now-time."—*Meyerbeer* was perhaps the least assailed on this side, simply because he had already been so clipped that little remained for assailing. At *Frankfort* I heard some remarkable extracts from the "Prophète," both musical and scenic: for one thing, the third act began without any orchestral prelude; the curtain rose (I anticipated the announcement of some contretemps) and chorus and orchestra fell plump into a bawling number; which made me suppose the Herr Kapellmeister had not discovered a suitable cut for patching the scene to an earlier one, here omitted. But who asks for such minutiæ? We here meet a whole family that appears to have adopted the motto of Francis Moor, not to concern oneself with trifles.

Dulled to a certain insensibility by the impressions received already, I felt no repugnance against attending a performance of my "Flying Dutchman" at *Mannheim*. It amused me in advance to hear that this music, scarce long enough to fill a regulation opera-bill, and once intended by me for a single act, had not escaped a quite peculiar style of clipping: I was told that the Dutchman's aria and his duet with Daland had both been cut, leaving nothing save their closing cadences. This I declined to believe, but it turned out true enough; and, after recognising the weakness of the singer of the title-rôle, my only regret was that the noisy closing sections should have been the ones retained. However, the omission spared me hearing the main body of these pieces rendered faultily and incorrectly, and I could console myself with the thought that these Moorish "trifles" were no concern of mine. It did concern me, on the contrary, to find that Senta's scene with Erik in the second act was *not* cut: a tenor who had the misfortune to spread fatigue all round him at his very entry, appeared to have insisted on a full performance of his part, for which the conductor seemed taking his revenge by stretching the tempo of Erik's passionate complaints to a truly distressing length, beating it out in strictest crotchets. Here I suffered from the conductor's conscientiousness, but he suddenly made amends by unbridling his whole subjective freedom at finish of the act: coming after an important climax in the situation, the extended close, the *peroratio*, has here a decisive meaning, and has always worked in this sense on the audience; but Herr Kapellmeister took upon himself to act as censor and cut the closing bars just because they annoyed him, whereas in the first act it would seem to have delighted him to cut everything *except* the closing phrases. With that I thought I had reached the end of my studies of this singular conducting character, and nothing could induce me to pursue them farther. But soon afterwards I heard of something lovely. A new conductor at the Mannheim theatre, to celebrate his entry into office, announced to the astonished public a performance of "Der Freischütz" for the first time *without cuts*. Whoever would have dreamt that cuts were possible in "Freischütz" too?

And in such hands, in such a care, reposes German Opera! If the French—so conscientious and exact in their reproductions—but knew of this, how they would rejoice at the triumphal entry of solid German culture into Alsace!—

For this utterly good-for-nothing German Kapellmeisterhood, hedged round with appointments for life and carefully nursed town-family coteries, and often retained by incompetent persons for half a century, there can only be one effectual corrective, namely the gifts and good sense of the singers themselves; who plainly are the first to suffer under that misrule, and after all are the only people to whom the public proper gives attention and applause.

Let us see, then, in what way these singers degenerate under that dishonouring régime.

On a recent occasion I said that, in seeking out competent singers for the stage-festivals (*Bühnenfestspiele*) purposed by me, I had much less anxiety about finding good voices than unspoilt manners of rendering.* I now must confess that not only have I met more reliable voices than might have been expected from their badness at our largest Court-theatres, but almost everywhere a better aptitude for dramatic speech than I had found ten years ago, when abominably-translated foreign operas ran rampant on the German stage. If one is to follow some of my friends and attribute this improvement to our singers having since appeared more often in my operas every year, whilst the juniors among them have mostly begun their career with learning my operas, my labours would thus receive a confirmation which really should move the Messieurs Singing-masters and Professors of our Conservatoria to a less hostile attitude towards my works.

Yet with these good qualities—nay, principles—of the singers, it at first was incomprehensible to me that their performances should be so vague and, strictly speaking, senseless. Not one of the singers observed by me had arrived at any true artistic finish. In the case of one tenor alone, Herr Richard, who sang the Prophet at Frankfort, did I remark that he had seriously aimed at artistic finish, and in a certain measure attained it. Beyond mistake this gentleman had tried for the method of the newer French tenors, as exemplified so temptingly by the amiable

* "*Actors and Singers*," page 203.—Tr.

Mons. Roger, and accordingly had devoted great diligence to the development of a somewhat stubborn voice: I heard the same volume that for long has characterised the tenors of French Opera, trained in the Italian school. Here one plainly had an *artist*; only, his art jarred upon me: it was the systematic "harangue" inseparable from all French art, which can never be applied with success to the German style of dramatic singing, since this style requires simplicity and naturalness of the whole demeanour. And yet such an artist would have every right to ask us where to find this style in practice, that he might mould his art thereon?

By side of this singer a Fräulein Oppenheimer, who played the Prophet's famous Mother, attracted my particular attention. An exceptional voice, faultless elocution, and a grand impassionedness of accent, distinguished this splendid lady. She, too, had unmistakably matured into an "artiste": yet, for all these advantages, her performance was wellnigh made repellent by the dramatic and musical caricature inherent in her task itself. Where must the singer of such a Prophet's-mother inevitably end, if, after all the fatuous extravagances of an enervating Pathos, she grasps at one effect the more? The representation of such a Meyerbeerian opera at our theatres, great and small, is the exercise of all the senseless tricks a tortured fancy can conceive; whilst the most appalling thing about it, is the stupid earnestness with which a gaping crowd accepts the rankest folly.

As I shall return to this point, I now pass over to the doings of those singers who have not yet attained that "artistic" finish, or merely in a minor degree. The only "culture" visible here, alas! was expressed in the hideous variety of efforts to produce an effect with that "harangue" at a phrase's close.

And this laid bare the whole mournful system of our present opera-singing, which may be summarised as follows:—

Entirely without a model, in particular of German style, our young people are mostly chosen for their pretty voices, often from among the members of the chorus, and employed for operatic parts in whose rendering they are completely dependent on the Kapellmeister's bâton. This gentleman, equally without a model, or perhaps instructed by the Professors of our Conservatories—who in turn know nothing of dramatic singing, or for that matter, of opera-music in general—proceeds as I have said before; he beats his time by certain abstract-musical theories: for common time he drags, for *alla breve* he scuttles, and the fiat is: "Singer, go by me! I'm the Kapellmeister, and the tempo is my affair." It has really touched me to note the suffering devotion evinced in the reply of a singer whom I had taxed with either galloping or drawling out his pieces; he said he knew it well enough, but that was how the Kapellmeister took things. On the other hand these singers have learnt a lesson from their only available models, those "artists" of the Meyerbeerian school, namely the whereabout to avenge themselves on the tyrant Kapellmeister's tempo and even soar to the glory of a storm of applause: i.e. the final *fermata*, where the conductor dares not lower his staff before the singer ends. This fermata with the closing-harangue is the grand bequest the departed Meyerbeer appears to have willed to our suffering opera-singers for a period long outlasting his natural life: into it is crowded all the blatant claptrap one ever hears from singers either good or bad. Levelled at the audience from the footlights, it has the special advantage that even when the singer has not to "make an exit" (so indispensable for giving the challenge full effect) he still can simulate one by a frantic retreat to his colleagues left within the frame.

Now all this hits its mark, especially in Meyerbeerian opera; though even there, as I later will prove by an example, it sometimes fails through overdoing. But the difficulty for our poor singers, is to apply this clap-trap to the honest music of our older composers. These people void of art and sense and counsel, maltreated by the Kapellmeister and his beat, can make nothing of their aria or phrase itself, and have to struggle through it like a lesson got by rote; as a final resource they rush at its last note, and stick to it, with a scream to warn the audience of its duty; and behold! the Kapellmeister shuts one cultured eye, and—pauses too.

Once I expostulated with a Kapellmeister for allowing the singer of Roger in Auber's charming opera "le Maçon" ("*der Maurer und der Schlosser*") to foist that clap-trap on the closing bar of his almost entrancingly spirited aria in the third act. The Kapellmeister excused himself on grounds of sheer humanity: the public was so spoilt, he said, that it would no longer dole out the least applause to a merely *correct* delivery of such an aria; if one singer were to submit to his (the conductor's) views, and simply sing the closing bar as the composer had written it—thereby most certainly going without applause—there soon would come another singer who would refuse to be robbed of his final hit, would bring off his round of applause, and be dubbed a success, against the former's failure. Indeed?—This time, however, I took upon myself to shew the Herr Kapellmeister that that obliging and very gifted singer of the performance just past could easily have gained the public's lively interest, even without that obnoxious Effect, had he himself but taught him—ay, simply made it possible to him by a proper tempo—to sing the *whole* aria *bar by bar* in such a way that the *aria* itself, not merely its closing bar, should compel applause. I proved it by singing him the theme in its proper tempo and with the right expression, following it with a reproduction of the singer's scampered rendering in false tempo; which had such a drastic effect upon him that for once, at any rate, I was declared in the right.

Reserving a statement of the grounds on which even our Kapellmeisters, particularly the younger ones, are as much to be pardoned for their ignorance of the true needs of Opera and dramatic music in general as the singers who suffer under them, I first must somewhat complete the picture of the ruin into which the representations at our opera-houses have fallen in consequence.

For this I may continue with the last-named performance of an opera of the most unassuming genre, that "Maçon" of Auber's. How I pitied both the work and our singers! To what man of judgment has this early opera of the last truly national French composer not formed a red-letter in his estimate of the amiable qualities of the French bourgeoisie? The German Theatre most surely ran no risk to its development, in making such a work as this its own; and for a time it seemed to have completely succeeded, as our native talent for the unaffected Singspiel here obtained a wholesomely assimilable food. But witness a performance of this work to-day, and that by singers so naturally gifted, I am bound to add, as those of the *Darmstadt* Court-theatre! The taste of high quarters having ordained that the very latest products of modern French Opera should be introduced at this court before any other place in Germany, this company had been accustomed to nothing but the most grotesque Effects, without the smallest practice in the Natural. Consequently not a creature was now in his proper place, in this bright and unsophisticated opera; the sparkling little vocal numbers, not one of which was taken in the right tempo or made intelligible by correct expression, slipped soulless through a dialogue defaced by "Grand Opera-singers" as if in lordly contempt. But since the dialogue, and especially its comic side, seemed raised in "le Maçon" to almost the main affair, they had to look about for tricks in substitution for the usual Operatic clap-trap; and so a creaking snuffbox and a sausage inadvertently drawn from the coat-pocket (traditional extempores of some former low comedian) became their models for enlivening a dialogue itself filled full with truly genial comedy, if one only gives it a little thought. 'Tis everywhere the same: the *text*, the true material substance of a work, our operists know no longer; like the rag-and-bone-man, they merely rake from here or there an obligato tag to trim their nightly plaudit-jacket.—That evening, though, I soon discovered how the wind lay: poor Auber's opera was nothing but the prelude to a *ballet*, where flower-fays and other mighty pretty things were to put in an appearance. The Intendant must have called me a barbarian, to turn my back on this!

The warmth with which I have defended Auber's harmless Singspiel must be my apology for the increasing chill with which I shall have to refer to other, higher art-doings at the theatres I visited. As the ratio of the reproduction to the task remained constant, the evils mounted higher with the higher pitching of the task itself, whilst the over-taxed sensitiveness of the hearer passed at last into insensibility. With the singers I found at the little theatre at *Wurzburg* I would wager to give an excellent dramatic performance, were I but allowed to choose a work in keeping with their faculties, and to see to its being properly directed. My inability to sit out more than one act of "Don Juan" here, was chiefly attributable to the conductor's misrule; coupled with a senselessness on the part of the régie beyond imagining, it made a further stay in the theatre obnoxious to me. Every one of the singers had natural ability; only the principal lady, Donna Anna, seemed somewhat spoilt—I fancy, not incorrigibly—though her warmth of feeling was much in her favour: but most of them were in presence of a task un-understood throughout and merely learnt in compliance with the common operatic scheme. A young man of exceptionally powerful voice and capital enunciation, but with the manners of a schoolboy and somewhat clumsy carriage, had to conjure up for us the fascinations of a seductive Andalusian cavalier, the title-rôle of Mozart's opera. But "Don Juan" it must be, and "Don Juan" was it beaten.—

It is easy enough to see that the singers do not really feel at home in such performances of classic works; another life thrills in their pulses when the "fermate" operas come along—which promises the works of Meyerbeer a life by no means measurable as yet. Hence there is something quite touching in their marked affection for my operas, seeing that they never arrive at a grand effect in them.

But how should they get an effect at all commensurable with that from Meyerbeerian rôles, since here success can dwell in nothing but the effect of the whole, whilst there each phrase has its own effect provided for it in the closing tirade? Now our singers distinctly have a presentiment of this *effect of the whole*, and it probably is that which attracts them to my operas; but this whole is chopped in pieces for them by the Kapellmeister. Whenever I have gone through one of the rôles of my operas with a singer who interested me, in course of the scene he was always obliged to stop short, for here came his Herr Kapellmeister's cut and he had learnt no farther. When I told him how the matter lay, explaining the importance to his entire rôle of just the passage elided, in his instant mortification I could see where to build my only hopes of a proper understanding. Yet the very best singers at our theatres are kept in this hazy state of wellnigh childlike ignorance of the nature of the tasks I set them: with what, then, are they left?

Into this we must inquire.

What the singers of operas such as mine will never perceive while their parts are given out to them in the mutilation beloved of our Kapellmeisters, is in any case the *dramatic dialogue*, the perspicuous building-up whereof was the author's chief concern—for which reason, also, he staked his whole musical art upon its working out. As I myself have almost entirely discarded Monologue proper—which erewhile, in the form of Aria, filled a whole opera with a series of soliloquies—it is easy to imagine the shifts the singer is put to, to weld the scattered fragments of the dialogue into the mould of monologue, with music whose whole character can only be understood through the animation of its discourse. There necessarily is nothing left for him but to hunt for effective operatic bits, and to take as such whatever he deems likely. Hence his perpetual stepping outside the frame, as he no longer finds the action knit together by its dialogue: instead of facing the person to whom his speech is addressed, he apostrophises the audience from the footlights—making me often disposed to ask, with the angry Jew: "Why does he say that to me, and not to his neighbour?"

Should anyone suppose that the ordinary effect of this ruling habit of our singers, namely a frequent interruption by applause, must at least be not without its profit to *my* operas, he would make a grand mistake: here nothing tells, but what is understood in due connection with the whole; what remains *unclear* in this sense, leaves the audience uninterested. Anybody may convince himself of this upon comparing the effect of a rightly rendered and undocked act, or even scene from one of my operas, with that of a maimed performance. At *Magdeburg*, a few years back, a Director had the courage to insist on "Lohengrin" being played in its entirety: the result was so successful, that in six weeks he was enabled to give the opera six-and-twenty times to the public of this middling town, and always to full houses. Yet as such an experience teaches no one, we can but infer a really bad and vulgar will on the part of theatrical managers.

Nevertheless even they are to be excused at times, on ground of a deep demoralisation of artistic affairs in general. The management at *Bremen* procured the written orchestral parts with the [printed] score of the "Meistersinger" from the publisher: the latter, presumably anxious to lighten the performance of my work for this little theatre, had had the parts copied from those in use at *Mannheim*, where they are so famous for their cutting. The able Bremen Kapellmeister soon discovered that quite a host of passages in the score had not been written out in these parts at all, and, as the date announced was drawing nigh, could only restore a few of them; the last act in particular—with exception of Hans Sachs's monologue, which the admirable singer had been able to rescue—had to remain in the Mannheim strait-waistcoat. Here again it was quite evident what consequences attend such a deed of maiming. To both the audience and myself it was possible to follow the relatively little-shortened first two acts with interest: the third, the very act which had made the liveliest impression at the first performances in Munich, so that its length was never noticed, here tired out the audience and plunged myself, who had lost all recognition of my work, into the most painful distraction. As the story is chiefly told in the thrust and parry of the dialogue,* these scandalous omissions made it vague and unintelligible; so that the performers got out of humour, and—most instructive point of all—the conductor, who till then had maintained an almost unexceptionably correct tempo, now fell from one misunderstanding to another: Eva's enthusiastic outpouring of her heart to Sachs was rushed, and therefore inarticulate; the Quintet was dragged, and thereby lost all suppleness and swing; whilst Walther's master-song, with the broader chorus built upon it, was rough and jerky. If this was done at *Bremen*, where at least there were many excellences in the rest of the performance, I might judge the character of the representations of my work at German theatres elsewhere.

Indeed it is particularly depressing to find the ineradicable vices of the German stage outcropping even in the doings of good and friendly artists. We are often on the verge of unalloyed delight, at seeing good material and ready will inclining to the right; all the more disheartened are we to see these good beginnings suddenly degenerate, and accordingly to find no vital consciousness of Art, but a blind submission to the havoc springing from an altogether spurious education.

To complete the hopeless picture, we find the theatre-going public in precisely the same attitude toward Opera. A dull insensibility lies stamped on every countenance: uninterested in all that happens on the stage or in the orchestra, the audience only wakens from its deafness to cap the singer's inevitable "harangue" with a round of applause, in token that it had not so far forgot itself as to really fall asleep. Not a face shews any feeling, save that of curiosity about its neighbours: the saddest or the

* "Die in einem theilweise exzentrischen Dialoge sich aussprechende Handlung" *etc.*—

merriest scene may be passing on the boards, not a muscle betrays the faintest sympathy. It is "Opera; which has nothing to do with either mirth or earnestness, but—simply *Opera*. Why doesn't the prima donna sing us something pretty?" And for this have they decked the theatre with untold luxury! The house is all aglow with gold and velvet, and the hospitable easy-chair seems upholstered for the evening's chief enjoyment. From nowhere can one get a view of the stage that does not include a large slice of the audience: the flaming row of footlights abuts on the middle of the proscenium-boxes; it is impossible to watch the prima donna, there in front, without taking in the glasses of the "opera-friend" who ogles her. One thus can find no line to part the putative artistic action from those before whom it is set. The two dissolve into one brew of most repulsive mixture, in which the Kapellmeister twirls his staff as magic-ladle of the modern witch's-caldron.

What specially disgusted me, was the shameless baring of the scenic mystery to the eyes of every gaper: that which can only operate through a well-planned distance, one thinks one cannot bring too near the glaring lamplight. As each organic link has been hewn from the tone-poet's work, one treats the scene itself no better; something must always be torn from the whole, and aimed at the audience from the footlights. At that Frankfort performance of the "Prophète" already mentioned, in the famous church-scene I saw the no less celebrated Fides quit her place in the extreme foreground and come down to the rail to vent her frantic imprecations on her son, which done she improvised a sensational exit behind the proscenium: as this did not extract the intended applause, came Fides humbly forth again and knelt beside the other worshippers, to be present, as needed, at the catastrophe's arrival. The astounding folly of this trick is manifest to anyone who knows that Fides should be among the people from the opening of this scene, with them should sink upon her knees at the litany "*salvum fac regem*," and in a pause of the chant should be heard muttering her unearthly curse; which, to fit the situation at all intelligibly, cannot be sung subduedly enough. To be sure, this time the lady failed in her effect; she was not applauded. But neither was she jeered: not a feature of the audience shewed a sign of ridicule; just as the utmost nonsense, the most grotesque exaggeration, throughout was felt by no one. Once a senior officer behind me laughed in fact: but it was merely at a Bishop stalking in the coronation-train, whom the laugher probably had recognised as his orderly, or what not.—

If this somnolence of all feeling for artistic truth but confined its degrading influence to our opera-houses, we perhaps might find release by giving up the Drama altogether. Unfortunately, it is only too true that the whole spirit of our public musical life is poisoned thence and led to shamefulest degeneration. At its Garden-concert and Change-of-guard the people proper is regaled with nothing but a re-warming of the opera-house stew. From thence our regimental bands obtain their musical pabulum, and in what that consists one may easily guess. The tempo and entire reading of the theatre passes on to the conductors of these popular orchestras, as only accessible model; and whenever we meet with grave misunderstandings here, we invariably receive the excuse that things were taken thus and thus at some great theatre. Of late I have often been honoured by military corps with a very friendly serenade of pieces from my operas: sincerely delighted and truly touched by their doings, for the most part, I have not been able to conceal from their excellent conductors my difficulty in accounting for certain omissions and faulty tempi which I had uniformly noticed in the first finale of "Lohengrin," for one thing: whereupon I learnt that they had based their arrangements on the reputedly authoritative score of the Dresden Court-theatre, for instance, in which the missing passages were left quite out, whilst one heard the tempo thus and not otherwise at all the theatres. Whoever has once arrived at hearing the closing Allegro of this first "Lohengrin" finale played properly in its entirety, may imagine my feelings at listening to the galloping stump of a tone-piece which I had laboured to make grow up before me like a well-formed tree, with branches, boughs and leaf-work!—When I explained this to the highly obliging, and for the most part excellent Kapellmeisters of those music-corps, they were utterly surprised and often disconcerted. "How were we to know any better? Indeed we nowhere hear it otherwise"—was their invariable reply.

And a whole nation that has its music played to it in none but this spirit?—Yet no! Our Conservatories and High Schools of Music now provide for the maintenance and nurture of the true musical spirit. It might be asked, who provides for these Schools themselves being conducted in the proper spirit and manned with really responsible teachers? But in the long run it always comes back to the question, how Music is plied with us in general; for the spirit in which the public is given its music, affords our only guarantee of a proper feeling on part of the leading authorities. And here we find that these institutes have absolutely no influence on the musical taste of the public, save this at most—they send incompetent conductors to our orchestras, and above all to our theatres. Forever in the position of the fox to the grapes, regarding Opera, which none of those majestic Conservators can reach with any measure of success, they ply their music by themselves. Their Trios, Quintets, Suites and Psalms are played behind closed doors, so strictly closed as to admit no one but the Messieurs Composers and executants. Now and again, however, the best-to-do, and therefore the most influential families in the town are busily invited, and even hospitably entertained in times of peril:* on them is then impressed that

* This forcibly reminds us of Wagner's experiences in 1834 at those Magdeburg "Lodge-concerts" about which he then wrote to Schumann: "During the Adagio of a Symphony one hears the rattle of plates. . . . When all is over, and respectable people are taking their hats, a mysterious door is opened, tempting vapours issue forth, the confederates troop into the inner chamber" (Glasenapp's *Das Leben Richard Wagner's*, 3rd ed. vol. i. p. 205). We also

what they have just heard is the only genuine article, whilst the music which goes on outside is bad tone. But if these well-to-do and influential families are appealed to, once in a way, to tender help in those regions of public music where a powerful aid alone can further a thing of service to the nation's spirit, then every avenue is blocked by pietistic sentries, and the great journals are impounded to see that nothing but systematic slander and abuse shall find a door or crevice open. If one asks these people, on the other hand, how they themselves propose to fulfil their promises of "pure" musical treats—without which, when all is said, no believer will truly pin his faith to them—one hears tell of a magnificent, quite classical Handelian "Solomon," to which the departed Mendelssohn himself wrote an organ-accompaniment for the English. An outsider like myself must have listened with his own pair of ears, to form a notion of the sort of thing these gentry of "pure music" compel their believers to swallow. But they do it, those believers. And glorious are the temples they build for their high priests: there sit they, pull no face,* and follow with the book, while their dear relations on the platform up aloft sing choruses and Jupiter himself beats time. I witnessed a specimen of this at *Düsseldorf*, whilst folk at other places much regretted that I had come too late for exactly the same thing there!— —

At *Cologne* I happened to say a few words among friends; my remarks were very kindly reported in a newspaper, but particular stress was laid on my expressing myself so much more mildly in private converse, such as this, than in my written lucubrations destined for publicity, where it would seem that I dipped my pen in venom. No doubt it makes a difference, whether I am speaking on the spur of the moment, or writing to the public: † there

hear of a grand concert "with supper," to celebrate the centenary of the Gewandhaus Concerts, March 9, 1843 (ibidem, p. 211).—TR.

* An evident parody of the author's own "Waltraute-scene" in *Die Götterdämmerung*, act i.: "So—sitzt er, sagt kein Wort" etc.—TR.

† "Gewiss ist es wohl etwas Anderes, wenn ich aus mir spreche, oder zur Öffentlichkeit schreibe."—

I have a pen to dip indeed, and public matters offer me by no means honey. However, to take my cue from a certain flask of Cologne venom that I wo'n't confound with sweet *Eau de Cologne*, I will close my "Glance" in right optimistic fashion with some well-meant advice—which I fancy myself better able to give than our Conservatories—to various Kapellmeisters; whence they may see that I find no pleasure in writing hopeless letters in the air.—

In the conductor of the "Magic Flute" at Cologne I made acquaintance with a really educated man, outside the theatre, who seemed to have taken up music as a profession, and the theatrical bâton as emblem of office, rather late in life. May he more and more arrive at a perception how hard it is to master the Theatre, and become familiar with the peculiar spirit that is the soul of a dramatic performance, from without. Should his musical training have issued from the sphere of our Conservatories, I beg him to particularly remark the woodenness with which the very soul of *Mozart's* music, its *singing quality*, is treated there, and thence to take a warning without the laying to heart whereof he can never attain a knowledge of the rendering required by Mozartian melody, and thus by all Mozartian music.

To the Kapellmeister of the *Mayence* theatre I take the liberty of expressing my delight at his eminent gifts as conductor: here was great precision without the smallest affectation, and the performance of "Fidelio" shewed many signs of correct conception as regards both tempo and dynamics. The more important I therefore think it, to direct his notice to the weakness common to all our conductors for scampering those Allegros which have only two beats to a bar: he *must* reflect that his tempo for the great Quartet in the second act, as also for the following Duet, not only turns the thing into a musical monstrosity, but robs the singers of all possibility of effective or even clear participation in the scene. Whilst the same remark applies to the closing chorus: "Wer ein solches Weib errungen," which was deprived of all its dignity by a too rapid pace, it is again to be deplored that the famous section preceding it in $\frac{3}{4}$ time—which seems to hover like a fleece of golden light above the surcharged situation—completely changed its character for that of painful rigidness, through a dragging of its tempo. By the conductor's fault the Quartet in act i. met an almost identical fate: could he not feel that we here have no set chant, but rather an *aside* by four persons soliloquising at once, and that its character is diffidence, embarrassment, musically expressed in staccato notes for the singers, and therefore at first accompanied by a *pizzicato* for the strings? Each speaks to himself; we hear them, but they do not hear each other. Nothing is farther from this piece, than the Adagio character; and only its sostenuto introduction can account for its being falsely classed by inexperienced conductors with the Adagio type of melody. But that introduction ranks as one of the noblest gems of Beethoven's genius for very reason that, before any of these characters begins to express himself in words, it enables us to plumb the unuttered inmost heart of each. And here the proper rendering was missed by all: each bawled and ranted at his fellow, whereas almost the entire piece should be sung with bated breath, and its fleeting accents little more than hinted.

This brings me to a last and capital offence of our conductors: with scarcely an exception, they have no sense of dynamic agreement between the singers and the orchestra; and for that matter, their disregard of the orchestra's connection with what takes place upon the stage is at the root of all their errors, even in respect of Tempo. I have repeatedly found that the orchestral nuances had been practised with diligence, consequently that the band played soft and low where needed, but hardly ever that the singers were held to a like expression, more especially in ensemble-pieces: the chorus in particular sings as a rule with all its force, and the Kapellmeister doesn't seem struck by its ridiculous and most disturbing contrast with his quiet orchestra. This utter obtusity of the conductor is perfectly incomprehensible when we hear the elfin chorus at end of the second act of "Oberon" murdered by the shrillest shouts of the common operatic chorus, as well-nigh universally, while the strings are playing with their 'mutes' on; and yet we are forced to assume that he hears nothing amiss.

My advice to friendly-disposed conductors of Opera might therefore be summed up as follows: *If you otherwise are good musicians, in Opera pay heed to nothing but what is happening on the stage, be it the monologue of a singer or a general action; let it be your prime endeavour that this scene, so infinitely intensified and spiritualised by association with its music, shall acquire the "utmost distinctness": if you bring that distinctness about, rest assured that you at like time have found the proper tempo and correct expression for the orchestra.* To the very able conductor of the operatic orchestra at *Bremen*—which delighted me, despite its smallness, by the unexpected excellence of its work in every respect—I offer the above advice in especial, since in this regard alone could he be said to fall short of mastership.—

It is impossible to close this account of my recent Glance at the Opera-stage of To-day, especially in the direction last taken, without referring to a theatre scarcely noticed by our newspapers, but which has been led on to deeds of exemplary perfection by the true artistic taste of one man at its head. In the little ducal capital of *Dessau* the Intendant of the Court-theatre, *Herr von Normann*, invited me to a performance of Gluck's *Orpheus*, since the illness of several singers forbade the representation of any opera that required a larger company. *I publicly declare that I have never witnessed a nobler and more complete performance at any theatre.* Certainly the misfortune suffered by the Intendant, in the laming of his personnel, had turned to the advantage of this evening; for it would have been impossible for a more numerous caste to achieve anything so thoroughly distinguished, as the impersonation of Orpheus and Eurydice by the two soloists. Naturally gifted, but in no uncommon manner, both these ladies were inspired by the most delicate artistic feeling, and so uniformly fine a portrayal of Gluck's creation I had never hoped to meet. As everything else was in such entire harmony with this portrayal, I could only conclude that the latter's perfection had been evoked by the studied beauty of every detail on the stage. Here the operatic mise-en-scène had taken life, and become an active element in the whole performance: each scenic factor, grouping, painting, lighting, every movement, every step, contributed to that ideal illusion which wraps us as it were in twilight, in a dream of truths beyond our ken. From the frequency with which the estimable Intendant left my side, in his consuming care lest any trifling fault should harm this fragile dream-life, I guessed to whose love of art was due the excellence of all I witnessed. And most surely I was not mistaken in ascribing the exceptionally brilliant execution of the whole musical ensemble, orchestra and chorus fully included, to the immediate influence of this wonderful care in the staging.

A truly encouraging example, and evidence of the truth that he who grasps the *whole* will recognise and rule the right in all its portions, even should he have no direct acquaintance with their technique. Herr *von Normann*, perchance without any knowledge of music, by his thoughtful stage-management led his Kapellmeister to a musical exploit of such beauty and correctness as I nowhere else have met at any theatre.

And this, as said, was in little *Dessau*.

III.

Letter to an Italian Friend* on the Production of "Lohengrin" at Bologna.

So deeply have I been touched by the gratifying reports from so many quarters about the production of my "Lohengrin" in Bologna, that I must take advantage of your knowledge of German to beg you to convey my heartfelt thanks to your honoured countrymen in your mother-tongue.

Perhaps I was not wrong in resisting the repeated invitations to attend that production ; by standing aside from the rehearsals of my work I have placed myself, and all who joined in this undertaking, in a position to clearly judge the mutual relations of all the forces coming into play. As everything here was due to the spontaneous impulse of Italian art-lovers, and nothing to my own initiative, I may well have wished to leave the issue entirely to the character in which my work was read and executed by your fellow-countrymen. Only thus could its success be an altogether free expression of Italian artistic taste.

That in my decision to remain away I had to battle with a truly great temptation, I will not conceal from you. In what that temptation consisted you will learn, to your astonishment, if I tell you my experiences with this very "Lohengrin" in Germany. You must know, then, that all the successes this work has won on the German stage have never been able to secure me a performance in complete accord with my directions. My offers to arrange for a thoroughly correct performance were evaded on every side,

* Arrigo Boito.—Tr.

and I only met with indifference when I pointed out that certain most important features of my musico-dramatic poem, such as the crisis in the second act, were not so much as brought to understanding on the stage. Folk stuck to a couple of orchestral preludes, a chorus, a "cavatina," and thought that sufficient, as after all the opera pleased. Once only, in Munich, did I arrive at rehearsing my work in full accord with my intentions, at least as regards its rhythmic architecture: those who attended the resultant performances, with true feeling and understanding, were astonished at one thing alone—namely that it remained the same to the public whether it obtained its "Lohengrin" thus or otherwise; if the opera was given thereafter in the old routine, the impression it made was identical—an experience most comforting to the Director of the theatre, but which necessarily must make me highly indifferent, in my turn, to any dealings with the German audience.

From many tokens I now know that with an Italian audience, in such a case, I should have met a very different grade of receptivity. Though, in a talk I had with him twelve years ago, *Rossini* blamed an effemination of his countrymen's artistic taste for the line he had adopted in his music, his words by no means warrant us in concluding that the Italians would prove insensible to nobler things when offered them. Moreover, after learning the impression made by Beethoven's music on *Bellini*—who previous to his stay in Paris had never heard a note of it—I have taken every opportunity of observing the Italian attitude to art, and hence have gained the most favourable opinion of its one main characteristic: to wit, an open mind and delicate feeling in all artistic questions. And thus, to overleap the singular castrato-singing and pirouetting century of Italian decadence, I understood again the matchlessly productive spirit to which the new world owes all its Art since the Renaissance.

I have told you how nearly the temptation touched me to appeal in person to this open-minded instinct of your countrymen, in order to enjoy for once the satisfaction of seeing a tenderly-prepared creation regarded and accepted with an equally tender sense. A peculiar fate has repeatedly withheld me from following in the steps of *Goethe*, from whom the lament was torn, on his visit to Italy, that he must torture his poetic Muse with the German tongue, when the Italian would so sweetly smooth her task. What drove Goethe back to our Northern climes, with sighs and deep regret, is certainly not to be wholly explained by his ties in personal life. If at various times I, too, have sought a second home in Italy, what always drove me back again was easier of explanation; yet it would come hard to me, my honoured friend, to name it to yourself. Perhaps I may best suggest it to you by saying that I heard no longer the naïve folk-song Goethe heard upon the streets, but in its place the workman on his homeward way at night would vent those mawkish and affected opera-phrases which I cannot believe were engendered by the manly spirit of your nation—or ever by the womanly! Yet even this might be ascribed to illness and a morbid mood. What made my ear so sensitive in Italy, may certainly lie deeper. Be it a good or evil genius that rules us in our hours of crisis—enough: stretched sleepless in a hostelry of La Spezzia, to me there came the prompting of my music for the "Rheingold"; at once I returned to the land of shadow, to carry out that bulky work whose fate, above all else, now binds me fast to Germany.

It has been remarked that the ground of a nation's original productiveness is less to be sought in what Nature has bestowed with lavish hand, than in what she has doled out to it. Physiologically considered, the fact that within the last hundred years the Germans have acquired so exceptional an influence over the development of *Music*, taken up by them from the Italians, may be partly explained by their lacking the temptations attached to a naturally melodious voice, and their thus being compelled to treat the art of Tone with somewhat the same deep-searching earnestness as their Reformers the religion of the Holy Gospels—a religion they were elect to recognise as not consisting in the pomp and glamour of church-ceremonies, in the intoxicating sheen of colours beneath a laughing sky, but in its serious promises of comfort to the human soul oppressed by deprivations of all kinds. If this necessarily led us to an idealistic explanation of the world, it also saved us from the effeminacy of an all-too-realistic self-abandonment thereto. From a beautiful, Music thus became more of a sublime art with us; and great must be the magical effect of this sublimity upon the mind, for none whose heart has been transfixed thereby has shewn himself amenable to the seductions of more sensuous beauty.

But we have still one yearning, which warns us that we do not embrace the whole essence of Art. The artwork wills to become in the end a full and physical deed; it wills to seize the human being by his every fibre of sensation, to flood him as with a river of joy. It has been proved that the womb of German mothers could receive and bear the loftiest geniuses of the world; what remains to prove, is whether the receptive organs of the German Folk are worthy of the noble issue of those chosen mothers. Perchance here is needed a new marriage of the genii of nations. For us Germans there could loom no fairer love-match, than a wedding of Italia's genius with that of Deutschland.

Should my poor "Lohengrin" have proved the groomsman, a glorious deed of love were his. The great, the truly touching zeal my Italian friends have devoted to the transference of this my work, a zeal my long experience teaches me to value to its utmost grain, might well awake in me that lofty hope. By my almost extravagant presage you may judge the importance I attach to this event, and how highly I prize the services of those artists and other friends of art to whom I owe that elating success.

RICHARD WAGNER.

Lucerne, 7. November 1871.

IV.

TO THE BURGOMASTER OF BOLOGNA.

MOST WORSHIPFUL SIR!

IT is difficult to relate in brief the feelings awoken in me by the honour shewn me by your glorious city. Not long ago I expressed to the Italian friends of my art the great joy I felt at the so auspicious success of my "Lohengrin's" production in Bologna: I now have to declare my profound astonishment at this success being regarded by the municipal authorities themselves as of the significance implied in their resolution to confer on me the freedom of their city.

As this significance must therefore be clear to the honoured representatives of the township of Bologna, it would seem superfluous to enlarge on it again from my side. The only thing for me, is to discover how I may contribute to the fulfilment of the hopes that fair success has roused in my new fellow-citizens. What obstacles I see before me, you may judge from the circumstance that for the next few years I am bound to Germany more firmly than ever, and indeed to devote my energies exclusively to carrying through an undertaking which at first appears restricted to the realisation of a purely national tendence. In fact, should my work succeed completely, it would be largely due to the independent evolution of those very seeds of a German-national art whose nurture and development upon the field of Musical Drama have hitherto been most injuriously retarded by the influence of Italian Opera. Moreover, having entirely withdrawn from that influence myself, I have felt compelled to shew its harmfulness under every aspect, and accordingly could not avoid an agitation which ended by placing me in the attitude of an antagonist to the very people to whom I now extend the hand of friendship and deep gratitude for adorning me with the title of an honorary freeman of Bologna.

Perhaps it might be wiser to clear up the contradiction just referred to, for, taken superficially, it may easily draw down on my Italian friends the reproaches of their sensitive compatriots. Now I should not like to expose my honoured fellow-burghers of Bologna to any accusation of unpatriotism; nevertheless I can only appeal for the present to their own feeling, which certainly will clear them of all charge of treachery in hospitably throwing wide to me the gates of their noble city. This feeling can but tell them that it was not the period of national prosperity and political esteem in Italy, when she sent her vocal virtuosi to every court of Europe to entertain with a seductive art-dexterity the very men who held her, no less than Germany, in bondage and division. On the other hand it was for us Germans a time of wakening from a no less ignoble subjection to evil influences, when a returning sense of seemliness forced our Princes to dismiss those castrati and prime donne, from whom we could learn nothing but a pitiful distortion of our natural idiosyncrasies. But if a German has now been permitted to shew you to what use and expression in the musical Drama he could turn those purely native qualities—so dear to him, however little glittering—it was you again, my honoured fellow-citizens, who determined that no base exchange had here been offered you; and as I spoke before of a marriage of the Italian with the German genius, I believe it could be celebrated under no happier sign than the motto of your city, emblazoned on whose scutcheon I see the word "Libertas."

This noble word I fain would read as symbol of my hearty wish to belong entirely to you.

In the French metropolis, too, my works once gained devoted and appreciative friends; yet I soon had to dismiss the hopes those friends had formed of my effect on Paris, for I recognised that in French taste and the institutions ruled thereby there dwelt no "freedom": what is not French, the Frenchman cannot comprehend, and the first condition for him who would try to please the French is to conform to their taste and its edicts.

A success such as that of my "Lohengrin" in Bologna is inconceivable in any town of France. Only under the sign of "Libertas" was it possible for a work so completely at variance with all the habits of an audience, as mine with those of the Bolognese, to be forthwith greeted as a long familiar friend. Thus the Italian proved that his own productive force is still unspent, that the mother-womb whence the Italian spirit once re-begat the world of Beauty is still susceptible of every noble fecundation: for he alone who can create, feels free to adopt without reserve the creation of another.

While heartily begging you, most worshipful Burgomaster, to convey my profoundest thanks to the honourable municipality whose generous resolution you have transmitted to me, I at like time assure you of my sincere desire to shew myself worthy of that high honour, and to leave nothing undone to achieve this end. In any event I hope to visit my esteemed fellow-citizens in the autumn of 1875,* if not earlier, and then to convince you all by a hearty hand-grip of what I write you to-day from afar:—that I am proud to be allowed to call myself an honorary freeman of Bologna!

With the most distinguished regard, I have the honour to subscribe myself

Your

devoted

RICHARD WAGNER.

Bayreuth, 1. Oct. 1872.

* The first Bayreuth Festival would appear at this time to have been fixed for the summer of 1875.—TR.

V.

TO FRIEDRICH NIETZSCHE,

PROFESSOR OF CLASSICAL PHILOLOGY AT THE UNIVERSITY OF BÂLE.

ESTEEMED FRIEND,

I HAVE just read the pamphlet you sent me of Dr.phil. *Ulrich von Wilamowitz-Möllendorff*, and this "Reply" to your "Birth of Tragedy from the spirit of Music" has left me with certain impressions which I fain would get rid of by asking you a few, perhaps surprising questions, in the hope of moving you to an answer as pregnant as was your explanation of Greek Tragedy.

Before all I should like you to explain an educational phenomenon which I have remarked in my own case. I believe there can have been no boy more devoted to classic antiquity, than myself at the time I attended the Kreuzschule in Dresden; though Greek mythology and history were my chief attractions, I also felt drawn to the study of the Greek language itself with a power that made me almost unruly in my shirking of the Latin. How far my case was normal, I cannot judge; but I may add that my favourite master at the Kreuzschule, Dr *Sillig*—still living, I hope—was so particularly pleased with my enthusiasm that he strongly urged me to adopt Philology as my profession. Now I well remember how my later teachers at the Nikolai and Thoma schools in Leipzig entirely rooted out these tastes and likings, and moreover can explain it by the manners of those gentlemen; yet in time I began to doubt those tastes and likings ever having had a deeper root in me at all, as they seemed to turn so soon into their opposite. Only in further course of my development did I grow conscious, through the constant outcrop of at least those likings, that something in me had indeed been stifled by a fatal plan of schooling. Again and again amid the most absorbing labours of a life entirely divergent from such studies I won my only breath of freedom by a plunge into the ancient world, however much I now was crippled by having wellnigh lost all memory of its speech. On the contrary, while envying *Mendelssohn* his philologic fluency, I could but wonder at its not having prevented him from writing just his music for dramas of Sophocles, since, with all my ignorance, I still had more respect for the spirit of Antiquity than he here seemed to betray. Other musicians have I also known, who could make no use of their fluent Greek in all their Kapellmeistering, composing, and musicing in general; whereas I myself (strange to say) had wrested from my hampered intercourse with the Antique an ideal for my every view of Mus-ic. Be that as it may, a dim feeling has arisen in me that the Antique Spirit must lie as little within the sphere of our teachers of Greek as an understanding of French history and culture, for instance, can be presupposed on behalf of our French-masters. But now comes Dr.phil. U. W. von Möllendorff, and quite seriously asserts that it is the object of Philologic science to train our youths in such a way "that Classical Antiquity shall yield them that only Imperishable which promises the favour of the Muses, and Classical Antiquity alone can give in equal purity and abundance, the Substance in their bosom and the Form in their mind."

With this magnificent apostrophe still thrilling through me, I looked round in the newly-risen German Empire for the blessings flowing from the culture of that Philologic science; blessings which surely should be manifest, since, hedged by its own inviolability, it hitherto has trained our German youth on principles none dared to question. Well, the first thing to strike me, was that everyone among us who lays claim to the Muses' favour, our whole artistic and poetic world in fact, jogs on without the faintest recourse to philology. At any rate that thorough sense of Speech, which should result from making philology the basis of all our classical studies, does not appear to have extended its functions to the treatment of our German mother-tongue; through the ever ranker spread of jargon from our journals to the books of our art-and-literature historians, one soon will have to rack one's brains with every word that comes to one's pen, to discover if it really belongs to German etymology or has been borrowed from a Wisconsin bourse-sheet. However, though things look black on the field of belles lettres, one might say that Philology has nothing to do with that, as she has pledged her service rather to the scientific than the artistic Muses. In that case we must seek her influence in the faculties of our High Schools? But theologists, jurists and physicians deny that they have aught to do with her. So the philologists must instruct each other, presumably with the one object of turning out philologists, i.e. Gymnasium-masters and University-professors, who will bake a fresh batch of Gymnasium-masters and University-professors in their turn? That I can understand; the motto is, to preserve the purity of the science, and teach the State such respect for it that substantial salaries to philological professors and such-like shall always be incumbent on its conscience. Yet no! Dr.phil. U. W. v. M. expressly states that it is a matter of training German youth by all sorts of "ascetic" methods for "that only Imperishable which promises the favour of the Muses." So there dwells in Philology, after all, the tendence toward a higher, a truly productive culture? Very probably—so I should say! Only, through a peculiar process in her present discipline, that tendence seems to be put quite out of sight. For thus much is evident, that the Philology of now-adays exerts no jot of influence on the general state of German culture; while the theologic faculty supplies us with parsons and prelates (*Consistorialräthe*), the juristic with lawyers and judges, the medical with doctors—all practically useful citizens—Philology gives us nothing but philologists, of use to no one but themselves.

You see, the Indian Brahmins were not of more exalted rank, and one therefore may await from them a sacred word from time to time. And indeed we are awaiting it: we await the man who for once shall step from out this wondrous sphere and tell us laymen, without learned terms and terrible quotations, *what* it is that the initiate perceive behind the veil of their incomprehensible researches, and whether it is worth the trouble of supporting so expensive a caste. For that must be something great and grand, something widely cultivating; not this elegant tinkling of bells with which they put us off from time to time in their fashionable lectures to "mixed" audiences. But that great and grand, for which we wait, seems very hard of utterance: here must reign a strange, a wellnigh ghastly dread, as though one feared that if one dispensed for once with all the mysterious attributes of philologic state, all quotations, notes and mutual compliments of major and minor colleagues, and let daylight shine on the plain interior, one must necessarily expose some mournful malady contracted by the science. I can conceive that nothing might remain for the man who undertook a thing like this, but to stretch forth a hand of might, and transfuse life into the purely philological profession from those fountains of human knowledge which have waited hitherto in vain for fertilising by Philology.

A philologist who resolved on such a deed, however, would presumably be treated much as you are treated now, my friend, after deciding to publish your luminous treatise on the genesis of Tragedy. At the first glance we could see that we here had to do with a philologist who was speaking to us, and not to his colleagues; so our heart beat high for once, and we regained a courage already lost completely through our reading the customary quotation-full and deadly context-empty philologisings upon Homer, the Tragic poets and the like. This time we had text but no notes; from the mountain-top we looked across the spreading plains, without disturbance by the brawl of peasants in the tavern down below. But it seems, we are not to be left in peaceful possession: Philology insists that you never have quitted her grounds, are therefore no emancipate, but a mere deserter, and the note-cudgel shall be spared neither you nor us. In fact its hail has begun already: a Dr.phil. has launched the rightful philologic thunderbolt. Yet at this time of year such a storm is soon over: while it rages a sensible person stops at home; one gives a wide berth to a bull let loose, and Socrates held it absurd to reply to the hoof of an ass with the toe of a man. Still, something remains to explain to us mere onlookers, something we cannot quite understand in all this affair.

For just that reason I address myself to you.

We had not believed there was so much rudeness in the "service of the Muses," nor that their "favour" left behind it such a lack of polish as we here perceive in one who possesses "that only Imperishable." A classical scholar who in the same sentence despatches a "*meinthalb*" on the heels of a "*meinthalben*," to us seems little better than a Berlin loafer of bygone days, with his stagger from beer to schnapps: yet this is precisely what Dr. phil. U. W. v. M. affords us on page 18 of his pamphlet. Again, if one knows nothing of Philology, like ourselves, one certainly defers with all respect to the statements of such a gentleman when they repose on huge quotations from the archives of the guild; but we fall into the direst doubt, not so much of that scholar's unintentional non-understanding of your essay, as of his capacity to understand the very simplest argument, when he attributes to you an optimistic meaning in your quotation from Goethe: "Das ist deine Welt! das heisst eine Welt!" ["Behold thy world! A world indeed!"] and therefore deems needful to explain to you (with indignation at your not even being able to understand your Goethe!) that "Faust is speaking ironically." How is one to call such a thing? A question perhaps too hard to answer on the public road of literature.

For my own part such an experience as I have reaped

in this instance is most disheartening. You know how earnestly I advocated the pursuit of classical studies a few years ago, in my essay on "German Art and German Policy," and how I foretold from their increasing neglect by our artists and writers a progressive deterioration of our national culture. But what is the use of taking pains with one's philology? From J. Grimm I took an ancient-German "Heilawac"; moulded it into "Weiawaga" (a form we still may recognise in "Weihwasser"), to make it more pliant to my purpose; passed on from that to its next of kin, in "wogen" and "wiegen," "wellen" and "wallen"; and thus built up a root-syllabic melody for my water-maidens, after the analogy of the "Eia popeia" of our nursery-songs. What befalls me? By our journalistic street-arabs I am hooted to the very doors of the "Augsburger Allgemeine," and upon this "proverbial wigala weia"—as he pleases to call it—a Doctor of Philology now founds his contempt for my "so-called poetry"! And this in the early-German orthography of his pamphlet, whilst no stage-compound of our modish writers is too washy and affected (as I lately discovered) to be regarded by Philological expounders of the Nibelungen-myth as a marvellous completion of our old Folk-poetry.

Of a truth, my friend, you owe us a word or two of explanation. For in those whom I mean by "we" you have people filled with blackest fears for *German culture*. What adds to these fears is the singularly high repute in which that culture stands to-day among foreigners, only recently acquainted with its former buddings; a reputation that reacts upon us like narcotic incense, which we take and waft before each other. Undoubtedly each nation has its germ of cretinism: with the French we see their absinthe finishing what their Académie began, to wit a foolish attitude of childlike ridicule of everything not understood at once, and therefore excluded by that Académie from their national scheme of culture. True, our Philology has not as yet the *power* of that Académie, nor is our beer as perilous as absinthe; but there are other qualities of the

German—such as his envy and its sister spitefulness, allied with an insincerity the more pernicious as it wears the look of an old-time sturdiness—which are so dangerous that they might easily rank as substitutes for the poisons we have not.

How stands it with our German educational institutes?

That question we address to you in special, whom a distinguished master of philology chose from many to take so young the chair of teacher, and since you there so quickly won your laurels that you could dare to boldly step from out a vicious circle and point its mischief with creative hand.

We allow you time in plenty. Nothing presses, and least of all that Dr.phil. who bids you descend from your chair; a thing you certainly would never do, even to oblige that gentleman himself, as there is little likelihood of his being chosen to succeed you in the place where you have worked. What we await from you is a lifelong task for the man we need the sorest, a man such as you have shewn yourself to all who ask from the noblest wellspring of the German Spirit—its deeply-inward earnestness in all it touches—enlightenment on the form to be taken by German culture if it is ever to help the re-arisen nation to its noblest goals.

Thus greets you from his heart your

RICHARD WAGNER.

Bayreuth, 12. June 1872.

VI.

ON THE NAME "MUSIKDRAMA."

E often read just now of a "Musikdrama," also hear of a society in Berlin, for instance, that proposes to help this Music-drama forward—yet without our being able to form an accurate idea of what is meant. I certainly have reason to suppose that this term was invented for sake of honouring my later dramatic works with a distinctive classification; but the less I have felt disposed to accept it, the more have I perceived an inclination in other quarters to adopt the name for a presumably new art-genre, which would appear to have been bound to evolve in answer to the temper and tendences of the day, even without my intervention, and now to lie ready as a cosy nest for everyone to hatch his musical eggs in.

I cannot indulge in the flattering view, that things are so pleasantly situate; and the less, as I don't know how to read the title "Musikdrama." When we unite two substantives to form one word, with any understanding of the spirit of our language, by the first we always signify in some sort of way the object of the second; so that "Zukunftsmusik," though invented in derision of me, had its sense as "music for the future." * But "Musikdrama" similarly interpreted as "drama for the object of music" would have no sense at all, were it not point-blank the old familiar libretto, which at anyrate was a drama expressly constructed for music. Yet this certainly is not what we mean: merely our sense of literary propriety has become so blunted through a constant reading of the farrago of our

* Namely, for a time when one could get it performed without bungling.—R. WAGNER.

newspaper-writers and other beaux esprits, that we believe we may put any meaning we choose to the nonsensical words they coin, and in the present case we use "Musikdrama" to denote the very opposite of the sense the word implies.

Upon closer inspection, however, we find that the solecism here consists in the now favourite conversion of an adjectival predicate into a substantival prefix: one had begun by saying "musical drama." Yet it perhaps was not solely that evil habit, that brought about the abbreviation into "Musikdrama," but also a hazy feeling that no drama could possibly be "musical," like an instrument or (in rare enough events) a prima donna. A "musical drama," taken strictly, would be a drama that made music itself, or was good for making music with, or even that understood music, somewhat as our musical reporters. As this would not do, the mental confusion thought better to hide behind a wholly senseless word: for "Musikdrama" was a name which nobody had heard before, and one felt assured that nobody would ever dream of wilfully misconstruing so seriously-combined a word by its analogy with "Musikdosen" [musical snuffbox] and the like.

Now the serious meaning, intended by the term, was probably an actual "drama set to music." The mental emphasis would therefore fall on the "drama," which one regarded as differing from the former opera-libretto, and differing in that a dramatic plot was not to be simply trimmed to the needs of traditional operatic music, but the musical structure itself was to be shaped by the requirements characteristic of an actual drama. But if the "drama" was thus the main affair, it surely ought to have been placed before the "music" which it governed, and, somewhat like "Tanzmusik" or "Tafelmusik" [dance, and banquet-music], we then should have had to say "Dramamusik." Into this absurdity, however, one did not care to fall; twist and turn it as one might, "music" remained the real encumbrance to the naming, though everybody dimly felt that it was the chief concern in spite of all appearances, and the more so when that music was invited to develop and put forth its amplest powers through its association with an actual drama.

The obstacle to devising a name for this artwork was accordingly, in any event, the assumed necessity of indicating that the new whole had been formed by welding two disparate elements, music and drama, together. And certainly the greatest difficulty is to place "music" in a proper position toward "drama," since it can be brought into no equality therewith, as we have just seen, and must rank as either much more or much less than "drama." * The reason surely lies in the fact that the word "music" denotes an *art*, originally the whole assemblage of the arts, whilst "drama" strictly denotes a *deed* of art. In coupling words together it is easy to tell by the intelligibleness of the resulting compound whether we really still understand its constituent parts, taken separately, or merely employ them after a conventional usage. The primary meaning of "drama" is a *deed* or *action*: as such, displayed upon the stage, it at first formed but a portion of the Tragedy, i.e. the sacrificial choral chant, but at last invaded it from end to end and thus became the main affair. By its name one now denoted for all ages an action shewn upon the stage, and, to lay stress on this being a performance to look at, the place of assembly was called the "theatron," the looking-room. Our "Schauspiel" [strictly "look-game" or "show-play"] is therefore a very sensible name for what the Greeks more naïvely still called "drama," for it still more definitely expresses the characteristic development of an initial part into the ultimate main object. But Music is placed in an utterly false relation to this "show-play," if she now is to form but a part of that whole; as such she is wholly superfluous and disturbing, and for this reason has at last been quite excluded from

* "Das Schwierigste hierbei ist jedenfalls, die 'Musik' in eine richtige Stellung zum 'Drama' zu bringen, da sie, wie wir dieses soeben ersehen mussten, mit diesem in keine ebenbürtige Verbindung zu bringen ist, und uns entweder viel mehr, oder viel weniger als das Drama gelten muss."

the stricter Play. Of a truth she is "the part that once was all," and even now she feels called to re-assume her ancient dignity, as very mother-womb of Drama. Yet in this high calling she must neither stand before nor behind the Drama: she is no rival, but its mother. She sounds, and what she sounds ye see upon the stage; for that she gathered you together: what she is, ye never can but faintly dream; so she opens your eyes to behold her through the scenic likeness, as a mother tells her children legends shadowing the mysteries of religion.

The stupendous works of their Æschylus the Athenians called not dramas, but left them with the holy name of their descent: "tragedies," sacrificial chants in celebration of the god inspiring them. Happy they, to have to puzzle out no name for them! They had the most unheard-of artwork, and—left it nameless. But there came the great critics, the redoubtable reporters; abstract ideas were found, and where these ran short came words for word's sake. The good Polonius edifies us with a handsome list of them in "Hamlet." The Italians capped it with a "*Dramma per musica*," which expresses much the same idea, though more grammatically phrased, as our "Musikdrama"; but one manifestly was not satisfied with this expression, and the curious outcome of the changes introduced by vocal virtuosi had to accept a name as nothing-saying as the genre itself. "Opera," plural of "opus," this new variety of "works" was dubbed; the Italians made a female of it, the French a male, so that the variety seemed to have turned out *generis utriusque*. I believe one could find no apter criticism of "Opera," than to allow this name as legitimate an origin as that of "Tragedy"; in neither case was it a matter of reason (*Vernunft*), but a deep-set instinct here expressed a thing of nameless nonsense, there a thing of sense indicibly profound.

Now I advise my professional competitors to retain the designation "opera," on second thought, for their musical works intended for the present theatre: it leaves them where they are, gives them no false colour, lifts them above all rivalry with their librettist, and if they are blest with good ideas for an aria, a duet, or even a drinking-chorus, they will please and give us something worth acknowledging, without having to overtax their strength to spoil their prettiest fancies. In every age there have been not only pantomimists, but cithern-players, flautists, and finally cantores: if some of their tribe were called for once to do a thing beyond their kind and custom, it was only very solitary units, whose unexampled rarity the finger of History underlines across the centuries and tens thereof; but never has a *genre* arisen thence, a genre in which, once given its proper name, the extra-ordinary lay ready for the common use of every fumbler. As for myself, with the best of will I should scarcely know what name to give the child that smiles from out my works a trifle shyly on a good part of the world we live in. Herr W. H. Riehl, as he somewhere has said, loses sight and hearing at my operas, for with some he hears, with others sees: how shall one name so inaudible, invisible a thing? I should almost have felt disposed to take my stand on its visibility, and abide by the "show-play," as I would gladly have called my dramas *deeds of Music brought to sight* (ersichtlich gewordene Thaten der Musik). But that would have been quite an art-philosophical title, fit to grace the catalogue of the future Polonii of our art-struck courts; since one may assume that, after their soldiers' successes, our Princes next will wish the Theatre led onward in a corresponding German sense. Only, in spite of all the "play" I offer, which many declare to touch the monstrous, there really would be far too little to see; as for instance I have been rebuked for not introducing into the second act of "Tristan" a brilliant court-ball, during which the hapless pair of lovers might hide themselves at the proper time in some shrubbery or other, where their discovery would create quite a startling scandal, with all the usual consequences. Instead there passes little more than music in this act, which unfortunately seems to be so very much music that people with the organisation of Herr W. H. Riehl quite lose their hearing through it; the more's the pity, as I give them next to nothing to see.

As folk would not let my poor works even pass for "operas," mainly because of their great dissimilarity to "Don Juan," I have had to console myself with handing them to the theatres without any designation of their genre at all; by this device I also think of abiding for just as long as I have to do with our theatres, which rightly recognise no other genre than "Opera," and, let one give them never so strict a "music-drama," would make of it an "opera" notwithstanding. To boldly emerge from the whole confusion, I lit, as known, on the thought of a *Bühnenfestspiel* [stage-festival-play], which I am hoping to bring about at Bayreuth with help from my friends. The name suggested itself through the character of my undertaking; for I knew of *Singing-festivals*, *Gymnastic-fêtes* and so forth, and could well imagine a theatre-feast—in which the *stage* and what takes place upon it, appropriately termed a *play*, would of course be the chief affair. But if any of the visitors to this Bühnenfestspiel shall chance to preserve a remembrance thereof, to him there may likewise occur a name for that thing I now propose to offer my friends as an unnamed deed of art.

VII.

PROLOGUE TO A READING OF THE "GÖTTERDÄMMERUNG" BEFORE A SELECT AUDIENCE IN BERLIN.

DESIROUS of your closer attention to a work which may have chiefly attracted your notice as a musical product, I believe I shall best attain that end by reading out a portion of the dramatic poem on which it is founded; for I thereby hope to shew you not only the character in which I view that work myself, but also that feature which compelled me to devise a plan of reproduction quite foreign to the habits of our Opera-house and its public.

People talk of innovations made by me in Opera: for my own part I am conscious of having, if not achieved, at least deliberately striven for this one advantage, the raising of the dramatic dialogue itself to the main subject of musical treatment; whereas in Opera proper the moments of lyrical delay, and mostly violent arrest of the action, had hitherto been deemed the only ones of possible service to the musical composition.

The longing to raise the Opera to the dignity of genuine Drama could never wake and wax in the musician, before great masters had enlarged the province of his art in that spirit which now has made our German music acknowledgedly victorious over all its rivals. Through the fullest application of this legacy of our great masters we have arrived at uniting Music so completely with the Drama's action, that this very marriage enables the action itself to gain that ideal freedom—i.e. release from all necessity of appealing to abstract reflection—which our great poets sought on many a road, to fall at last a-pondering on the selfsame possibility of attaining it through Music.

By incessantly revealing to us the inmost motives of the action, in their widest ramifications, Music at like time makes it possible to display that action itself in drastic definition: as the characters no longer need to tell us of their impulses [or "grounds of action"—*Beweggründe*] in terms of the reflecting consciousness, their dialogue thereby gains that naïve pointedness (*Präzision*) which constitutes the very life of Drama. Again, whilst Antique Tragedy had to confine its dramatic dialogue to separate sections strewn between the choruses delivered in the Orchestra—those chants in which Music gave to the drama its higher meaning—in the Modern Orchestra, the greatest artistic achievement of our age, this archetypal element goes hand in hand with the action itself, unsevered from the dialogue, and in a profounder sense may be said to embrace all the action's motives in its mother-womb.

Thus, besides the restoration of its naïve pointedness, it became possible to give the dialogue an extension covering the entire drama; and it is this that enables me to read to you to-day in guise of a bare dramatic poem a work that owes its origin to nothing but the feasibility of carrying it out completely in music: for I believe I may submit it as a play in dialogue to the same judgment we are wont to invoke with a piece indited for the Spoken Play.

The quality I thus have claimed for my work not only emboldens me to shew it you from this one side without alarm, but has also been my principal reason for the unusual steps I am taking to place it before the German public in its entirety; in the one case as in the other I wish to commend it, not to an assemblage of opera-lovers, but to a gathering of truly educated persons earnestly concerned for an original cultivation of the German Spirit.

Bayreuth.

*　　*
*

Under this heading I have assembled all that to me seemed worth recording anent the plan for a performance of my stage-festival-play "*Der Ring des Nibelungen*" under exceptional circumstances, a plan at last nearing its realisation. I accordingly begin with the "Final report on the fate" of my work and its plan, to impress once again on my readers' attention the character in which I wish my undertaking judged.

R. WAGNER.

I.

FINAL REPORT ON THE FATES AND CIRCUMSTANCES

THAT ATTENDED THE EXECUTION OF THE STAGE-FESTIVAL-PLAY "DER RING DES NIBELUNGEN" DOWN TO THE FOUNDING OF WAGNER-SOCIETIES.*

HE kindly reader will have recognised the hopeless mood in which I wrote the closing words of the preface to the publication of my Bühnenfestspiel, reprinted at the end of the sixth volume of my Collected Writings and Poems †: as that mood had prompted me to launch my poem as a piece of literature, it also made me act at last with not much greater pity toward the finished portions of my musical composition. If I trimmed up an excerpt or two from my scores for a concert-performance, I might flatter myself with the same idea as suggested that publication, namely that it perhaps would be not impossible to attract by this means the notice I needed for my work and the tendence it followed. In fact, considering that the music had been penned, as no other,

* While it may be necessary to explain that "execution" (*Ausführung*) here simply refers to the author's own part of the work, and not to its public performance, the word "final" must be taken in reference to the two earlier pamphlets, written in 1871, from which Richard Wagner compiled the present article (1873). The re-arrangement of their contents, part of which had been embodied in the "Epilogue to the Nibelung's Ring" (see Vol. III.) involved his making certain additions, omissions and verbal alterations in the text. To detail these changes, would simply confuse the reader without serving any conceivable purpose: the chief particulars, however, will be found in my notes on pages 256, 260 and 274 of Vol. III. and page 318 of that in hand. I may add that both this and the following article are to be regarded as addressed, in particular, to the early "Wagner-Vereins."—TR.

† Volume III. of the present series.—TR.

with a single eye to a great dramatic whole, it was astonishing to see even these desultory fragments received by the public with the liveliest favour: an experience which, given a little rightmindedness, should have effected a striking alteration in the current opinion that with my conception of this work I had fallen into a chaos of unintelligibleness and impossibility. Nevertheless the old story went on, that it was well to have nothing to do with me.

These impressions so preyed on my mind at last, that I felt driven to take something in hand which should lift me out of all the atmosphere of wishes, hopes, imaginings, and especially exertions, surrounding my opus magnum. I drafted the "Meistersinger von Nürnberg."—The musical composition of this new work had made but little headway, however, when there came into my actual life the "Prince" I had asked of Fate in those closing words.

No poetic diction, nor a whole poetic dictionary, could possibly convey the moving beauty of the event that entered my life through the summons of a noble-minded King. For indeed it was a King who called to me in chaos: *Hither! Complete thy work: I will it!*

The remoter future—should my work be then still living—cannot be spared a knowledge of the circumstances which have hindered my work from becoming a full-fledged deed, from that decisive meeting to the present day. Now that I and my unusual artistic project had been placed in broad daylight, it really appeared as if all the ill-will that had lurked before in ambush was determined to make an open attack in full force. Indeed it seemed as though no single interest, of all those represented by our Press and our Society, was not stung to the quick by the composition and plan of production of my work. To stay the disgraceful direction taken by this feud in every circle of society, which recklessly assailed alike protector and protected, I could but decide to strip the scheme of that majestic character which my patron had accorded it, and turn it into a channel less provocative of universal wrath.* Indeed I even tried to divert public attention from the whole affair by spending a little hard-won rest on the completion of the score of my "Meistersinger," a work with which I should not appear to be quitting the customary groove of performances at the theatre.

But, for all its favourable reception by the public, the experiences I made with the fate of this very work, on the one hand, on the other with the spirit of our German stage, determined me to hold unflinchingly aloof from any further dealings with the latter. Owing to the peculiar nature of the German sense of art, whoever has had serious dealings with the German theatre in the hope of meeting some power of discrimination, some support by an energetic expression of will, on the part of public taste, must have perceived at once that his efforts were totally fruitless and could only stir up strife against himself. Thus nothing could persuade me to take a share in the attempts at performing single sections of my larger work, though I myself had taken the first step thereto in my earlier bending to the storm. I am even ignorant of the exact way in which those attempts fell out, since my friends fully recognised that I should be spared a report of the details.†

Through the sacrifice herein involved, however, it became possible for me to obey the first command of my exalted benefactor: *Complete thy work*! Arrived once more in

* In rendering the latter half of this sentence I have been obliged to slightly paraphrase it, to make its meaning clearer. What our author alludes to, is obviously the grandiose project entertained by Ludwig II. in 1865, of building a monumental theatre for the *Ring*, to be connected by a bridge across the Isar with a new avenue extending to the royal palace in Munich. This plan fell through, as is commonly known, owing to the bitter jealousy of courtiers, place-hunters, and the press. In fact it was not until 1871, after the epoch-making reconsolidation of Germany, that Richard Wagner's hopes of getting even a "provisional theatre" built for his work, no matter in what German "nook," revived at all.—TR.

† *Das Rheingold* and *Die Walküre* were produced in Munich on Sep. 22, 1869, and June 26, 1870, respectively. Through an oversight, in my note to Vol. IV. p. 305 of these translations the year of the first performance of *Das Rheingold* is erroneously given as "1868."—TR.

that peaceful refuge whence I once had gazed upon the soundless world of Alps while mapping out that overweening plan, remote from every clamour I was at last to be permitted to bring its composition to an end.*

Now the same faithful guardian who watched over the completion of my work, has also made it possible for me to tread in hope and confidence the path that shall lead to its performance in the mode first planned. For if a whole community (*Gesammtheit*) once set itself against the mandate of one master mind, with a work completed under shelter of this mighty one I now have found a fresh community to whom, by its own will, to commit the realisement of that scheme. I found it through *an appeal addressed to the friends of my art*, commencing with the exposition of my plan as contained in that Preface to the poem of my Bühnenfestspiel, and concluding with a statement of the character of my present enterprise and the benefits I believed it would offer to the German Theatre in general, as quoted below.

"In the republication of my older plan I have already indicated that the special nature of my larger work makes it essential for me to secure it a completely correct performance, since experience has taught me that the most lamentable feature in the modern German Theatre is the criminal incorrectness of all its mode of reproduction, with perhaps the solitary exception of the very humblest class. The reason I have frequently explained elsewhere, and here will merely define it as residing in the *unoriginality* of what our theatres take in hand: for the fact of our stage-performances being simply imperfect, and often quite defacing imitations of a non-German theatric art, can least of all be cloaked from sight by our German authors them-

* The orchestral sketch of *Die Götterdämmerung* was completed on Feb. 9, 1872, though the full score was not finished till Nov. 21, 1874. See H. S. Chamberlain's "*Richard Wagner*," page 312.—Tr.

selves deriving both style and conception of their works for the stage from nowhere save abroad. Therefore whoever knows no other Theatre than ours, must necessarily form a false idea of theatric art in general; which leads the truly educated to despise that art, the larger public of less reflecting theatre-goers to a decadence of taste whose reaction on the spirit of our stage is bound to drive it to yet deeper depravation.

"Hence the sole hope of profiting our Theatre itself, in course of time, to me appears to be this: not to commit to it in the first place works whose very originality demands the highest correctness if they are to make the right impression on the public, since this Theatre can only maim or utterly efface the tendence they embody. By withdrawing them entirely from its baleful influence, on the contrary, such works could be made to help our Theatre as well; for, upheld to it in full correctness and unspoilt purity, they now would constitute intelligible models of what it could not understand before.

"The German Theatre can never be helped by a mere injunction of artistic maxims, for it has become a habit as it stands, and thus a power. Its faults lie rooted in its whole organism, which has settled to a vicious copy of the foreign, just like our French fashions in dress. As we can but rate ourselves too weak to shake it, and if we have at heart the unfolding of the German spirit's individuality on this incomparably influential field of art, we must therefore take in eye an altogether novel institution, as remote as possible from the operation of that Theatre. The outlines of such an institution were suggested to me by my own sore need. As prefigured in that Preface, it would admirably match the national body politic now evolving in the re-arisen German *Reich*, since its operative forces would continue to belong to the single parts of the whole. *At first it should offer no more than the localised point of periodic meeting of Germany's best theatrical forces for practice and presentation of a higher German Original-style in their art, an exercise impossible in ordinary course of their labours.*

"For the bringing about of stage-performances of this stamp I rely in the first place on the interest taken in my own dramatic works by the German public, since I assume that it would be granted in still larger measure to my longest work when the public heard that it was written in a style whose justice I could only prove by a performance of such correctness as nothing can ensure, at present, save the execution of the plan proposed. And here it is not the success of my work as such, but of the complete propriety of its stage-portrayal, on which I reckon to awake the desire for a periodic repetition of similar performances; a series to be gradually extended perchance to every class of dramatic products, and for which one would always have to choose such works as possessed a special claim to correctness of representation in virtue of their originality of conception and sterling German style.

"As I have fully discussed in other places the benefits that would spring from a fulfilment of this fond presumption, from every point of view, I here will merely add my notion of the way in which the progressive scheme may be practically carried out.

"In the first instance I must limit myself to an appeal to true friends of my art and art-tendences for their active assistance in the attainment of my immediate object, namely a performance of my grand Bühnenfestspiel according to my mind. I therefore hereby formally request them to simply send me in their names as approvers of my enterprise. If I am so fortunate as thus to win sufficient hope, these favourers of my undertaking shall then be notified of the simple means of forming themselves into a Union (*Verein*) of promoters and attenders at the performances to be prepared by me. Further, I should consider the project as stamped with a still more eminently national character, if non-German friends of my art announced their adhesion to this voluntary alliance; for I may assume that the great attention paid by educated foreigners to the German art-spirit in this direction, and the hopes they cherish of its beneficial influence on their own country too, are mainly concerned with the *purity* and *originality* of that spirit's evolution, and therefore with the very thing that so especially concerns ourselves in the best national sense.

"Should this first and voluntary enterprise be attended with a happy issue—an issue which I imagine would throw a favourable light on my ulterior aim—measures would next have to be devised for consolidating the single transient undertaking into a really national-artistic institution. As I already have stated my views of the character and tendence proper to such an institution, and particularly the points which should distinguish it from any of our standing theatres, for the moment there only remains to say that it might best be figured as arising from a second union, that of all existing German theatres, or at least the well-endowed among them. If I have left this second union altogether out of count in my immediate plan, it has been because of my rooted conviction that, with the present tendence of these theatres and their managers, any appeal addressed to them by me would in the best event have led to the greatest misunderstandings, and consequently to a dire confusion. Only the correct impression, which I hope to see produced by a favourable outcome of my undertaking, could spread the needful light on this side too; and in any case a good effect upon these theatres could be expected from that permanent institution only in the event of its having been called for and supported by themselves.

"To give it the right foundation, might then become an earnest object of some imperial authority nobly anxious for the nation's moral weal. For it is positive that a nation's public morality may fitly be gauged by the character of its public art: but no art has so strong an influence on a people's heart and fancy, as that which every day is set before it in the Theatre. Though we may comfort ourselves that the highly dubious action of the Theatre in Germany has not been caused by a decline in the nation's morals, and if we admit that it so far has led to nothing worse than a perversion of public taste, yet it is certain that an improvement of taste, and necessarily thereby of manners [or "morals"—*Sitten*], must be started and sustained with the utmost energy by the Theatre. To have moved the nation's leaders to weigh these thoughts, would in nowise be the smallest satisfaction I could reap from a happy result of my undertaking announced herewith."

If I may take it that the foregoing leaves no doubt as to the light in which I view the undertaking for whose furtherance I appealed to the friends of my art, I now should like to define the character I ascribe to that "other *community*" addressed above.

For this purpose I must first be allowed to quote from my account of the fate of my "Nibelungenring"* an expression by which I tried to explain my decision to turn back from Paris to Germany for all my future artistic plans. There I said: "It was my very perception of the unparalleled disorder and confusion of its *surface* art-affairs,† that sharpened my sight for the *secret* lying deep beneath." This "secret" I now had to seek beneath the covering of that sorry surface, to bring it into open daylight together with the secret living clear in my own breast. After desperate excursions which brought me into the strangest company, it has been to me a great, nay a redeeming privilege, to find this sought-for outer secret as the *genuine Essence of the German Spirit.* Amid troubles of every kind had I to gain my knowledge that the hideous aspect under which this spirit met the outward eye was merely its disfigurement; that the very poorness, nay in many respects the absurdity of the figure it presented, might

* At the close of the sixth volume of these Collected Writings and Poems. —R. WAGNER.—Vol. iii. page 271, of the present series.—TR.

† The "its" refers to Germany, whilst the word "öffentlich," which I have rendered as "surface" in this and the following sentence, literally means "open, or public."—TR.

upon closer consideration be held as witness of its native truth (*ursprüngliche Tugend*). History teaches us the deeply earnest stake for which the German sacrificed his outward independence during more than twice a hundred years; that for over two centuries he at once was recognised by other European nations as a "German" for reason of the shyness of his outward bearing, the clumsiness, in fact the ridiculousness of his public actions—is less disgrace to him, considering the wretched circumstances in which his life dragged on, than if he had worn his livery with a grace and assurance that would have transformed him past all recognition, somewhat as French Culture has transformed the Pole. From the very blunders he committed in public it was to be concluded that his genuine nature here never came into play, for its disguise was palpable at every instant. Not to lose heart in face of so doleful a deception, required a faith wellnigh as strong as that the Christian has to maintain in face of the deceptive semblance of the world itself. This faith inspired a German statesman of our day with the stupendous courage to disclose to all the world in valiant deeds his secret of the nation's Political power. The secret to whose disclosure I long to contribute, will consist in the proof that the now-feared German is henceforth also to be respected in his Public Art.

Of a truth the faith in this secret's power, and in the possibility of its disclosure, demanded scarcely smaller courage than that statesman's, who had only to take the measure of the force stored up in an organisation which had never ceased developing, to make that force his own; whereas in the very sphere from which the most important influence might be exerted on the public—because it touches it the most effectively—the artist finds the absolute epitome of all that harms the sense-of-art hedged in behind an organisation of almost equal strength with that the statesman found in the defensive forces of the land.*

This "sphere" I believe I now have sufficiently indi-

* "Die männliche Wehrkraft der Nation," i.e. the "*Landwehr.*" For the second "organisation" see my footnote to the next paragraph but one.—TR.

cated: its perversion of the German spirit, not merely as regards æsthetic feeling, judgment, and receptiveness of mind, but extending even to the moral sense of all concerned in maintaining such a perverse state when once established—this was the bitterest foe to vanquish. An art not truly understood by anyone concerned therewith, and therefore neither respected nor loved for its own sake, in its every contact with the nation's life must spread a miasm of unworthiness; and the more general the influence of that art, the wider the poison's range of infection.*

Under that cloak whose folds descend to the very depths of our confederate officials' moral consciousness,† where was I to search for that "secret" answering to my own? It seems impossible to get the statesman to cast his glance this way. We should soon discover how absurd and frivolous the whole affair appears, if we asked one of our Parliaments to take it into discussion. That everything here [i.e. in Press and Theatre] is as disreputable as was our German Policy itself before its great arousal, can scarcely be perceptible to those who "want to take their sup in peace" after their exertions with the business of the State. We are only sorry that the gentlemen are given such bad and un-nutritious cooking; but if for once we

* In the pamphlet from which this portion was taken ("Bericht an den deutschen Wagner-Verein über die Umstände *etc.*," dated Lucerne Dec. 7, 1871) here followed: "It was in Paris that the treacherous conduct toward me of an 'artist' compatriot [Meyerbeer] roused universal indignation, even among the section of the French public most hostile to me, and prompted one of my friends to ask in despair if that marvellous Arnold Ruge was not right in declaring point-blank that the German was contemptible."—Tr.

† "Unter der bis in die Tiefen des sittlichen Bewusstseins dringenden Gewandung unserer giltigen und machtvoll organisirten Öffentlichkeit"—literally, "under that garment, reaching to the very depths of the moral consciousness, of our authorised and mightily organised Publicity." This most tantalising clause appears to refer to the alliance between the standing theatres and the Jew-led press, as self-styled representative of "the public," for a similar reference to a "fully-organised opposition" occurs in the article on Judaism in Music (the 1869 appendix—see Vol. III. pp. 108 and 114), where mention is also made of Wagner's Paris experiences of 1859-61. From the first words of the preceding paragraph it is obvious that the allusion here was purposely veiled by the author.—Tr.

cater for them with trouble and self-sacrifice, we can't prevent their swallowing the vilest stew to-morrow with no less gusto than the choicest food to-day; which justly annoys us again, and makes us leave their kitchen to the scullions.—

In search for the ideal side of German nature, I necessarily must turn to the community of executant artists, before the so-called Public. Here I began with the musician proper [i.e. the bandsman], and won encouragement from his ready apprehension of the right, so soon as duly shewn him. Next to him, though far more encased in bad habits, I found the musical mime; who, with any real talent, at once perceives and gladly treads his art's true sphere, if but the right example is held up before him.

Arguing from these two hopeful symptoms, I then inferred that an excellent performance by the artists could scarcely lack intelligent acceptance; and thus my further task was to awake the presentiment of such a higher satisfaction in all whose help I needed to promote my scheme. If alike by setting the example of good performances, as by supplying the key to artistic problems first clearly worked out by myself, I shall have roused the active attention of a sufficient number of the German public to enable me to reach my goal—in *that* I must recognise the "new community" I had to find. 'Twould be the core beneath the husk, which I believed in from the first: belonging to no special section of society, but permeating its every class, in my eyes it would represent the latent receptivity of German Feeling become responsive to original expression of the German Spirit on that domain which hitherto had been abandoned to the most un-German abuses.

II.

THE FESTIVAL-PLAYHOUSE AT BAYREUTH

WITH AN ACCOUNT OF THE LAYING OF ITS FOUNDATION-STONE.

To Baroness Marie von Schleinitz.*

Honoured Madam,

In drafting the following report for the patrons and well-wishers of my undertaking I singled out one name alone from those of all my aiders: it was his, whom an early death snatched from us; my living helpers I denoted by nothing but the characteristics of their contribution to the work itself. If to you I dedicate to-day a statement of affairs to none known better than to you yourself, it again is with the wish to breathe aloud the name of one to whose untiring zeal and energy my undertaking owes wellnigh exclusively its furtherance; a name pronounced by all my art's true friends with that sincere esteem in which forever I remain

Your grateful servant

RICHARD WAGNER.

Bayreuth, 1. May, 1873.

* Now Countess von Wolkenstein-Trostburg.—The article was also published separately by Fritzsch of Leipzig in 1873.—TR.

ITH the appeal I lately published to the friends of my art, to join me in the undertaking I had planned, I was addressing in the strictest sense a question to an unknown quantity, with whose constitution I was first to gain aquaintance from its answer.

Only to a handful of more intimate friends did I express my views as to the precise mode in which a solid form might be given to the interest I asked for. The youngest of these friends, the exceptionally talented and energetic *Karl Tausig*, embraced the matter as a task peculiarly falling to himself: together with a lady of distinguished rank and earnestly inclined towards my art, he sketched the plan of obtaining for my enterprise a sufficient number of patrons to subscribe the sum we estimated as the minimum required for building a provisional theatre, equipping a first-class stage with faultless scenery, and compensating the artists who were to be specially selected and assembled for our performances; a sum amounting to three hundred thousand thalers, to be collected in patronate-subscriptions of three hundred thalers each [£45,000, and £45]. Hardly had he begun to set his scheme in motion, than a sudden death removed him from us in his thirtieth year. My last word to him was committed to his gravestone: the present seems a not unworthy place to repeat it.

Epitaph on Karl Tausig.

"Reif sein zum Sterben,
"des Lebens zögernd spriessende Frucht,
"früh reif sie erwerben
"in Lenzes jäh erblühender Flucht,
"war es Dein Loos, war es Dein Wagen,—

"wir müssen Dein Loos wie Dein Wagen beklagen."—*

Deeply awed, to me the question erst addressed to a "community" had now become a question to Fate.

The little band of friends, so seriously lessened, worked on undaunted in the spirit of the friend deceased: a man of sovereign power was won as Patron, and unexpected readiness displayed itself among less powerful, ay, even among the powerless, to raise for me a new and vital power through association. At *Mannheim*, with the support of comrades just as earnestly disposed, a pre-eminently active friend of my art and tendences—a gentleman till then unknown to me in person †—called into life a union for the furtherance of my published project; a union which boldly took the name of "Richard Wagner Verein," and bore it in defiance of all scoffers. Its example soon was copied: under the same title a second Verein arose in *Vienna*, and similar societies were quickly formed in an ever-increasing number of German cities. Nay, from across the German frontiers, from Pesth and Brussels, London ‡ and at last New York, unions of like name and tendence conveyed to me their promises and greetings.

It then appeared high time for me to make the needful preparations for carrying out my enterprise. Already in the spring of 1871 I had chosen *Bayreuth* for my goal, after a quiet visit of inspection: all idea of using the famous opera-house of the Margraves I abandoned as soon as I had seen its interior; but the character and situation of the kindly city were all that I had wished for. So I repeated my visit in the winterly late-autumn of that year; this time to open direct negotiations with the Bayreuth town-authorities themselves. I have no need to here re-

* Tausig died July 17, 1871.—The epitaph may be roughly rendered:—

"Ripe for Death's harvest,
harvest of Life's last lingering fruit;
ripe all too early,
culled in the flower-fleet springtime of youth:
this thy endeavour, this was thy lot—
thy lot, thy endeavour, we cherish and mourn."—Tr.

† Emil Heckel.—Tr.

‡ Due to the exertions of Ed. Dannreuther.—Tr.

iterate the earnest thanks I owe those true and honoured men; in excess of every expectation, their courteous hospitality now gave my daring enterprise the friendly soil whereon to thrive in common with my livelong home. An unrivalledly beautiful and extensive freehold, hard by the town itself, was bestowed upon me for erection of the theatre I had in mind. Having arranged the structural scheme with a man of eminent experience and proved inventiveness in the internal disposition of theatres,* I agreed with him to commit to an equally practised architect † the preparation of the further plans and execution of the provisional building. And thus, despite the many difficulties occasioned by the unusual nature of our task, we were able to announce to our friends and patrons the 22nd of May in the year 1872 ‡ as the date for laying the foundation-stone.

For this event I conceived the notion of giving my supporters an artistic reward for their trouble of meeting at Bayreuth, in the shape of as perfect a performance as possible of *Beethoven's* great Ninth Symphony. The simple invitation which I addressed to our best orchestras, choirs and famous soloists, sufficed to procure me a body of such admirable executants as scarcely ever can have been assembled for a similar purpose.

This first success was of most encouraging augury for the future prospering of the grand theatrical performances themselves. It set all concerned in so excellent a temper, that even the drenching storm which maimed the rites of laying the foundation-stone was unable to damp our spirits. In the capsule to be buried in that stone we placed a message from the illustrious defender of my best endeavours, together with various records and a verse indited by myself:

* Wilhelm Neumann, of Berlin; perhaps, however, the reference is to Karl Brand of Darmstadt, the expert stage-machinist who had so much to do with the building of a theatre in which the stage was the main consideration.—Tr.

† Brückwald, of Leipzig.—Tr.

‡ R. Wagner's birthday.—Tr.

"Hier schliess' ich ein Geheimniss ein,
da ruh' es viele hundert Jahr':
so lange es verwahrt der Stein,
macht es der Welt sich offenbar." *

To the assembly itself I addressed the following speech.†

"My Friends and valued Helpers!

"Through you I to-day am placed in a position surely never occupied before by any artist. You believe in my promise to found for the Germans a Theatre of their own, and give me the means to set before you a plain delineation of that Theatre. For this is to serve, in the first place, the provisional building whose foundation-stone we lay to-day. When we see each other on this spot once more, that building shall greet you, that building in whose characteristics you will read at once the history of the idea which it embodies. You will find an outer shell constructed of the very simplest material, which at best will remind you of those wooden structures which are knocked together in German towns for gatherings of singers and the like, and pulled down again as soon as the festival is over. How much of this building is reckoned for endurance, shall become clearer to you when you step inside. Here too you will find the very humblest material, a total absence of embellishment; perchance you will be surprised to even miss the cheap adornments with which those wonted festal halls were made attractive to the eye. In the proportions and arrangement of the room and its seats, however, you will find expressed a thought which, once you have grasped it,

* A secret here I deep have lain,
for centuries there may it rest:
while e'er the stone shall this contain,
its meaning may the world attest!—Tr.

† This address, originally intended for the ceremony itself, was actually delivered to the great gathering in the old opera-house at Bayreuth after the return of the little party that had braved the elements to assist in laying the stone. The performance of the Ninth Symphony was given later in the day.—Tr.

will place you in a new relation to the play you are about to witness, a relation quite distinct from that in which you had always been involved when visiting our theatres. Should this first impression have proved correct, the mysterious entry of the music will next prepare you for the unveiling and distinct portrayal of scenic pictures that seem to rise from out an ideal world of dreams, and which are meant to set before you the whole reality of a noble art's most skilled illusion. Here at last you are to have no more provisional hints and outlines; so far as lies within the power of the artists of the present, the most perfect scenery and miming shall be offered you.—

"Thus my plan; which bases what I just have called the enduring portion of our edifice on the utmost possible achievement of a sublime illusion. Must I trust myself to lead this artistic exploit to complete success, I take my courage solely from a hope engendered by despair itself. I trust in the German Spirit, and hope for its manifestment in those very regions of our life in which, as in our public art, it has languished in the sorriest travesty. Above all I trust in the spirit of German Music, for I know how glad and bright it burns in our musicians so soon as e'er a German master wakens it within them; and I trust in our dramatic mimes and singers, for I have learnt that they could be as if transfigured to new life when once a German master led them back from idly playing at a harmful pastime, to true observance of their lofty calling. I trust in our artists, and aloud I dare to say it on a day which, at my simple friendly bidding, has gathered round me so select a host of them from points so distant in our fatherland: when, self-forgetful for very joy in the artwork, they presently shall sound their festal greeting to you with our great Beethoven's wonder-symphony, we all may surely tell ourselves that the work we mean to found to-day will also be no cheating mirage, though we artists can only vouch for the sincerity of the idea it is to realise.

"But to whom shall I turn, to ensure the ideal work its solid lastingness, the stage its monumental shrine?

"Of late our undertaking has often been styled the erection of a 'National theatre at Bayreuth.' I have no authority to accept that title. Where is the 'nation,' to erect itself this theatre? When the French National Assembly was dealing with the State-subvention of the great Parisian theatres a little while ago, each speaker warmly advocated the continuance, nay, the increase of their subsidies, since the maintenance of these theatres was a debt not merely due to France, but to Europe which had accustomed itself to receiving from them its laws of intellectual culture. Can we imagine the embarrassment, the perplexity into which a German parliament would fall, had it to handle a similar question? The debates perhaps would terminate in the comforting conclusion that our theatres required no national support at all, since the French National Assembly had already provided for *their* needs too. In the best event our theatre would be treated as the German Reich was treated in our various Landtags but a few years back: namely, as a pure chimera.

"Though a vision of the true German Theatre has built itself before my mental eye, I have had to promptly recognise that I should be abandoned from both within and without, were I to step before the nation with that scheme. Yet I may be told that, though one man might not be believed, the word of many would perhaps find credence: that one really might succeed in floating a gigantic limited company, to commission an architect to rear a sumptuous fabric somewhere or other, which one then might dub a 'German National Theatre' in full confidence that a German-national theatric art would spring up in it of itself. All the world now pins its faith to a continual, and in our latter days an extremely rapid 'progress,' without any clear idea of what we are advancing towards, or the kind of step we are marching; but those who brought a really new thing to the world have never been asked what relation they bore to this 'progressive' surrounding, that met them with naught but obstacles and opposition. On a holiday like this we will not recall the undisguised complaints, the deep despair of our very greatest minds, whose labours shewed the only veritable progress; but perhaps you will allow the man you honour to-day with so unusual a distinction, to express his heartfelt joy that the thought of a single individual has been understood and embraced in his lifetime by so large a number of friends as your gathering here and now attests.

"I had only you, the friends of my peculiar art, my deeds and labours, for sympathisers with my projects: only asking your assistance for my work, could I approach you. To be able to set that work intact and pure before those who have shewn their serious liking for my art in spite of all adulteration and defacement—this was my wish; to you I could impart it sans presumption. And solely in this almost personal relation to you, my friends and helpers, can I see the present ground on which to lay the stone to bear the whole ambitious edifice of our noblest German hopes. Though it be but a provisional one, in that it will resemble all the German's outward Form for centuries. 'Tis the essence of the German spirit, to build from within: the eternal God lives in him, of a truth, before he builds a temple to His glory. And that temple will proclaim the inner spirit to the outer eye in measure as that spirit has matured its amplest individuality. So I will call this stone the talisman whose power shall unseal to you the hidden secrets of that spirit. Let it now but bear the scaffolding whose help we need for that Illusion which shall clear for you life's truest mirror, and already it is firmly, truly laid to bear the prouder edifice whene'er the German Folk desires, in its own honour, to enter its possession with you. So be it consecrated by your love, your benisons, the gratitude I bear you, all of you, who have sped, enheartened, given to and helped me!—Be it consecrated by the spirit that inspired you to hear my call; that filled you with the courage, taunts unheeding, to trust me wholly; that found in me a voice to call you, because it dared to hope to recognise itself within your hearts: the German Spirit, that shouts to you across the centuries its ever young Good-morrow."—

I scarcely need relate the course of that fair feast whose tenour I believe the speech above sufficiently expresses. With it was begun a deed that can endure the scoffs and calumnies of all to whom its underlying thought must forever stay incomprehensible, as is only to be expected of those who hang about life's market-place to glean the fodder for an ephemeral art or literary existence. However hard our undertaking prove, my friends and I will therein merely recognise the selfsame hardships that have weighed for years, for centuries, upon all healthy evolution of a culture truly native to the German. Whoever has followed with sympathy my demonstrations of those hardships, as viewed from my particular standpoint, will not require me to explain them once again. My hopes in this regard, however, I here will finally denote by one sole name, that "Bayreuth" which has already become a byword for something unknown or misinterpreted, by the one side, and awaited with fond expectance by the other.

For what our not always very brilliant wags had formerly made merry over with the senseless term, a "Zukunftsmusik," has now exchanged its cloudy shape for the solid masonry of "Bayreuth." The cloud has found a resting-place, whereon to take material form. The "theatre of the future" is no longer the "preposterous idea" I tried to force on our standing Court and City theatres for sake, we will say, of becoming General-Musikdirektor or even General-Intendant;* but (perhaps because I nowhere saw a chance of getting appointed?) I now appear to wish to graft my notion on a definite locale, which therefore must be reckoned with. This is the little, out of the way, forgotten Bayreuth. It thus must be allowed, in any case,

* As the music-historian in Brockhaus' Konversationslexikon has recently insinuated.—R. WAGNER.

that I had no desire to frame my undertaking with the glitter of a crowded capital—which would not have come so hard to me as some profess to fancy.* But whether those wits direct their jests at the place's smallness, or the extravagance of the idea it stands for, they cannot do away with its localisation of what was but a thought before, and I accept the sneer with greater satisfaction than was possible to me with that idiotic "Zukunftsmusik." If my friends were able to adopt the latter designation of their tendences with the same pride as the valiant Netherlanders once wore their nickname "Gueux" [beggars], I willingly adopt "Bayreuth" as a title of good omen, a collective term for all the life that gathers now from widest circles round the realising of the artwork I had planned.—

Who, buffeted from place to place, attains the spot he chooses for his final rest, examines all its signs for happy augury. If my *Hans Sachs* in the "Meistersinger" lauds Nuremberg as lying in the heart of Germany, with still more right I now could claim that kindly lot for Bayreuth. Hither once stretched the vast Hercynian wild, in which the Romans ne'er set foot; to this day its memory lingers with us in the appellation "Frankenwald," that wood whose gradual uprooting we may trace in countless names of places shewing "Rod" or "Reut." Of the name "Bayreuth" itself there are two different explanations. Here the Bavarians (*Bayern*) are said to have cleared the forest and made a habitation, their Herzogs having once upon a time received the land from the King of the Franks: this theory flatters a certain sense of historical justice, restoring the land, after many a change of rulers, to those to whom it owed a portion of its earliest culture. Another, a more sceptical explanation declares that we here have simply the name of an ancient castle, situated "near the clearing" ("*beim Reuth*"). In either case we

* In his "*Richard Wagner*" Mr H. S. Chamberlain tells us that a society in Berlin offered the master "a million" (£50,000) in 1873, if he would transfer his project to that city, and that a similar offer reached him from Chicago.—TR.

keep the "Reuth," the place reclaimed from waste and made productive; reminding us of the "Rütli" of old Switzerland *—to gain an ever fairer, nobler meaning from the name. The land became the Franconian Mark [border-land] of the German Reich against the fanatical Czechs, whose more peaceable Slavonic brethren had already settled in it and so enhanced its culture that many local names still bear alike the Slavic and the German stamp; here first were Slavs transformed to Germans, without a sacrifice of idiosyncrasy, and amicably shared the fortunes of a common country. Good witness of the German spirit's qualities! After a long dominion over this Mark the Burggraves of Nuremberg took their road to the Mark of Brandenburg, to found in time the royal throne of Prussia, and finally the German Empire. Though the Romans had never pushed so far, yet Bayreuth was not left without Romanic culture. In the Church it stoutly threw aside the yoke of Rome; but the old city, burnt so oft to ashes, assumed the garment of French taste at bidding of parade-struck princes: an Italian built its great opera-house, one of the most fantastic monuments of the roccoco style. Here flourished Ballet, Opera and Comédie. Yet the Burgomaster of Bayreuth "affected"—as the high dame herself expressed it—to address his welcome to the sister of Frederick the Great in honest *German.*

From these few traits who might not paint a picture of the German character and history, a picture which enlarged would mirror back the German realm itself? A rugged soil; tilled by the most diverse of tribal settlers; with local names often scarce intelligible; and distinctly recognisable through nothing, at the last, but its victorious loyalty to the *German language.* The Roman Church imposed on it her Latin, Gallic Culture her French: the scholar and the gentleman used none but foreign lingo, yet that bumpkin of a burgomaster still "affected" to speak his Deutsch. And "Deutsch" it after all remained. Eh! and looking closer at that scene between the Bay-

* Where Tell and his companions met to found Swiss freedom.—TR.

reuth burgomaster and the Prussian princess, we see that not only was German spoken here, but one even affected a "purified" German; which must have much annoyed the lofty dame, as in her meeting with the Empress of Austria the two ladies had been unable to understand one another in German, through the opposing rankness of the only patois known to each. Thus we here find German *culture* too: plainly the educated burgesses of Bayreuth took an active interest in the re-awakening of German Literature, enabling them to follow the unparalleled up-soaring of the German spirit, the feats of Winckelmann, Lessing, Goethe, and finally Schiller; so that at last the town itself produced a far-famed contribution to the culture of that spirit, in the works of its native Friedrich Richter — self-styled "Jean Paul" in mirthful irony— whilst the folly of high quarters, disowning home for foreign dictates and French influences, fell victim to a ghastly impotence.

To whom must not the strangest thoughts have flocked, when he took his seat on that 22nd of May 1872 in the selfsame place once filled by the Margrave's court and guests, great Frederick himself at their head; from the selfsame stage that once had offered these a ballet, an Italian opera or French comédie, to hear the forces of that marvellous Ninth Symphony unchained by German bandsmen gathered to the feast from every district of the Fatherland? When at last from those tribunes where gold-laced trumpeters had blown the banal fanfare, for reception of their mightinesses by a fawning household, impassioned German singers cried to the assembly now: "Embrace, ye millions!"—before whom did there not float a living vision of the sounding triumph of the German Spirit?

This meaning was it granted me to attach to our inaugural feast without dissent; and to all who kept it with us the name Bayreuth has come to mean a precious memory, a stirring thought, a pregnant motto.

In sooth it needed such a motto, to hold out in daily

war against the undermining of the German nation by a deeply alien spirit.

The question "What is German?" has long and earnestly engaged me. Forever it would shape itself anew: did I deem it answerable for certain in the one form, straightway it stood before me in another, till I often gave it up in utter doubt. A patriot driven to undisguised despair, the wonderful Arnold Ruge, at last pronounced the German "despicable." Who once has heard that awful word, cannot prevent it coming back to him in moments of revulsion, and it perhaps may then be likened to those potent drugs which doctors use to fight a deadly malady: for it speedily brings home to us that we ourselves are "the German," the German who recoils in horror from his own degenerate image; he perceives that only to himself is this degeneration visible as such—and what else could have made that knowledge possible, save the indomitable consciousness of his own true nature? No trick can now deceive him any more; no longer can he dupe himself with pleasant words, cajole himself with semblances; over him they have lost all power. In no accepted phase of life, no current form, can he recognise Germanity, but where it often positively sins against that form. Even his language, that one hallowed birthright of his race, laboriously preserved and handed new to him by greatest spirits, he sees insensately abandoned to the openest abuse: he sees how almost every preparation is on foot to verify the boastful saying of the President of the North American States, that soon but *one* tongue will be spoken over all the earth—which, taken literally, can only mean a universal-jargon blent of all ingredients, whereto the modern German may at any rate flatter himself on having already furnished a right handsome contribution.

Whoso had shared with me these painful thoughts, must alike have felt the power of the promise, "Embrace, ye millions!" upon that day in the strange roccoco opera-house at Bayreuth, and perchance divined that the saying of General Grant might fulfil itself in another way than loomed before the esteemed American.

It surely also dawned on everyone that the redeeming German word, in the sense of the great master of tones, required another dwelling-place than that Franco-Italian opera-house, to become a concrete plastic deed (*That des fest sich zeichnenden Bildes*). And hence we laid upon that day the foundation of a building with whose peculiarities I now will try to familiarise the reader, foreshadowing by their very character the *example* of what I long have yearned for as a meet and fitting habitation for the German Spirit.

To explain the plan of the festival-theatre now in course of erection at Bayreuth I believe I cannot do better than to begin with the need I felt the first, that of rendering invisible the mechanical source of its music, to wit the orchestra; for this one requirement led step by step to a total transformation of the auditorium of our neo-European Theatre.

The reader of my previous essays already knows my views about the concealment of the orchestra, and, even should he not have felt as much before, I hope that a subsequent visit to the Opera will have convinced him of my rightness in condemning the constant visibility of the mechanism for tone-production as an aggressive nuisance. In my article on Beethoven I explained how fine performances of ideal works of music may make this evil imperceptible at last, through our eyesight being neutralised, as it were, by the rapt subversion of the whole sensorium. With a dramatic representation, on the contrary, it is a matter of focussing the eye itself upon a picture; and that can only be done by leading it away from any sight of bodies lying in between, such as the technical apparatus for projecting the picture.

Without being actually covered in, the orchestra was therefore to be sunk so deep that the spectator would look right over it, immediately upon the stage; this at once supplied the principle that the seats for the audience must be ranged in gradually ascending rows, their ultimate height to be governed solely by the possibility of a distinct view of the scenic picture. Our whole system of tiers of boxes was accordingly excluded; beginning at the walls beside the stage itself, their very height would have made it impossible to prevent their occupants looking straight down into the orchestra. Thus the arrangement of our rows of seats acquired the character obtaining in the antique Amphitheatre: yet the latter's actual form, with arms stretched out on either side beyond the full half-circle, could not be seriously thought of; for the object to be plainly set in sight was no longer the Chorus in the Orchestra, surrounded for the greater part by that ellipse, but the "scene" itself; and that "scene," displayed to the Greek spectator in the merest low relief, was to be used by us in all its depth.

Hence we were strictly bound by the laws of *perspective*, according to which the rows of seats might widen as they mounted higher, but must always keep their front towards the stage. From the latter forward the *proscenium*, the actual framing of the scenic picture, thus necessarily became the starting-point of all further arrangements. My demand that the orchestra should be made invisible had at once inspired the genius of the famous architect * whom I was first privileged to consult in the matter with a scheme for the empty space between the proscenium and the front row of seats: this space—which we called the "mystic gulf," because it had to part reality from ideality—the master framed in a second, a wider proscenium, from whose relation to the narrower proscenium proper he anticipated the singular illusion of an apparent throwing-back of the scene itself, making the spectator imagine it quite far away, though he still beholds it in all the clearness of its actual proximity; while this in turn gives rise

* Gottfried Semper.—TR.

to the illusion that the persons figuring upon the stage are of larger, superhuman stature.

The success of this arrangement would alone suffice to give an idea of the spectator's completely changed relation to the scenic picture. His seat once taken, he finds himself in an actual "theatron," i.e. a room made ready for no other purpose than his looking in, and that for looking straight in front of him. Between him and the picture to be looked at there is nothing plainly visible, merely a floating atmosphere of distance, resulting from the architectural adjustment of the two proscenia; whereby the scene is removed as it were to the unapproachable world of dreams, while the spectral music sounding from the "mystic gulf," like vapours rising from the holy womb of Gaia beneath the Pythia's tripod, inspires him with that clairvoyance in which the scenic picture melts into the truest effigy of life itself.*

A difficulty arose in respect of the side-walls of the auditorium: unbroken by any tiers of boxes, they presented a flat expanse, to be brought into no plausible agreement with the rows of seats. The famous architect at first entrusted with the task of building the theatre in monumental fashion had all the resources of his art to draw upon, and made so admirable a use of the noblest renaissance ornament that the bare surface was transformed into a perpetual

* As to the scandalous thrusting-forward of this picture, so that the spectator can almost touch it, I recently expressed myself in my *Glance at the German operatic stage of to-day*; I have only to add that, to my sincere relief, I found that this evil had already been felt by a builder of theatres—though, to my knowledge, by this one alone—namely the architect of the playhouse at *Mannheim*. So far as possible in the present Theatre, he had isolated the scenic picture by abolishing the proscenium-boxes and leaving in fact an empty recess at either side, behind a second proscenium. But unfortunately the orchestra occupying this space was unconcealed, and the towering boxes still jutted hard on the proscenium; whereby the good effect was lost, nothing remaining but the excellence of the builder's idea. Governed by an equally proper feeling, the artistic Intendant of the *Dessau* Court-theatre kept the proscenium mostly in half-light, to throw the picture back as by a rim of shadow; which had the additional advantage that, finding themselves but poorly lighted in the extreme foreground, the performers preferred to stay in the vivid relief of the middle distance.—R. WAGNER.

feast for the eye. For our provisional theatre at Bayreuth we had to renounce all idea of a like adornment, which has no meaning unless the material itself be precious, and were once more faced with the question how to treat these walls that stood at variance with the actual space for holding the audience. A glance at the first of the plans contained in the appendix * shews an oblong narrowing towards the stage, as the space to be employed for the spectators, bounded by two unsightly wedges that widen as they approach the proscenium. While the side-walls flanking these wedges were obliged to be rectangular on account of the structural requirements of the building, and although the space thus left on either hand could conveniently be utilised for stairways giving access to the seats, the visual effect of the whole would have been ruined by those two empty corners. Now, to mask the blanks immediately in front of our double proscenium, the ingenuity of my present adviser had already hit on the plan of throwing out a third and still broader proscenium. Seized with the excellence of this thought, we soon went further in the same direction, and found that, to do full justice to the idea of an auditorium narrowing in true perspective toward the stage, we must extend the process to the whole interior, adding proscenium after proscenium until they reached their climax in the crowning gallery, and thus enclosing the entire audience in the vista, no matter where it took its place. For this we devised a system of columns, answering to the first proscenium and broadening with the blocks of seats they bounded; at once they cheated us of the square walls behind them, and admirably hid the intervening doors and steps. With that we had settled all our internal arrangements, as outlined in the accompanying plans.—

As we were building a merely *provisional* theatre, and

* These architectural plans and elevations, six in number, I have omitted as now unnecessary; the theatre itself has so often been sketched and photographed since our author published his ninth volume of the *Ges. Schr.* (1873) that, even to the few who have never visited it, there can scarcely be a building in the world whose aspect and construction are so familiar.—Tr.

therefore had only to keep in view its *inner* fitness for its end, we might congratulate ourselves on being relieved, for the present, of the task of furnishing our edifice with a beautiful exterior in architectural harmony with the inner idea. Had we even been supplied with nobler material than our estimates allowed of, we should have shrunk in terror from the task of erecting a monumental pile, and been obliged to look around us for assistance such as we could scarcely anywhere have found just now. For here presented itself the newest, the most individual problem, and, since it could never yet have been attempted, the most difficult for the architect of the present (or the future?) day. Our very poverty of means, however, compelled us to think of nothing but the sheer objective fitness of our building, the absolutely essential for our aim: and aim and object here resided in the inner relation of the auditorium to a stage of the largest dimensions necessary for mounting perfect scenery. Such a stage requires to be of three times the height it presents to the spectator, since its scenery must be able to be raised alike and lowered in its full extent. Thus from floor to roof the stage needs twice the height required by the auditorium. If one consults this utilitarian need alone, the outcome is a conglomerate of two buildings of totally different form and size. To mask the disproportion of these two buildings as much as possible, most architects of our newer theatres have considerably increased the height of the auditorium, and above that, again, have added rooms for scene-painting and sundry managerial purposes—though such rooms have generally been found so inconvenient, that they are very seldom used. Moreover one could always fall back on the expedient of adding another tier or two of boxes, even allowing the topmost gallery to lose itself high up above the opening for the stage, since it was only meant for the poorer classes, upon whom one thought nothing of inflicting the inconvenience of a bird's-eye view of the goings-on below them in the parterre. But these tiers are banished from *our* theatre, nor can an architectural need dictate that we should lift our gaze on high, above blank walls, as in the Christian dome.

The opera-houses of former days were constructed on the principle of an unbroken roof-ridge, consequently in the form of long chests; whereof we have a naïve specimen in the Royal Opera-house of Berlin. The architect had therefore only one façade to care for, that of the main entrance, at the narrow end of a building whose length one was very fond of tucking away between the houses of a street.

Now, by treating in the very baldest way our task of erecting an outwardly artless and simply provisional theatre, to be placed on a high and open site, I believe we have at like time reduced the problem itself to its plainest terms. It now lies naked and distinct before us, the tangible diagram, so to speak, of what a theatric structure should outwardly express if it have no common, but an altogether ideal purpose to reveal. The main body of this structure thus represents the infinitely complex apparatus for scenic performances of the greatest possible perfection of technique: its annexe, on the other hand, consists of little more than a covered forecourt, in which to accommodate those persons for whom the performance is to become a visual play.

To ourselves it is as if the mere necessitously plain and simple statement of this principle in our building, uninfluenced by structures built for ends quite other—as palaces, museums and churches—will yield the genius of German Building a not unworthy, perchance its only truly individual task to solve. But if anyone thinks that for sake of the inevitable grand façade the main object of the theatre must be concealed by wings for balls and concerts, or the like, he will also ban us forever to the unoriginality of their usual ornament; our sculptors and carvers will then fall back on all the motives of the renaissance, with figures and scrolls that tell us nothing we can understand—and we shall end by having everything go on again exactly as in the opera-house of the "now-time"; whence the question already put to me by most people, why I really want a special theatre at all.

Yet he who has rightly understood this want of mine, as well, cannot but perceive that Architecture itself might win a fresh significance from the spirit of Music, which mapped for me alike my artwork and its habitation, and thus that the myth of a city built by Amphion's lyre may not as yet have lost its meaning.—

We finally might extend our view to what the German nation wants in general, if it is ever to be led into the path of an original development, unconfused by wrongly-understood and ill-appropriated foreign motives.

Many an intelligent observer has been struck with the fact that the recent prodigious successes of German Policy have not contributed one jot toward diverting the sense and taste of the German people from a foolish hankering for the Foreign, toward arousing the wish to cultivate those native aptitudes still left to us. Our great German statesman puts forth all his strength against the pretensions of the Romish spirit in the province of the Church: the French spirit's eternal pretensions to govern and dictate our taste, with the manners influenced thereby, remain unheeded on all hands. If it occurs to a Parisian wanton to give her bonnet an extravagant form, that suffices to bring every German woman beneath the selfsame bonnet; or a lucky speculator on the bourse makes a million overnight, and straightway orders a villa in the St. Germain style, for which the architect has all his plans in readiness. So we may think at times that things are going too smoothly with the German, and only some dire want (*Noth*) can turn him back to that simplicity which well becomes him, a simplicity only intelligible to him through recognition of his genuine inner need.

Though we leave this thought upon a nation's broader life but hinted at, let us abide by it in the realm of Ideal Want. What characterised the evolution of the plan for our theatre-building was this: in answer to an altogether ideal need we had piece by piece to discard each traditional arrangement of the inner space in favour of a new one, for which in turn we were unable to accept a single traditional ornament, either on the inside or the out; so that we must keep our building, for the nonce, in all the naïve simpleness of its emergency. But confiding in the inventiveness of Want in general, and in the ideal need of beauty in particular, we hope that our propounding of the problem may itself incite to the discovery of a German style in architecture; which style would certainly make no unworthy commencement by displaying its first distinctive features in a building devoted to German Art, and indeed to that art in its most nationally popular of dramatic forms. We have ample time to develop a monumental style of ornament that shall rival the renaissance or roccoco, let us say, in wealth and variety: haste is absolutely needless, for in all probability we shall have leisure enough before the "Reich" decides to take an interest in our work. So, albeit our provisional building may only very gradually become a monument, let it rear itself for now as admonition to the German world to ponder what has grown quite clear to all whose sympathy, whose trouble and self-sacrifice, it has to thank for its erection.

There may it stand, on the fair hill by *Bayreuth.*

SUMMARY.

POEM. *To the German Army before Paris* (2).

PREFACE TO "A CAPITULATION."

French taunts before the war, and German playwrights' stupid skits; no originality in the German of to-day. The "Capitulation" intended for music, to be composed by a young friend; the piece offered to a Berlin theatre, rejected; its music never written, as it needed the genius of Offenbach himself. It really shews the Germans in a more ridiculous light than the French, whom they invariably imitate (6).

A CAPITULATION.

A burlesque comedy, dealing with the Siege of Paris, Victor Hugo's bombast, Gambetta's balloon-trips, the trumped-up accounts of French victories, etc., etc., and ending with Offenbach triumphant over the German Court-Theatres (33).

REMINISCENCES OF AUBER.

His recent death and burial; oration by Dumas; the Frenchman's empty phrase. How Wagner sought to champion Auber against Rossini in Paris, 1840; the French editor's objection, politics and art. The *Muette de Portici* (Masaniello) took greater hold on the Germans than Rossini's *Tell*; the first real drama on the lyric stage, and with a tragic dénouement! Spontini et al., with their "satisfactory ending" (39). Here it was the *whole* that worked, and its music gained a quite new form, vital, drastic and distinct; the *plastic* rather than the picturesque (40). Starch and chill of earlier French Grand Opera, which was really more Italian than French; the *Muette* pulsed warm with life. German composers' bewilderment, for here was nothing imitable; Marschner's progressive confusion, his attempt at the new "stretta" and "furia." The *Muette* a strictly isolated moment, both in French operatic music and in Auber's own career (42). Innovations made by Auber in scoring etc.; his constant attention to the progress of the plot, thus enriching means of dramatic characterisation; but the artistic fire of this work he never touched again. His comparison of his Muse to a mistress cooling down to wife does not account for the warmth of a work written later than the epoch alleged for that cooling (44). Auber's subsequent operas fell flat in Germany, as did Hérold's *Pré aux clercs* after *Zampa*. The build of these works explained by the square dance; their secret in the *cancan*. National dances as depicting national character; Auber's music at its zenith in the *Muette*, like the cancan-dancing gamin glorified by the daring of the barricades; he seized the roots of national character laid bare by these revolutions (46). Boieldieu still was "gallant," Auber became outspoken; even the Cancan could be treated artistically, i.e. as a mere game of play; Music, like the wife in many a French comedy, rewon her husband by learning all the arts of the cocotte. Auber's candour in saying of a Beethoven Symphony, though then Director of the Conservatoire, "Je n'y comprends mot": only great natures, sure and whole, can waive aside, like himself and Rossini, the misconceptions of their worshippers (49). The ouvrier and "Voilà mon publique." Wagner meets Auber in 1860; *Tannhäuser* and "il y aura du spectacle"; reminiscences of *Lestocq*, contrasted with the *Circassienne* (50). No force or fire in Auber's character—frigidity in all French art: how came he by the music for the *Muette?* A revolt against the Government that chid the French for their national vices and wounded their amour propre (52). The July Revolution of 1830 stood in close relation with the *Muette*: each was an "excess," and the Parisians soon grew shy of both; Napoleon III. and Auber's *Premier jour de bonheur* (53). Could Auber have written a Mass or Symphony, even when kindled to fever-heat? Bach and Beethoven the only great musicians whose music appears to have arisen without incitement by Drama: yet even here we find the true dramatic element at work (54). That the *Muette* had no lasting effect on French Grand Opera shews us a plague-spot in the national character. What hope is there for the German nation, whose Theatre takes everything from Paris? (55).

BEETHOVEN.

Preface.—Fiction of a speech to be delivered on Beethoven's Centenary. A contribution to the philosophy of Music. Written in the stir of great national events (the Franco-German war), may it bring the German heart into closer touch with the German Spirit (60).—

The relation of great artists to their native land: its speech influences the poet's thought, its form and colour the painter's picture; but, though natural advantages of voice have given Italian music another direction than that taken by German, the real difference must lie deeper. Goethe and Schiller have left us written data of their inner life, up to a certain point, but what can we learn of the relation of Beethoven the musician to Beethoven the man from his letters and biography? (63). The poet stands midway between plastic artist and musician: Goethe and his leanings toward painting, Schiller more inclined to the inner world, Kant's Thing-in-itself—his saying that the Epos leans toward Plastic art, the Drama toward Music (64). Schopenhauer the first to clearly distinguish Music from the other fine arts: the "Ideas" the 'object' of the other arts, but Music itself a world-Idea: "he who could translate it into abstract concepts would have found a philosophy to explain the world itself" (65). According to Sch., to really seize an Idea there must be temporary preponderance of Intellect over Will, but only through our inner Feeling do we arrive at the *character* of things, through our self-consciousness at the essence of things, the Will itself, of which we are but an individual part (67). Sch. and clairvoyance: his dream-theory. As there are two worlds, a waking and a dreaming, similarly there is a sound-world distinct from the light-world (68). Events of the inner organism translate themselves into dreams; from the dream we wake with a *scream*, thus entering the sound-world before the light-world: the Cry as origin of Music. Music thus differs from all the other arts, which arise from tranquil contemplation of the outer *show.* The effect of Beauty sheer pleasure in the semblance: "Where seize I thee, o Nature infinite?" Answer given by Music, which reveals the oneness of all being (71). Music's nature as an art: silenced in the plastic artist, the individual will awakes in the musician as Universal Will, above all bounds of individuality. The inspired musician's state thus one of ecstasy, only comparable with that of the Saint; but the saint's is lasting, the musician's alternates with the suffering attendant on all individual consciousness. Music stands to all the other arts as Religion to the Church: 'tis an organ like the dream-organ, but created by the Will to *directly* convey the vision of its inner self, the One and All (73). A sleepless night in Venice and the gondolier's cry; a mountain solitude and the herdsman's jodel; the mother crooning to her babe; the sounds of Nature speaking to man: the ear reveals the essence of what the eye had held suspended in division. This dreamlike state experienced in the concert-room, where the brain loses consciousness of its visual surroundings under influence of the musician's magic from the other world (75). Music as Harmony has nothing to do with time or space, but as Rhythm she makes contact with the visual world by resemblance to the laws of motion governing tangible bodies: analogy with dream of deep sleep passing into "allegoric" dream that precedes waking consciousness (76). Wrongness of judging Music by canons of Plastic art and the Beautiful: her category the Sublime. What other arts only gradually effect, a will-freed contemplation, Music effects at her *first entry*—pure Form set free from Matter; empty music never ceases toying with this first effect. Beethoven shews these forms in nothing but their inner meaning: thus archetype of the Musician. The musician's eye for the In-itself becomes an ear when facing outwards. Palestrina and his timeless, spaceless music: his music gives us Religion free from dogma (79). In dance-music, the Symphony, or Opera, *plastic* element the chief factor; periods arranged symmetrically and architecturally; called "secular," as against the spiritual, for Music here quits her lofty innocence and becomes entangled in Appearance—one here wants something to *see* (80).

Evolution of Beethoven's genius.—Effect on young musician of the music going on around him; B. brought more into contact with pfte-works than any other class; virtually remained a sonata-composer (81). The Sonata-form had then become a fixed and ruling type, through E. Bach, Haydn and Mozart. Haydn, the greybeard born, repudiated by Beethoven the born adult; his improvising to Mozart and the latter's prophecy. Beethoven had a treasure to guard, and defied the world. Schopenhauer's dictum that the Musician speaks a tongue his reason does not understand (83). Musical forms of eighteenth century compared with Jesuit architecture and French "classic" poetry. B. never overthrew the traditional forms, but moulded them anew from within—the German spirit: Wolfram von Eschenbach and the old French epics (85). Works of his forerunners a transparency seen by daylight; B. sets his painting in the hush of Night, and brings behind it the light of the clairvoyant. Here each convention becomes a direct outpouring of his spirit: the whole is melody, even to the pauses (87). Whence did he gain this power? From force of character: contrasted with Haydn and Mozart;

no prince's musical servant. Reason could not have guided him in choice of life more surely than his natural instinct: defiance of a world that asks for naught but usefulness and sweets. Strength of skeleton and density of skull defending a brain of utmost delicacy; solitude and wellnigh boorish tastes—Spinoza's glass-cutting and Schopenhauer's parsimony (90). Despotic treatment of his patrons; nothing to be got from him save what and when he pleased. The outer world had still less charm for him when deafness became total; his life now given wholly to the inner—Tiresias the blinded seer. And now his eye grew bright within, his works are steeped in full serenity: Pastoral Sym., "To-day shalt thou be with me in Paradise;" but the Seventh and Eighth transcend all Beauty—no other word but the Sublime (93). As thinker an optimist: he feels that Love is god, and writes down, God is love. Though fascinated all his life by Goethe's *Faust*, he worshipped Klopstock: rigorous morals. Born and bred a Catholic, living in gay Vienna, his whole tendence that of German Protestantism; Bach's works became his bible. A "saint" and the penance for his optimism (96). A day from his inner life: the C-sharp minor Quartet (97). Striving to find the melody for the "good man" of his belief: follows Haydn to the folk-dance; Eroica, C-minor, Seventh Sym. a dance of Nature to celebrate the birth of a planet (99). Sublime gladness shewn in works of period when total deafness arrived; though a sadder mood recurs, it is as expression of the world itself, for the Artist can only conceive in a state of profound serenity. Beethoven *the man* included in this world; thus his doubts too find expression in Ninth Sym., but are silenced by the cry with which he wakes from a tortured dream and insists that "man *is* good" (101). Never has the highest art produced a thing more simple than this final melody, the *cantus firmus* of a new communion, a revelation of the purest universal Love (102). Beethoven's music, having advanced from mere Beauty to the Sublime, will be understood when his predecessors are wellnigh forgotten. The new meaning he gave to the voice in its conjunction with instruments: his Missa Solemnis a symphonic work; relation of music to poetry an illusion (104). In Opera sight and hearing excited in turn, but the poet's *thought* unheeded. Beethoven required a *passionate* plot, to match his music; the opera *Fidelio* eclipsed by its greatest overture. Drama towers above Poetry as Music above the other arts; Music man's qualification *a priori* for fashioning the Drama. Shakespeare and the "poet"; his world of shapes coequal with Beethoven's musical world of motives (107). Coriolanus according to Shakespeare and Beethoven: the motives set forth equally clearly by both, merely their laws of operation differ. Shakespeare a Beethoven who goes on dreaming though awake, and he too abrogates the formal laws of his art in fulfilling them; a "ghost-seer" conjuring up the spirits of the past, he gives them flesh (110). As in dreams an inner stimulus travels through the brain to the senses in inverse fashion to ordinary mode of sense-perception, so the musician might reach from the world of Sound to that of Light, and union of Sh. and B. thus become complete; B.'s deed for art in his Last Sym. would thus beget the perfect Artwork (112).

Beethoven's lesson to the nation.—Great change in the present generation: just previously the age had been confessedly "critical"; now Goethe and Schiller are thrust aside in favour of the "modern" spirit. This modern spirit governed by French taste and its changing fashions, e.g. our women's dress; a veritable curse fallen on the nation, which needs an entire new-birth (115). Gradual decline of feeling for *plastique* since invention of writing, printing, and finally journalism: who buys a paper, buys its opinion. The very ruins of Greek art teach us how man's life might yet be fashioned into something bearable; but the revival of art passed from Italians to French, a people unproductive save for making *itself* a work of art—in this it is original and badly copied by all others (118). Here the furniture ranks above the house; taste of the *demi-monde* supreme; medley of styles, Chinese, renaissance, roccoco etc. "Modern art" a new watchword of Æsthetics, its unoriginality and vulgarising of noble types; our Civilisation at end of all true productiveness (120). But a world of Music has risen beside this world of Mode; potent as Christianity itself against Roman emperors, it melts this world of semblances to naught. Music ruled the Greeks in all their art and life; the great Italian painters were almost all musicians; then came the Jesuits and Mode (121). Beethoven, in his wrath against "the Mode," strengthens an epithet of Schiller's *Ode to Joy*: the German's calling, as against our modern civilisation (123). Goethe and Schiller seek to raise the German's nature to the grace of his Romanic neighbours. Wilhelm Meister is led through all the fairer forms of life to a career of usefulness; Faust is wed to Helena, the archetype of beauty; but in Mignon and Gretchen the Eternal-womanly is the redeeming power. This Eternal-womanly we may call the spirit of Music, the new religion preached by Beethoven's Symphonies. As the German has shewn his "bravery" in war, let him be brave in peace, cast off his false and borrowed show, and cleave to the Sublime (126).

THE DESTINY OF OPERA.

Preface.—Written for an Academic lecture; agreeing in substance with *Opera and Drama*, it offers new points of view in details. Correct performances of my stage-works would afford a better proof, but hitherto I have been condemned to theorise. The stage alone contains the living elements for a higher Artwork (130).

Cry that Opera has ruined the Play. Yet foundations of Opera were laid with the very beginnings of modern Theatre. Effect of Goethe and Schiller on our actors: the task out of proportion to their talents, "false pathos" resulted; rhetorical mode of diction lent itself to "effect"; exit-tirades counted off as in the Opera (133). These opportunities for applause being more plentiful in Opera, priests of Thalia and Melpomene are envious, for a play composed of nothing but declamatory phrases is as yet unthinkable; yet even Opera requires a plot, and borrows those of Shakespeare, Goethe and Schiller. The actor still further incensed; but if he could have held his audience with Faust's monologue, the public would never have run away to Gounod's aria. Something thus still lacking in our Play, if it is ever to influence public life: if Opera has made palpable the Theatre's downfall, through it alone can the Theatre be restored to the Ideal (136). Stage "pathos" shews the modern Drama as having always aimed at ideality: Italians' attempt at the antique drama; Calderon's pieces wellnigh operatic; Shakespeare's genius alone could *realise* with success. Goethe and Schiller perceive that the task of idealising Drama is reserved for the musician: the poet, merely as such, is insufficiently equipped for Drama. Plato's dialogues and didatic poetry, but Greek Tragedy enthralled through the Dionysian element, not through "poetic diction" (139). What moved Goethe and Schiller in Gluck's *Iphigenia* and Mozart's *Don Juan* was the idealising effect of Music on the drama; here no need of apothegms, for all revealed by Melody. What room was left for the "poet"? Who would care to give up his rank and become "librettist"? Again, even the poorest "book" and sickliest music could in Opera be transfigured by a great dramatic artist, e.g. Schröder-Devrient (141). Goethe and Schiller's other problem, Shakespeare: no commentator has yet discovered Shakespeare's secret. Was he a poet? He was an actor who wrote plays for his troop; like Lope de Vega, Molière and Æschylus, an *improviser* of the highest poetic value—cf. Beethoven's wonderful impromptus; the "poet" is silent, but his work the only genuine Drama (144). It strictly belongs to class of *effective stage-pieces*, such as the French turn out from year to year, the difference lying in its poetic worth. Scarce imaginable that Shakespeare's players could have risen to level of his work, but it was in full accord with the possibilities of mimetic art. To attain that possibility the aim of Goethe and Schiller, and they believed it to lie in *music* (146). The humblest incident of life transfigured by art of mimicry; and this again when dipped in magic well of Music, becomes the purest Ideality, pure Form set free from Matter. Music's *form* is Melody: the old Italians from the tiresome recitative of first lyric dramas evolved the Aria; developed by Gluck, the far greater musician Mozart gave it a wealth of dramatic characterisation; but Beethoven vitalised every particle of musical form. His humour, for instance, is that of Shakespeare: relationship of musician to poet-*mime*; for both the Poet merely drafts the plan (148). The highest Artwork would combine the factors of Beethovenian music and Shakespearian drama, its sublime irregularity recalling a scene from Nature, not a work of Architecture: an impromptu of the musician which the greatest dramatist has taught us how to "fix"; and whereas "poetic diction" falls victim to caprice of the declaimer, *melodic* utterance of feelings can be placed beyond all risk of error (150). Spoken Drama would thus be removed from competition with "Opera," for it would leave to that the idealising tendence, and confine itself to the more realistic side of life: e.g. in *Fidelio* the spoken word of Schröder-Devrient where material horror takes us from Music's ideal sphere (152). Leaving the lessons of History to the spoken Play, the "Musically-conceived" dramatic Artwork would fulfil the destiny of Opera by realising all the possibilities long perceived therein by earnest minds. We thus appeal to all educated persons, to whom the Theatre's present tendence is abhorrent, and to those whose natural instincts alone can restore our German Theatre to a place of honour befitting the nation's military triumphs, the actors, singers and bandsmen (155).

ACTORS AND SINGERS.

The Mime as Actor, Singer, and Bandsman. A good performance will disguise the worthlessness of a dramatic work, but the best stage-poem ineffective f badly played: the performers are thus the only *artists* here. Mimetic art an epitome of all the others, and its effect unrivalled, thrilling in exact degree as the performer loses himself in the character he represents—Ludwig Devrient as King Lear, and the Berlin public motionless: here was the Sublime, and issuing from the *mime*, whether L. D. or Shakespeare (161).

Ordinary performances at Theatre a mere trade, the actor trying to set his personality in most becoming light. Art ceases to be art when it strikes the mind as such: in France the Drama was given an academic cut, and rules invaded the acteur's art; in England Garrick reawoke dramatic art and rescued Shakespeare (163). Apart from natural gifts, essence of mimetic art lies in the actor's passing entirely outside himself. In France was matured a stage-convention, the art of "playing comedy," whereby both actor and audience are never to forget that the thing is make-believe: Louis XIV., like Augustus, a good "comedian"; the Germans too "play comedy," but badly—a German Louis XIV. inconceivable, yet our theatres are ruled by canons of French taste (165). The German's "talent" is scanty, owing to lack of an established national Culture: our actors, wanting talent, play to the audience, not like Garrick forgetting the world in his soliloquies; they consequently rant and overdo their parts. The Frenchman's talent for social intercourse gives his pieces the air of a polished conversation: the German has a passion for "asides" (168). Glaring instance in Hebbel's "Nibelungen," with Münchhausen-like self-ridicule of its poet and players—much as "Pyramus and Thisbe" in *Midsummer-night's Dream*: a picture of modern German Theatre; and all this both given and taken in solemn earnest! (170).

Stage-system of to-day. E. Devrient's attempt to get Actors officially recognised as a civic "class," and Holtei's preference for a dissolute band of strolling players (173). Both tendencies combined at other theatres, always on the supposition that something here was to be *learnt*; but Genius alone can teach, and all we can do is to sharpen our eyes for its appearance, i.e. to train our Judgment (175).

The German has no talent for acting, because all our dramatic art is borrowed from abroad, like cut of clothes. Distinction between Genius and Talent: the German has the former, and certainly will acquire the latter when our Theatre is made *original*. Earlier proposals for an Original German Theatre, and their reception: there would have been no dearth of self-styled "poets"; if revived to-day by a wealthy limited company, the poets would hail it with "patriotic" glee; but the Originality of their work? Get it tested by asking our actors to behave as in actual life: its stiltedness at once apparent (178). This same unnaturalism in all our public speaking: funeral oration by a professor of philology; Goethe and Schiller reading aloud: "comedianism" a fatal feature in German plan of culture; in the actor it takes the form of airs and graces instead of a faithful impersonation of his rôle (180). When the whole of life is filled with this Comedianism, 'tis difficult for the mime to find aught natural to copy; his art is thus original only in pieces of the humblest sphere; even from this stronghold it now is being driven, till we are left with little but the puppet-stage—encounter with a genius in this street-show. *Faust* the only truly original German play, yet impracticable with a Theatre so degenerate as our modern (183).

Faust a test for native acting-talent: no ranting here avails, for every line is true to nature. An experience at Vienna; advice to Director to make his actors speak twice as fast, timing them by his watch—"German conversational tone!" (184). Career of German Theatre from its beginnings in Folk-play to modern Court and Tivoli Theatres: "the German lies when he is courteous." Can our actors still play Kleist's or Raymund's pieces? If not, let them leave Schiller, Shakespeare and the "higher drama" alone, for Genius is a rarity and all we can do is to prepare the ground for it by honest toil, like that of Schröder, Iffland etc. before the coming of L. Devrient (187). If all our theatres confined themselves to sound and unpretentious work, at periodic national festivals their choicest forces might be tried for higher tasks in combination—resembling present constitution of German Reich: then most careful experiments would have to be made in the rendering of Schiller's pieces, whose ideal has only once been realised, by the genius of Sophie Schröder and *musical* tone of voice (189). The stage erected in Shakespeare's day, in midst of the spectators, made any attempt at "rhetorical pathos" ridiculous; thus freedom from affectation the first law in acting his dramas, but the true *passion* they need is rare among our actors. His dramas the antithesis of Greek Tragedy: between these two opposites, and equally independent, must come the hoped-for German Artwork and its own original style of acting (192). Task before the genius that one day shall spring from German Theatre: to plan the house and stage in such a way that the Shakespearian or realistic drama may be brought quite close to us, whilst dramas such as Goethe's *Faust* may be given the full illusion of distance; simplicity of the Shakespearian architecture enriched by all modern improvements in mechanism. If this cannot be done for the Recited Drama, the Theatre can only be rescued by Music (194).

Our theatres are strictly *opera*-houses; the building shews it. Modelled on a misconception of antique amphitheatre, they yet have given the orchestra its preponderant place. In this modern theatre the Play has fallen to such *flatness* that it is powerless before Opera (196). The Orchestra with its Chorus stood in very heart of Greek audience: Shakespeare's "Chorus" had become the drama itself, and moved in the Orchestra with such realistic freedom as at last to fancy *itself* the audience and get a second play performed to it, in *Hamlet* and *Midsummer-night*; but academic taste prevailed, and this inner hinder stage became the stage itself. Then the instrumental orchestra began its idealising mission; nonsense about "pedestal and statue," for Music is the very mother-womb of Drama (198).

The German opera-singer.—Originally he had to act in spoken Play as well, and the opera was merely a *Singspiel*: Weber and first "German Opera"; Genast and the two brothers Devrient as actors *and* singers. Advent of the "coloratura" lady and gentleman: they became the poles of Opera and ruin of its German type; for presently the whole troop had to sing coloratura and mangled what little spoken dialogue remained (200). If Goethe and Schiller could only hear a German performance of the *Prophète* or *Trovatore*! Origin and development of Italian Opera; what has our honourable German singer in common therewith? If Italian singing is practicable in a German throat, it can only be through acquisition of Italian tongue. French influences and Gluck; but the *Singspiel* the only truly native German product (202).

Style of singing proper for German musical drama. Italian *bel canto* inexecutable in this tongue; the words become an inarticulate jumble, and the singers therefore never seize the character of their rôles. Vocal cramp resulting from effort to sing "finely": the German must learn to speak naturally in singing; instruction on the *mental* plane (204). *The right example to be set by the dramatic composer*; interpreting the Ideal the higher evolution of bent to imitate reality. Earlier German opera-composers and their oscillation from Italian *canto* to French *recitative*: the difficulty to be overcome is the turning of the whole dialogue into music; this will be the true German style (207).

The German composer hitherto confused by division of Opera into two halves, a dramatic and a lyrical, e.g. Kaspar's scene in *Freischütz*; had the dialogue been made main subject of musical treatment, there would have been no need of a closing aria—how this might have been done, by thematic development and combination (208). Evolution of my own scores: folk said I had "killed the singer," but the singers took a great liking for my works; *Meistersinger* at Munich—not a "continuous fugue," but a continuous *dialogue* (210). Success of *Tannhäuser* due to lyric details: I had not marked the "example" sufficiently plainly. Cry of shallow critics that these expressional marks and elaborate scorings rob singers of all freedom; but if the poet's image is not made lifelike for the mime, the latter cannot convert it into actual Drama. Wealth of metre and choreographic detail in Greek Tragedy even surpassed by second part of *Faust*, yet it remains a riddle because Goethe had no means of "fixing" its type for the mime to follow. Our great German musicians have given these means into our hands (213).

The *dignity* of Histrionic art a question purely of the ideal height to which the dramatic poet is able to guide the mime's natural gifts: nothing to do with official "respectability"—an old Margrave of Bayreuth and the drunken buffoon. The gifted mime not self-denying, but self-divesting: the consciousness of self he never quite recovers even in daily life; Ludwig Devrient (216). This self-divestment common to both Mime and Dramatist, but latter becomes master of former through his mental "self-control": nothing more genial than comradeship of these two (217). The mime saved from raving madness by consciousness that his art is only play: Wilhelmine Schröder-Devrient and a playful scene behind the wings in midst of tragic situation; but nothing could distract her from her rôle when on the boards; this great artist had no exceptional "voice," but let a true womanly soul stream forth in such wondrous sounds that no one thought of voice or singing—here the "example" given by mime to poet (219). This example taught me the nature of Mimetic art, truthfulness; sincerity the wall dividing histrionic genius from bad comedian always on the watch for gain. This noble woman would have died of shame, had she owed applause to claptrap; yet enthusiasm of audience the only element to bear this sublime Illusion safely; from *you* must the actor's relinquished soul make answer to him, or he slinks away a lifeless shade (220).

"Self-denial" as enforced on the mime by some Directors: the virtue-master and his high-and-mighty airs; the manager diverting all attention to the "total" of his productions; the virtuoso tumbles down the house of cards (222). And why should the actor be robbed of his due applause? The fleetingness of his renown is tragic: S.-Devrient in vapid "Swiss Family" at Nuremberg; no monument could preserve the wonders of that evening (223).

The poet forgetting himself in joy at the mime's achievement, the mime's affectionate enthusiasm for the poet: thus do the two become one, and afford the only surety of the healing of Dramatic Art (224).

The mime's true dignity: German statesmen consider the Theatre outside the province even of an Art-ministry; let the mime show his spiritual rank, and teach the "cultured" what their unaided eye could never see (226).

Tribute to the memory of an actress as noble in her life as in her art, a woman glorified by the Spirit of Music, great Wilhelmine Schröder-Devrient (228).

THE RENDERING OF BEETHOVEN'S NINTH SYMPHONY.

Certain difficulties in giving due distinctness to the master's intention.—While his conceptions vastly outstrip those of Haydn and Mozart, he knew no orchestra but theirs, and consequently exacted of his bandsmen the feats of virtuosi, e.g. his crescendo ending suddenly in a *piano,* where two separate bodies of instruments really needed to give due effect; the same difficulty in his last Quartets, which, when perfectly performed, give the idea that more musicians are playing than the actual four (233). Drastic *marking of the melody* the first principle in rendering Beethoven—Paris Conservatoire and this Sym., Bülow and the Sonatas. Obstacles caused by master's deafness; he somewhat lost consciousness of relative dynamic values of instruments, pitting wood-wind against strings as equal forces; but 'natural' horns and trumpets his gravest hindrance. Obvious remedies in latter case (236). Adding horns and trumpets to second theme of Scherzo: the question, in all such cases, is whether one prefers to go without distinctly hearing what the master meant, or to get it judiciously brought out (239). Fanfare at beginning of last movement, an unintended rhythm given it by gaps in nature-scale of same brass instruments: make them take the wood-wind's theme throughout; a rhythmic chaos preparing us for light of the "word" (241). Other difficulties due to instrumental compass observed in those days, sometimes causing Beethoven to drop his melody an octave lower, or give the highest 'voice' notes not contained in melody of the lower 'voices': instances from Eighth Sym. and the *espressivo* of first movement of Ninth (243). Proposals to amend last-named by trifling alterations in flute part (247). Importance of eliciting the meaning of every word or note in the message of genius, not fearing outcry of pietists (248). Nuances of dynamic expression in *crescendo* etc.; the sense of these signs must be studied as closely as the theme itself; but no excuse for the "piquant" mode of rendering now coming into vogue since "Conducting" was written (250). Difficulty in final Quartet of the vocalists solely due to tenor part commencing its figured phrase a bar too soon; amending this, the beautiful effect intended by master is assured. Betz and "Freude," against the English Oratorio school and two strict crotchets (253).

LETTERS AND MINOR ESSAYS.

I. *Letter to an Actor.*

Invitation to write for an "Actor's Almanac." What can a layman know of the actor's mind beyond that state of ecstasy into which mimetic genius falls? An artistic exercise originally reserved for rare festivals, and practised by every educated man, now made daily avocation of a class. The boldest layman might shrink from disguising himself and facing an audience in cold blood; and what a disguise! An actor's dressing-room; the horrible impression only vanishes under spell of music. A similar spell must be exercised on the actor, even in non-musical drama, by fascination of audience's expectant gaze; but something else is also at work, viz. the object given him to portray (259). The average actor and mixed motives that bind him to the stage. To cultivate the artistic element, actors should refuse to play bad pieces; to sharpen their sense for really 'acting' pieces, let them practise *improvising* scenes themselves; thus they would both weed out incompetents and regenerate their profession from within (262).

II. *A Glance at the German Operatic Stage of To-day.*

A tour in western Germany in search of singers for projected Bayreuth Festival; dread inspired by many years of abstention from theatre-going; gloomiest forebodings outdone. Mozart and Meyerbeer as much maltreated as myself—e.g. Tannhäuser and Leporello. A military bandmaster promoted to conduct *Don Juan* at Wurzburg; the Magistrate and financially "solid" lessee. Stage-managers no better than the Kapellmeisters: "chassé croisé" in *Tannhäuser* March; Archbishop of Antwerp and Elsa; Elisabeth's retreat after praying to the prompt-box (265). Kapellmeister's beat in *Magic Flute* and cuts in *Prophète*: motto of Francis Moor, not to concern oneself with trifles. *Flying Dutchman* mangled at Mannheim—importance of closing scene in act ii.; cuts even in *Freischütz* (267). Singers now declaim better than ten years ago; friends attribute this improvement to more frequent appearance in my operas: but the performances are vague and hazy; why? The best "artists" have aimed at French method, and lesser singers take them as model: hence prevalence of "harangue" and scream directed at the audience; on the other hand the Kapellmeister ruins them with his false tempo (270). Expostulating about Auber's *Maçon*, I convince the conductor by singing him the aria in right tempo; but the Darmstadt Intendant had only meant the work as prelude to a ballet (272). *Don Juan* defaced by conductor and regisseur at Wurzburg: the singers not at home in such classical performances; another life thrills through them with the Meyerbeerian operas' Effect (273). Touching, that they should care for my works, where nothing but the *whole* can make effect, and yet that whole is chopped in pieces by the Kapellmeister, leaving them nothing but to search for operatic bits and aim them at the audience. Interruption by applause is *no* advantage to my operas: an unmutilated *Lohengrin* was given 26 times in 6 weeks to full houses in middling Magdeburg, but this experience teaches no one (275). Mutilated orchestral parts of *Meistersinger* supplied to Bremen theatre; results (276). Attitude of audience: accustomed to raw effects, it sleeps in its easy chair till they arrive. The Prophet's Mother and an Effect that failed; but no one laughed! (278). Popular performances, at Garden-concerts and Change-of-guard, demoralised by the theatres whence the military bandmasters take their cue. And our Conservatories do nothing to improve public taste, ply music for themselves behind closed doors: a musical 'treat' with relatives for chorus and Jupiter for time-beater. Remarks in the press on words I had spoken in private: venom versus eau-de-Cologne (281). Advice to various conductors: the spirit of Mozart's music its *singing quality*; tempo in *Fidelio*, and correct expression for its great Quartet; dynamic agreement between band and singers, e.g. in elfin chorus of *Oberon*; make the *scenic action acquire utmost distinctness through its orchestral exposition* (283). A perfect performance of Gluck's *Orpheus* brought about by infinite care of one artistic manager who had grasped the effect of the *whole*: and this in little Dessau (284).

III. *On the production of "Lohengrin" at Bologna.*

Invitations to assist in production declined: by leaving it entirely to Italians we all could better judge the opera's relation to your country. Fate of *Lohengrin* at German theatres: Rossini's estimate of modern Italian art-taste; but I have remarked a keen artistic appreciation in your countrymen. Advantages of Italian language tempted even Goethe; in Italy the first theme of *Rheingold* came to me, but nature of *Ring* binds me fast to Germany. A nation's productivity measurable rather by what Nature has doled out to, than by what she has lavished on it: Italian voice denied to Germans; but we yearn for what we have not, and there could be no nobler marriage than that of the genii of the two nations (288).

IV. *To the Burgomaster of Bologna.*

Apparent contradiction in an opponent of Italian Opera receiving honorary freedom of an Italian city; but it was not in Italy's flowering-time that she sent her virtuosi to sing at all the courts of Europe to those who held both Italy and Germany in bondage and division. The word "Libertas," on your scutcheon, better understood in Italy than France: only he who can create, feels "free" to welcome the creation of another. Looking forward to personal visit after the *Ring* shall have been performed in Germany (291).

V. *To Friedrich Nietzsche.*

An educational phenomenon: no boy more fond of Greek antiquity than myself, yet a fatal plan of schooling stifled the liking till later in life; perhaps the Antique Spirit beyond the sphere of our teachers of Philology. But a Dr.phil. comes forward to assert that this science "promises the favour of the Muses;" little evidence in our modern art and literary doings; the philologists seem to do nothing but bake fresh batches of unproductive teachers of Philology. What mysterious malady does the caste conceal behind its terrible quotations and mutual compliments? (295). Your "Birth of Tragedy" a breath of mountain air in this dismal science: but the Commentator storm is rising; Socrates and the hoof of an ass. The Dr.phil. cannot even understand your argument: in my case he falls foul of a strictly etymological "Weia waga," and these professors hound my "so-called poetry" while applauding the washiest stage-concoction of the Nibelungenlied (297). Each nation has its germ of cretinism, the Frenchman his Académie and absinthe, the German his spitefulness and beer. Our German Culture, now receiving such flattering attentions from abroad, requires a man like yourself to point it to its proper educational path (298).

VI. *On the name "Musikdrama."*

A senseless name, apparently invented in honour of my later works, and now usurped by imitators. Meaning of German compound words; this one a solecism, condensed from equally incorrect "musical drama." Music an *art*, Drama a *deed*. Music the part that once was all; Greek "Tragedy," Italian "Opera," and German "Schauspiel." Let my rivals stick to "opera," which will confuse no one, nor spoil their prettiest fancies. I should like to call my dramas "deeds of Music brought to sight," but people say I give them too little to see. Let "Bühnenfestspiel" serve for the nonce, for at Bayreuth the *stage* will be the main object of the *festival* (304).

VII. *A reading of "Die Götterdämmerung."*

My only innovation in Opera is the raising of dramatic *dialogue* to the main subject of the musical treatment; this enabled by prodigious development of Music by great German masters. By incessantly revealing the action's inmost motives music makes it possible to give it drastic definition and concision, and to extend the dialogue, unlike Greek Tragedy, over all the drama. This quality of my work calls for a representation outside the groove of present German stage-system (306).

BAYREUTH.

I. *Final Report on Fate of the Ring.*

Hopeless mood when Preface to public issue of *Ring* was written in 1863; concert-excerpts also simply to attract attention to my larger plan. Despairing of success, I began *Meistersinger*; but the dreamt-of Prince appeared: "Complete thy work! I will it." All the ambushed opposition now burst forth, attacking both protector and protected (310). In loyalty to the King I dropped original project, completed *Meistersinger*, and allowed *Rheingold* and *Walküre* to be performed at Munich: how the latter really fared I know not, for my friends spared me the details. Returning to Switzerland I finished *Ring* composition by my Prince's favour, and appealed to a "new community" to help forward its performance, as follows (312):—

Owing to criminal incorrectness of performances at German theatres the special nature of my *Ring des Nibelungen* makes it imperative to have a special locale, a place of periodic assemblage of Germany's best artistic forces for practice in truly German style. Not the success of my work, but of its correct performance, is what I care for: I therefore appeal to unknown friends to send me their names as promoters of my undertaking. In this special building a series of dramatic works of every really *German* class might thereafter be performed; in any case the performances should have wide-reaching influence on our standing theatres by example, and perhaps would incite them to combine in a permanent organisation, which then might properly receive the State's support as a power for good of public morals through improvement of national taste (316).

The "secret" lying hid beneath the German's outward semblance: despite poor figure he cut in public, a German statesman believed in his latent power—result the recent German victories. But Bismarck had a splendid organisation of force behind him, whilst *we* are fronted with a powerful organisation for evil

—the press and theatres. The canker of German stage-system eating into nation's manners: yet our Parliamentarians are content to take "their sup in peace." I therefore must begin with the executant artists, and trust through result of their labours to reach the "new community" in the heart of German nation (319).

II. *The Festival-Playhouse at Bayreuth.*

Dedication to Baroness Marie von Schleinitz (320).

Karl Tausig's scheme for collecting the necessary funds: his sudden death; epitaph. First Wagner-Verein founded at Mannheim, second in Vienna: soon followed by other German cities and even foreign ones, e.g. London and New York. High time to prepare the site: visits to Bayreuth, generosity of town-authorities; architectural plans and builders. Invitation to artists to assist in performing Ninth Symphony to celebrate laying of foundation-stone; alacrity of response; a drenching storm that damped no spirits (323).

Speech after the ceremony.—"This theatre a sketch of what we hope the German Theatre will some day be: its building will be but provisional, though the very arrangement of seats will shew you that you have entered a new relation to what is set before you; but the stage and miming are to be as perfect as can be got in Germany to-day—this the enduring portion of the edifice whose stone we now have laid. I trust in the German Spirit, which hitherto had pined in hideous travesty, but now shines bright in those who have gathered round me; our Beethoven's great wonder-symphony, "Embrace ye millions." A "national theatre at Bayreuth": would that it were so! (326). The world of "progress" has always hindered those who brought it a new thing: I had only *you*, to help me. Essence of the German's spirit to build from within; the eternal God lives in him of a truth, before he builds a temple to His glory. So be this building consecrated by that Spirit, which shouts to you across the centuries its glad Good-morrow" (328).

"Bayreuth" snapped up as nickname by cheap wits: but better than "Music of the Future," for the cloud has now solidified; like the "Gueux" we will adopt the title as good omen (329). Ancient history of the town, and derivation of its name; a Burgomaster "affecting to speak purified German" in address to sister of Frederick the Great; the burghers' interest in revival of German Literature; Jean Paul. Contrast between Margrave's court in that roccoco opera-house and German musicians lately there assembled to perform Ninth Symphony, the sounding triumph of the German Spirit (331). We needed such a motto as *Bayreuth*, to hold out against degenerate modernism; General Grant and a universal language—but that language is Music (333).

Explanation of plans of Festspielhaus: concealment of the orchestra led step by step to transformation of whole auditorium; "mystic gulf," no boxes possible; ascending rows of seats; second proscenium giving illusion of distance, idea carried out by a series, enclosing whole audience and masking the empty corners (336). Its exterior necessitously simple, but the very disproportion between stage-building and auditorium-annexe would need an architectural style not yet discovered; the baldness of the problem's statement may incite to that discovery, and give us in time a German Architecture unborrowed from abroad; haste is needless, for it probably will be many a year before the new "Reich" decides to take interest in our work and build a monument. So let our simple building stand on the fair hill by Bayreuth (340).

INDEX

As in former volumes, the figures denoting tens and hundreds are not *repeated* for one and the same reference unless the numbers run into a fresh line of type. Certain references will be found enclosed by brackets, the object being to distinguish my own footnotes &c. from the author's text. —W. A. E.

A.

C.

E.

G.

H.

I.

M.

P.

Q.

R.

T.

Y.

Z.